Saturn
from Antiquity to the Renaissance

Saturn
from Antiquity to the Renaissance

Edited by

Massimo Ciavolella
and
Amilcare A. Iannucci

University of Toronto Italian Studies 8

Dovehouse Editions Inc.

1992

Canadian Cataloguing in Publication Data

Main entry under title:
   Saturn from antiquity to the Renaissance

(University of Toronto Italian Studies ; 8)
Includes bibliographical references.

ISBN 1–895537–01–0 (bound) — ISBN 1–895537–00-2 (pbk.)

1. Saturn (Roman deity).   2. Saturn (Roman deity) in literature. I. Ciavolella, Massimo, 1942–   . II. Iannucci, Amilcare A.   III. Series.

PN57.S34S27 1992   398.2   C92–090199–0

This book copyright ©Dovehouse Editions Inc., 1992

For orders write to:
   Dovehouse Editions Inc.
   1890 Fairmeadow Cres.
   Ottawa, Canada
   K1H 7B9

For information on the series write to:
   University of Toronto Italian Studies
   c/o The Department of Italian
   University of Toronto
   Toronto, Canada, M5S 1A1

No part of this book may be translated or reproduced in any form, by print, photoprint, microfilm, microfiche, or any other means, without written permission from the publisher.

Typeset by the HUMANITIES PUBLISHING SERVICES, University of Toronto

TABLE OF CONTENTS

Foreword   ix

Gianni Guastella
   Saturn, Lord of the Golden Age   1

Maurizio Bettini
   Iacta alea est: Saturn and the *Saturnalia*   23

Giuseppe Pucci
   Roman Saturn: The Shady Side   37

Amilcare A. Iannucci
   Saturn in Dante   51

James F. Burke
   The Polarities of Desire: Saturn in the
   Libro de buen amor   69

Donald A. Beecher
   From Myth to Narrative: Saturn in
   Lefevre and Caxton   79

Roberto Guerrini
   Saturn at Città di Castello   91

Leatrice Mendelsohn
   Saturnian Allusions in Bronzino's London *Allegory*   101

Frederick A. de Armas
   Saturn in Conjunction: From Albumasar to Lope de Vega   151

Massimo Ciavolella
   Saturn and Venus   173

Foreword

With one exception, the essays in this book were presented at a conference held at the University of Toronto in 1988. The objective of the conference was to bring together a group of classical, medieval and Renaissance scholars from various disciplines to explore those aspects of the complex and ambiguous figure of Saturn which had remained largely unexamined in Klibansky, Panofsky, and Saxl's monumental *Saturn and Melancholy*. One area which warranted further study was the relationship between the Greek Kronos (whom some contributors prefer to call Cronos) and the Roman Saturn. Another was the exact nature and meaning of the *Saturnalia*. These important topics are addressed in the first three essays in this volume.

Especially provocative is Pucci's paper, which questions the claim in *Saturn and Melancholy* that the Roman Saturn was originally not ambivalent but good, and that he inherited his negative traits from his Greek counterpart. Supposedly these characteristics were greatly accentuated when the notion of the mythical deity merged with that of the planet called Saturn. Pucci demonstrates that from a very early date the Roman god was an awesome and terrible figure, a chthonic divinity who ruled over the dead. With this in mind, Pucci re-examines the significance of the *Saturnalia*. Regardless of the origins of the Roman Saturn's "dark side," it is also true, as Guastella points out, that the Roman literary tradition generally preferred to emphasize Saturn's positive qualities as a divine benefactor and to stress his role in the "historical" beginnings of Italy as sovereign of Latium. Thus, Virgil, for instance, sets the Golden Age not just in a mythic past but also in a legendary one, remote yet connected to history.

The medieval and Renaissance group of papers is more specific, focusing on a single author, text, or work of art either not addressed in Klibansky, Panofsky, and Saxl, or mentioned only in passing. There are detailed treatments of Saturn or saturnian elements in Dante, the *Libro de buen amor*, Lefevre's *Recueil des Troyennes Ystoires*, and Lope de Vega, through the curious mediation of Albumasar. The latter's role in the propagation of Saturn as a negative astral deity in the Middle Ages and the Renaissance is documented by de Armas. It is worth noting in this regard that in the *Genealogy of the Gods* Boccaccio cites Albumasar as his sole source for his presentation of the astrological Saturn as a dark, malefic, and destructive force.

Several papers deal with that dark and cold star's influence on the affairs of men, especially in amorous affairs. It would appear, as Burke points out, that many of the hero-poet's difficulties with women in the *Libro de buen amor* can be traced to his birth under the double influence of Venus and Saturn. This stellar dilemma is portrayed in even more dramatic terms by Girolamo Cardano in a horoscope which he cast for himself. The mixing of the rays of Saturn and Venus provided Cardano with "a profound yet lascivious mind" and inclined him toward a "shameful and obscene libido." Forever torn between the demands of the mind and the flesh, he suffered throughout his tormented life from erotic melancholy. In his paper, Ciavolella discusses Cardano's plight, invoking medieval and Renaissance medical texts to define the exact nature of his malady, universally known as *amor hereos*.

But the planet Saturn is as ambivalent as the ancient god of the same name. A few turns in the sky and his complexion and influence can change completely. In Dante's *Paradiso*, much of Saturn's malignant character is mitigated by the fact that the planet is "in exile" in the sign of Leo, i.e. in the sign opposite Saturn's usual domicile. When this happens, as Jacopo della Lana, one of Dante's early commentators, explains, the planet's nature is altered quite dramatically: "Leo is hot and dry, Saturn is cold and dry. Now mix these two constitutions, and you produce an excellent dry." This fortunate celestial coincidence permits Dante to retrieve the Neoplatonic tradition of Saturn as overseer of the contemplative life. Thus, his seventh sphere hosts those religious souls endowed with a meditative and mystical temperament. Dante's extraordinary portrayal of the planet-god had an enormous impact on Florentine Neoplatonism (mainly through Landino) and helped to establish the notion of Saturn as a star of sublime contemplation. Yet Ficino, who was a child of Saturn, saw this as both a blessing and a curse—an index of the unresolved tension in Saturn's powerful character.

Of the two art history papers, one brings to our attention a bold representation of Saturn in the Palazzo Vitelli alla Cannoniera in Città di Castello, part of a fresco cycle which until very recently had attracted little critical attention. The other, much longer, piece deals with Bronzino's

London *Allegory*, which has certainly not suffered from neglect. Since the painting's meaning is unclear, it has generated a number of contradictory interpretations. The paper dealing with this enigmatic work is the only one which was not part of the original proceedings. Other essays on Saturnian manifestations in works both obscure and famous could, of course, have been added to the collection, but it was never our intention to strive for completeness. Mendelsohn's Bronzino paper was included because it provides an interesting and ironic twist to our theme. Panofsky, who was the first to conduct an iconographical analysis of the painting in his essay tracing the origins of "Father Time," identified the bald-headed, grey-bearded figure in the upper right hand corner of the painting as "old Chronos." Surprisingly, he did not stress the saturnine aspects of the image. By doing so, Mendelsohn finds the key to unlocking the allegory's meaning. Iannucci also engages Panofsky's essay on Time, appealing to it in order to uncover yet another trace (previously unnoticed) of Saturn in Dante, and one, moreover, that has a significant bearing on our understanding of a theme — exile — which is at the very core of Dante's great Christian epic of conversion.

One thing is certain: Saturn had staying power. His ambivalent personality and complex history guaranteed this. In fine, his story contained something for everyone. So in the Renaissance, as Beecher notes, the myth of Saturn was variously fragmented and redeployed "by court poets in celebrating their patrons through flattering associations with the Golden Age of Saturn and the return of Astraea, by Neoplatonic philosophers as the basis for a doctrine of poetic fury and intellectual inspiration, or by astrologers and physicians as the basis for a codification of the melancholy temperament." But there was also an attempt — and this is perhaps one of the most interesting manifestations of Saturn in the Renaissance — to reconcile the various conflicting elements of the Saturn myth and organize them into a coherent narrative, guided by the conventions of romance realism. And, although in the end this was not entirely possible, Raoul Lefevre's *Recueil des Troyennes Ystoires* enjoyed wide popularity in the Renaissance and was translated into English by William Caxton. Lefevre produced an everyman's version of Saturn. Among Renaissance intellectuals and erudites, Saturn may have become identified with extraordinary characters and destinies, but his story appealed to everyone, even the common reader.

The volume and the conference on which it is based would not have been possible without the help of many people. Special thanks go to Maurizio Bettini, who co-ordinated the Italian end of the conference, which was organized within the context of a scholarly exchange agreement between the Universities of Siena and Toronto. This explains why many of the contributors are affiliated with these two institutions. Others who contributed significantly to the project are Donald Beecher, Douglas Campbell, Michael Dunleavy, Andrea Fedi, Hiroko Fudemoto, and Susan Iannucci. We would also like to thank the libraries and museums that kindly allowed us to reproduce illustrations from their collections.

Massimo Ciavolella
Amilcare A. Iannucci
Toronto, April 1992

Gianni Guastella

Saturn, Lord of the Golden Age

The subject I would like to discuss concerns the constant connection that the extant Greek and Roman versions of the legend of the Golden Age established between blissful primitive mankind and the sovereign deity of those remote days. I will try to show how these legends linked the mythical past, its "culture" and its gods, with the history of human civilization, and most of all, with the civilization and religion of the people who produced and read such stories. Therefore, I will briefly consider the "morphology" of this mythical theme, and then I will try to determine the part played in it by Cronos-Saturn. First I will examine a short passage from Tibullus, which is both schematic and exemplary, and then I will discuss ampler versions such as the one taken from the first book of Ovid's *Metamorphoses*. Particular attention will be paid to the presence of the theme in Virgil's works (especially in the *Georgics*). Finally I will consider more specifically the character of the Roman Saturn.

Ancient authors described the Golden Age as a fantastic world where primitive mankind lived a near perfect existence akin to that of the gods,[1] which precluded the need for culture and its arts. Since the various versions of this myth cannot be analyzed in detail here, I will try to focus on some of their narrative constants, in particular, the use of inversion to describe life in the Golden Age, and on the more complex ways by which the remote past and the present were linked together in these tales.

How then was the world of these early people described? They were depicted as living in a natural condition amidst the richness of a bountiful nature (Gatz 74, 204). Beyond this information, ancient authors provided just a vague outline of that primitive world, the enlargement of whose boundaries could be achieved by means of the rhetorical figure of synecdoche. In other words, only a few features of this fantastic world were presented as a partial picture of an entirely happy life.

Let us see now how the features that synthesized the whole Golden Age were described. For this purpose, I will discuss a short passage from

Tibullus, where the poet, lying ill in a distant country, curses the necessity of travelling:

> quam bene Saturno uiuebant rege, priusquam
> tellus in longas est patefacta uias!
> *non*dum caeruleas pinus contempserat undas,
> effusum uentis praebueratque sinum,
> *nec* uagus ignotis repetens compendia terris
> presserat externa nauita merce ratem.
> Illo *non* ualidus subiit iuga tempore taurus,
> *non* domito frenos ore momordit equus,
> *non* domus ulla fores habuit, *non* fixus in agris
> qui regeret certis finibus arua, lapis.
> Ipsae mella dabant quercus, ultroque ferebant
> obuia securis ubera lactis oues.
> *non* acies, *non* ira fuit, *non* bella, *nec* ensem
> immiti saeuus duxerat arte faber.
> *nunc* Ioue sub domino caedes et uulnera semper,
> *nunc* mare, *nunc* leti mille repertae uiae.
>
> (1.3.35–50)[2]

[How well man used to live with Saturn as king,
Before the earth was laid open for faraway campaigns!
The pine tree had not yet shown contempt for sky-blue waves
And yielded its spanking sails to the winds.
Nor had the roving sailor, questing for gain in unknown lands,
Laden his galley with foreign wares.
In those days the powerful bull had not bowed to the yoke
Nor the horse champed the bit in a docile mouth,
No house had doors to lock, no stones, set in the fields,
Marked fixed limits to the farms.
Of their own accord, oak trees dripped honey, and ewes,
Voluntarily coming forward, gave free-flowing milk.
No armies, no rage to kill, no war existed;
Nor had the cruel smith with brutal skill yet forged a sword.
But now in the reign of Jove, slaughter and wounds are
                                          ever-present,
Untimely Death comes now by sea, by a thousand other ways.]

The former age, under the reign of Saturn, was the opposite of that under the reign of Jupiter. The temporal succession of the two ages coincides, so to speak, with the contrast between their respective elements and cultural values. During the Golden Age, the suffering, pain, toil, that typifies the human condition did *not* exist at all. The "before" is described by inverting some of the main characteristics of the "today";[3] by synecdoche, it can be thus imagined as the entire opposite of contemporary times. The Tibullian description is a sort of continuous litotes, denying every negative feature of reality (according to a linguistic mechanism whose function has been illustrated by Weinrich) and by extension reconstructing a fabulous and perfectly happy world.

While the Golden Age staged the inversion of the negative features of the human condition, the Iron Age was usually described as a sort of "world turned upside-down" and represented the opposite of the most primitive age.[4] All the positive elements and values of the Golden Age were inverted during the Iron Age, with every kind of bad habit, fault, and evil (such as war, privation, greed, and so on) dominant. We can consider the cycle of ages, opening with the golden period and closing with the iron one, as comprising the entire range of the possibilities of civilization, from an initial perfection of mankind to its complete degeneration. At the "neutral point" between these two stages of utmost perfection and total downfall lies the cultural system of those people who both compose and read such tales (Avalle). This cultural system has its own inextricable blend of positive and negative elements and presents to its members absolute models illustrating both conditions. Thus the two extremes in the cycle of the ages represent two imaginary — we could say theoretical — perspectives: by denying the negative values of civilization, one may return to the almost godly condition of primitive happiness; on the other hand, by denying the positive values of culture, one may point out the ultimate fate of a completely wicked mankind.[5]

Let us now pass to another question. How was this cycle of ages placed with respect to the most recent period of mankind's history? Ancient authors gave different answers, which were nonetheless organized according to a definite structural logic. Either the cycle of ages could be neatly severed from history and located in the remote mythical past, or it could, in various ways, include history.

A clear presentation of a distant and already concluded cycle of ages may be seen in Ovid's version of the myth in *Metamorphoses* 1.89–113 (Gatz 70 ff.; Bömer, *Metamorphosen* 48 ff.; Schwabl, *Zum Mythos* and "Weltalter" 801 ff.). By means of the usual inversion device (Bömer, *Metamorphosen* 1.48 ff.), the poet describes a sequence of four progressively degenerating ages. The Silver Age, which began when the world was under the rule of Jupiter (Saturn having been banished into Tartarus), was already worse than the Golden Age. Actually, it declined from the original natural condition because Jupiter brought in the seasons, and then many difficulties arose (such as cold and hot weather, scarcity of food, and so on) that had to be overcome by means of cultural arts, such as agriculture. The people of the ensuing Bronze Age, devoted to war, were even worse. Eventually, during the Iron Age, *omne nefas* spread over the world, until the angry Jupiter decided to sweep mankind away by the Flood. Later on, Deucalion and Pyrrha revived mankind on earth.[6] The path that led from perfection to degeneration then ran through a remote mythical past that had no relationship to the present.[7]

What happened, then, when the present entered explicitly into the story? The cycle of ages did not undergo substantial changes; only the representation of the Iron Age was modified, according to different procedures. The present could be described:
a) as a central phase in the Iron Age, before its culmination, when everything would be turned upside-down;
b) as quite simply the Iron Age;
c) as the final period of a whole age cycle (in which case the present immediately precedes the beginning of a new Golden Age, i. e., of a new age cycle).

A well-known passage from Hesiod's *Works and Days* (ll. 90 ff.) can be considered in order to illustrate the first point. In this passage, four races follow one another, not in a progressive degeneration (as in the case of Ovid's *Metamorphoses*), but according to an alternation of unequal values, which have been examined by J. P. Vernant in a famous book. After three metallic ages (golden, silver and bronze), the fourth age, the Age of Heroes, is inserted before the present appears in the story. *Nūn gàr dè ghénos estì sidéreon*, says Hesiod at l. 176. It is only during the present that the inversion of values begins to become apparent. It will be total in the future, when the world will be "turned upside-down," and only evil will be left to mankind (ll. 200 ff.: *kakoū d'ouk éssetai alké*). Thus the present clearly becomes the pivot upon which the paradigmatic opposition between human perfection and final degeneration hinges, since it occupies an intermediate position between the two extremes.[8] Thence originates the moral later on drawn by Hesiod (ll. 274 ff.), who showed his brother the model of justice (the same justice that characterized the Golden Age and the Age of Heroes), trying to dissuade him from *hybris*, whose "model" would ruin mankind (West, *Works* 49).

The most common way of relating the present to the past in such texts was the one we have seen in the example from Tibullus, who neatly opposed the age of Saturn to that of Jupiter (i. e. the present; the *nunc*).[9] Various negative characteristics of real life were absent from the fabulous past, conceived as a sort of screen upon which to project unsatisfied aspirations as well as beautiful utopias.

In the context of utopias we still have to mention those texts in which two cycles of ages follow each other. In such cases the present is considered to be the Iron Age of a concluding cycle, which eagerly waits for a new Golden Age to come. Probably the most famous example of this way of conceiving the Age cycle is Virgil's *Fourth Eclogue*, which opens with the messianic prediction: *redeunt Saturnia regna* (Lovejoy and Boas 85 ff.; Gatz 87 ff.). Here the Golden Age occupies not only the past, but the future, too: instead of a remembered fantasy, one now has the expectation of imminent happiness.[10]

There also existed the possibility of envisaging a contemporary golden age. I am referring particularly to descriptions of fabulous places, such as the Islands of the Blest, provided with the characteristics of the primitive natural world that existed during the Golden Age. Such places were not located in a remote past, but in *a remote space*; they were located at the boundaries of the earth, in a country that could not be reached by mortals. The different condition of blissful mankind during the Golden Age as well as on the Islands of the Blest, after death, needed either a spatial or a temporal context in which to be shown. To be imagined, such men had to remain distant and inaccessible, like the dream of their happiness (cf. the chapter "Jenseits und Wunschraum" in Gatz 174 ff. and Gelinne 237 ff.). Traces of Cronos-Saturn's sovereignty were left in such fabulous pictures: it would not be surprising to find him king of the Islands of the Blest too.[11]

So far we have dealt with a few of the narrative devices through which the mythical theme of the Golden Age is set up, and we have done so only in a very general and schematic way. However, it must be clear that the oppositional principles we have been talking about cannot always appear in such a definite way.[12] Sometimes the past is connected with the present in a quite complicated, even contradictory manner. Everybody is familiar with the case of Virgil's *Georgics*, where the Golden Age is described in two passages, each with different connotations.

In the so-called "Theodicy of Labour" (1.125 ff.) Virgil contrasts an unnamed age with Jupiter's reign. The first one is simply said to have occurred before the second one; but it is, however, structured according to the Golden Age pattern.[13] During it, *artes* were not necessary, because the earth spontaneously offered everything. In any case, this stage is not exactly presented in positive terms. In fact, Virgil describes nature's perfection as a motionless world, subject to the risk of *torpere graui . . . ueterno* (l. 124), becoming torpid through a dull sluggishness. In order to remove this sluggishness from his kingdom, Jupiter introduced into nature some flaws that could rouse human *artes*. Since cultural progress is now looked upon as a positive phenomenon, the evaluation of primitive mankind has changed perceptibly. Therefore the natural condition is now marked with a strange flaw: torpid sluggishness, the *ueternus*.[14] The function of the natural perfection theme has been completely turned upside down (Lovejoy and Boas, 369 ff.).[15]

A new variation occurs in the second book. Virgil is now praising the life of *agricolae* (ll. 458 ff.), who get an easy living from the earth (Johnston, "Saturnia" 49; Novara 754 ff., esp. 756), and do not know the troubled life of the town where people are distressed by war. While praising that kind of life, Virgil likens the condition of farmers at the present time to that of the ancient Italians, making the two appear almost identical:

> hanc olim ueteres uitam coluere Sabini
> hanc Remus et frater; sic fortis Etruria creuit
> scilicet et rerum facta est pulcherrima Roma,
> septemque una sibi muro circumdedit arces.
> Ante etiam sceptrum Dictaei regis et ante
> impia quam caesis gens est epulata iuuencis,
> aureus hanc uitam in terris Saturnus agebat.
> (ll. 532–38)

> [Such a life the old Sabines once lived,
> such Remus and his brother. Thus, surely,
>   Etruria waxed strong,
> thus Rome became of all things the fairest,
> and with a single city's wall enclosed her seven hills.
> Nay, before the Cretan king held sceptre, and before
> a godless race banqueted on slaughtered bullocks,
> such was the life golden Saturn lived on earth.]

Virgil is here suggesting a well-defined cultural pattern: i.e., traditional ethics "disguised" as the agrarian life, and thus opposed to contemporary ethics, which have given rise to civil war (La Penna 235 ff.; Barchiesi 161 ff.). The Golden Age still retains its oppositional meaning: its description has been set up as an inversion of certain negative values of the present. Moreover, an historical-legendary description has been juxtaposed with the mythical one, and has almost intermingled with it. Etruscans, Sabines, former Romans, have appeared beside the unnamed men of the Golden Age. And so Saturn has become the "guarantor" of the merging of the two pictures. What is more, this complex scenario has been projected on the present, fitting into the idealized (if not thoroughly utopian) picture of rural life. Therefore, it appears as a kind of *actual* Golden Age.[16] This model was all the more legitimate in that it conformed to a tradition going back to the origins of the Roman people.[17]

Let us come back to Saturn, who has until now remained in the background of the mythical pictures we have been dealing with. I have only hurriedly said that the Golden Age existed *epì Krónou, Saturno rege*; but our main question is still unanswered. Let us pose it again. What are the characteristics of Cronos-Saturn that justify his presence as a sovereign in such a context?

I will continue to consider Cronos-Saturn's mythical life, since there is only patchy evidence regarding his cult, especially in classical Greece; and so, it would be difficult to interpret his distinguishing features as a religious character.[18] However, while his western cult was quite widely diffused,[19] since Cronos was identified with various local deities,[20] the Greek god seems to have existed chiefly in myth. Basically he was the sovereign "before Zeus" and, in a certain sense, anti-Zeus. The heart of his mythical life is the struggle against his son, with the final attainment of power by Zeus.[21] In brief, we can say that Cronos is a deposed king, linked to the past of Greek "theology," i.e., to a somehow concluded religious stage (Lovejoy and Boas 24 ff.; West, *Theogony* 204 ff.; Briquel 149 ff.).

If we then consider the seat of the other Greek gods, Cronos' location seems to be in a fringe zone. He does not live on Olympus, whence he had been banished once and for all. We can find him either in Tartarus (where he was precipitated with the Titans: Hom. 14.203, 274, and 15.224; Hes. *Theog.* 851),[22] or, exceptionally, in the Islands of the Blest, at the limits of the earth (Hild 1083, Pohlenz 2007 ff.).[23]

Cronos' figure is thus generally connected with either a time or a space *different* from the ones that are occupied by the gods ruled by Zeus. His *different* location in mythical space and time goes together with the contrasting ways of evaluating his figure. On the one hand, Cronos is the god who devoured his children; he is also the sovereign who had seized power after having castrated his father.[24] His "dark side" might be connected, in a religious sense, with recurring data regarding human sacrifices made in his honour in various areas (always records of customs that had subsequently been abandoned: Macrob. *Sat.* 1.7.28 ff.; Hild 1087; Pohlenz 1993 ff.).[25] On the other hand, charitable qualities were also ascribed to Cronos' sovereignty, at least toward mankind. I am referring to Cronos' image as a seemingly benign king during the Golden Age.[26] We could probably see a reflection of Cronos' benevolent nature in the Greek feast of *Cronia* (despite the fact that not much is known about it) and in the more complex and important Roman version of the same feast, the *Saturnalia* (Nilsson "Saturnalia"; Lovejoy and Boas 65 ff.; see also Bettini's paper in this volume).[27]

While outlining these two values of Cronos' figure, I am following the "classical" statements of Klibansky, Panofsky, and Saxl. They insisted on the ambiguous, sometimes even contradictory, characteristics of this ancient god, going so far as to define him as "the god of opposites" (133). Let us consider the ambiguous elements that really surround this "remote" god with regard to the narrative mechanism of the theme of the Golden Age.

If we consider again Hesiod's passage from *Works and Days*, we can observe that Cronos' presence is hardly mentioned. The only hint can be found at line 111: *hoì mèn epì Krónou ēsan, hot' ouranō(i) embasíleuen*.[28] Nothing else. No effect of this sovereignty on men's life is either visible or explicit (Baldry 84).[29] The reference seems to be simply a temporal indication. The origins of mankind are said to have occurred when Cronos was king,[30] while the rest of human history is said to be under the rule of Zeus, who several times is described as interfering in human life (Hes., *Erga* ll. 137 ff., 143 ff., 156 ff., and 167 ff.).

Generally, the most ancient Greek authors did not worry about defining precisely the relationship between Cronos' sovereignty and the Golden Age.[31] It was rather the Romans who significantly developed the idea of Saturn's reign as having had beneficial effects on human life; the *Saturnia regna* lost their mostly temporal meaning and became a legendary landscape provided with more precisely definable characteristics. This point will be taken up at a later moment.

Let us now come back to Hesiod's text. Even the "temporal" indication of Cronos' reign has a definite oppositional value. Cronos' time is to Zeus' time as the "natural" life of primitive mankind is to the following "cultural" ages. From a pessimistic point of view, Hesiod shows us the spread of civilization, and in particular its degenerative effects. In the end, a black picture of the human condition is painted. In contrast with an age characterized by unchanging perfection another one is presented during which imperfection becomes absolute, in various stages. The oppositional nature of Cronos, as well as that of the mythical time "represented" by him, seems to match the oppositional nature of the Golden Age. Outside history, Cronos ruled as a sovereign in a remote and concluded past when mankind enjoyed a natural condition on earth. Zeus was contrasted to him as the sovereign of cultural times.[32]

In most of the texts where this mythical theme appears we can find the same contrast between a perfect past and either a single epoch or a succession of epochs (often including the present) that become more and more imperfect. The temporal succession, respectively marked, at the level of mythical actors, by Cronos' and Zeus' sovereignties, is just a way of making a story out of an opposition among paradigmatic values. In such cases the "better" is connected with the "before," the "worse" with the "after." In this context, Cronos acquires those positive connotations that contrast with his "dark side." Even his presence in the Islands of the Blest could be considered from the same point of view.[33]

Till now we have seen the possible values of the "otherness" that characterizes the "golden" Cronos, the rejected god of the past. But Cronos' functions and, even more, Roman Saturn's functions were determined not only according to such an oppositional scheme. In Roman literature Saturn's figure is also connected with the history of the land of Italy through legendary tales about the primitive past (Verg. *Aen.* 8.319 ff. and Serv. *ad Aen.* 319, 322; Ovid. *Fast.* 1.235 ff.; Herodian. 1.16.1; [Aur. Vict.] *Origo* 1.3, 3.1 ff.; Macrob. *Sat.* 1.7.21 ff.).[34] I will consider only the effects of this situation on the relationship between Saturn and the Roman way of conceiving the Golden Age (Gatz 122 ff., 205).

Whereas the Hesiodic scenario was quite indistinctly determined, the Golden Age depicted by Roman authors was much more clearly described, as was Saturn's presence in it. The *Saturnia regna* were set in the *Saturnia tellus*, still retaining the distinguishing features of a bountiful nature (Wissowa 434).[35] The god himself was represented as living on earth amongst the aboriginal people. His character as beneficent "hero" with agricultural connections (Hild 1086; Wissowa 427; Briquel 143 ff., 149 ff.; Leglay 464; Brelich 83 ff., 91 ff.; Johnston, "Vergil's Conception" 57 ff., and "Vergil's Agricultural," 62 ff., 69)[36] must be considered to be part of this legendary conception of Italy's origins. Even the Euhemeristic version of Saturn's history, which was known in Rome at an early date (Pohlenz 2010 ff.; Johnston "Vergil's Conception" 58 ff., 68 ff. and "Vergil's Agricultural," 64 ff.),[37] seems to have been structured according to a similar pattern.

The characteristics of the cultural model connected by Roman authors to the Golden Age theme can be defined more precisely than those of the model suggested by Greek authors. Some poets, in particular, such as Virgil, laid down a definite paradigm of values explicitly attributable to the Italian tradition (Johnston, "Saturnia" 75 ff.), instead of exalting in general terms a range of positive values realized in the fabulous context of primitive life. The image of Saturn's reign acquired a new significance within the mould of Roman tradition.

The consequences of this state of affairs are remarkable. Actually, the contrast between Italian past and Roman present could hardly be considered simply in terms of nature versus culture, since the "re-proposed" model was already provided with well-defined cultural values. Generally, Romans did not represent the original perfection as a natural model; rather it, too, was a cultural model which had gradually degenerated. This conception of men's origins seems to be consistent with the well-known Roman idea of the historical past as a sort of repertory and paradigm of cultural models. Thus, the opposition "nature versus culture" does not disappear, but it certainly changes. In texts such as the second book of *Georgics* the "natural" culture of the *agricolae* is contrasted to the degenerate culture of the town. Agriculture is picked out as the "natural" art through which nature and culture can merge.[38] Therefore, the agricultural character of Saturn is emphasized, for example, by ascribing to him the introduction of agriculture in Italy (Varro *R. r.* 3.1.13; Plut. *Quaest. Rom.* 42; Macrob. *Sat.* 1.7.25, 1.10.19 ff.).

The Golden Age as visualized by the Romans was also peculiarly related to the past, even if not always in a well-defined way. Sometimes it is not possible to tell how the succession and the struggle between Saturn and Jupiter was imagined by some authors; neither is it clear how the same authors connected the most primitive stage of human life to the "golden" condition introduced by Saturn into the land of Italy as well as into Italian legend. In general, Saturn's story seems divided into two periods: the epoch of remote human origins (which is common to the Greek versions of the myth of the ages), and the "historical" period of Italy's origins. Usually, the latter is presented as a stage occurring during Saturn's flight or exile, after he had been sent away from Olympus (Verg. *Aen.* 8.319–58; Ovid. *Fast.* 1.235 ff.; Iuven. 13.38 ff.).[39] Having been either put to flight or set free from Tartarus by Jupiter, Saturn was seeking refuge in Italy (more precisely in Latium, according to some sources: Serv. (and Serv. Dan.) *Ad Aen.* 8.322), where he eventually reproduced the conditions of the Golden Age, introducing also the benefits of agriculture or even of culture in general (Verg. *Aen.* 8.314 ff., esp. 321 ff.: cf. Taylor 263; Dion. Hal. 1.38.1; Plut., *Quaest. Rom.* 42; Macrob. 1.7.21 ff., esp. 24 ff., 1.10.19 ff.; Brelich 100 ff.; Gatz 125; Klibansky Panofsky and Saxl 135). Thus this beneficent god whose most ancient history, as far as we can see, remains in the background,[40] entered into the world of indigenous deities such as Janus (Ovid. *Fast.* 1.233 ff.; Macrob. *Sat.* 1.7.21 ff.).[41]

Saturn's positive characterization in this particular context can be related to the more general Roman conception of this god. The "hellenized" deity who appears in the best known literary version of this story was a figure in which various characteristics had been gathered: the Greek god (whose theogonic story, as well as his reign during the Golden Age, we already knew from the Greek texts) had merged with the indigenous chthonian god of agriculture. However, the Roman sources from the "classical period" seem reticent about the "dark" outlines of this god. If it is true that this "dark side" remains the basis of the cult as well as of the Roman conception of Saturn,[42] it is also true that the literary texts are quite evasive about this specific point, preferring to emphasize the positive qualities of the divine benefactor. As far as the legend of primitive mankind is concerned, these characteristics of the ancient god are absolutely predominant. Seemingly, the Romans tried not only to keep separate Saturn's sovereignty among the gods from his sovereignty in Latium, but also to confine the complex of his "dark features" to the remotest and most indistinct past.[43] The god that had castrated his father and had devoured his children was thus committed to a theogonic past, which was both distant and vague.[44] At the same time, the Romans tried to ascribe the positive characteristics of this deity to their own tradition, and stressed his importance within their legendary past. Thus it is that Saturn's features have been divided into two "sides" and that his history has acquired an ambiguous setting (Brelich 94 ff.). If we come back to the passage from the second book of the *Georgics*, we can detect the embarrassment of the poet, who sets the Golden Age both in a mythical past, opposed to Jupiter's sovereignty (*ante etiam sceptrum Dictaei regis*), and in a phase of legend, remote yet connected to history and the present by a thread of continuity (Johnston, "Vergil's Conception" 61 ff., esp. 69).

Obviously, the separation of the two "sides" of Saturn is not clear-cut and mechanical. Sometimes the two images seem to overlap to the point that, in the conflicting versions of literary sources, the opposition between Saturn and Jupiter does not seem to make any sense within the "Italian period" of Saturn's story;[45] and, in some other cases, the Golden Age itself could seemingly have existed only in the land of Italy (Dion. Hal. 1.36.1). The uncertain overlapping of the two characters has left on Latin texts traces of an unsolved ambiguity.[46]

The symbolic function of the figure of Cronos-Saturn mostly depends on the position of his story within myth (Brelich 100 ff.).[47] He represented an original period that had been overcome by the age of Zeus, and he also represented a divine model that had been rejected after Zeus-Jupiter's accession to the throne. This godly figure seems to be susceptible of two different interpretations. If Zeus' accession to the throne is positively considered, then the dark side of the story of a cruel deity surfaces more decidedly: he was a father who devoured his own children, a son who castrated his own father. But if the succession of the two sovereigns is evoked in a story based upon the deprecation of the "cultural" trend of present times, then negative aspects are attributed to the most recent epoch, while the Golden Age acquires, by contrast, a positive characterization. The benign qualities of the figure of Cronos-Saturn as king of the Golden Age have to be considered in this context. It is in such a way that the Romans have mostly developed the positive image of the god of the origins, who was also connected with agriculture (Brelich 90; Coarelli 373 ff.).[48] The ambivalence of this figure has been passed on to the subsequent heritage of Saturn, as is well-known. In some cases, the difficulty of distinguishing between the different qualities attributed to the ancient divine figure has led to the creation of a contradictory character, in which the wicked deity and the beneficent one, the sovereign of the theogonic myth and the traditional benefactor of Italians, co-exist.

It can be instructive to quote a passage from Fazio degli Uberti's *Dittamondo*, where Saturn's Italian reign is described as follows:

> Di qua fuggio, come t'ho detto; in pria
> nascoso stava e, quando Gian morio,
> rimase solo a lui la signoria.
>   E, benché fosse tanto avaro e rio
> nondimeno era scaltro e intendente
> e sottil molto a ogni maestrio.
>   Costui mostrò di far nave a la gente,
> scudi, moneta e di terra lavoro,
> che prima ne sapean poco o niente.
>   Questa età si disse età dell'oro,
> perché la gente viveano a comuno,
> sobria, casta e libera fra loro,
>   semplice, pura e senza vizio alcuno.

(1.12.79–91)

> [From here he ran, as I told you; first
> he hid and then when Janus died,
> he alone remained ruler of the land.
>   And, although he was greedy and mean,
> nonetheless he was a great master and conaisseur
> of every kind of art.
>   He taught man how to build ships,

shields and money and how to work the land.
Of these things before man knew little or nothing.
This time was called the Golden Age,
because man lived together in harmony,
sober, chaste and free,
pure and without vice.]

The lines of this fourteenth century poet, which are based upon the Eumeristic version of Saturn's story, assemble all those characteristics we have found one by one in more ancient texts about the former king of the gods and of the Golden Age.[49] From a radical inversion of the traditional picture, a diffuser of every cultural art eventually emerges.[50]

In the course of two thousand years, many features have been added to the bare Hesiodic description of the *chryseon ghenos*, living blissfully in a simple manner—*epì Krónou*, in the time of Cronos, when he was king in heaven.

University of Venice

NOTES

1 I will always use the expression "Golden Age," though the theme could be indicated in different ways, according to the various texts (*ghenos, stirps, aetas, saecula*, etc.): see Baldry 88, 91 ff.; Gatz 73, 128 ff., 205 ff.
2 See Flower Smith's notes and loc. (244 ff.).
3 Gatz (74) notes that Ovid's version is full of "Verneinungen der Gegenwärtigen Lebenssphäre. Die Vorzeit kann nicht aus sich selbst verstanden werden, kann nicht autonomer Begriff sein. Sie erhält ihre Farben durch den Kontrast zur Gegenwart." This statement could be referred to almost every ancient version of the Golden Age. Even the "positive" description of nature (according to Gatz, such a systematic description can be found only in Aratus' and Hesiod's versions) is to be considered in contrast with the negative one: actually, the context in which the "positive" features are stressed is always an oppositional one (Gatz 204). About the use of negation in such descriptions see Avalle 80 ff.
4 A comprehensive study of this popular theme from antiquity to recent times is Cocchiara (with an interesting foreword by Camporesi). Much less useful is Kenner, whose only concern is "die griechisch-römische Antike."
5 A renowned specimen of the "didactic" use of this theme is in Hesiod's *Erga*; Vernant 44 ff., 61 ff., 75 ff.
6 In view of what we will say further on, it is interesting to note how the sequence of epochs described by Ovid seems to contradict Vergil, *Ecl.* 6.41 ff.: *hinc*

lapides Pyrrhae iactos, Saturnia regna, / Caucasiasque refert uolucris furtumque Promethei.

7 The "present" was absent from Aratus' version too (Gatz 63).
8 The tale itself is narrated in order to explain the original closeness of the human race to the gods (l. 108: *hos homóthen ghegáasi theoì thnetoí t'ánthropoi*; a line wrongly bracketed by some editors). Cf. Gatz 35; West, *Works* 49, 178; Vernant 92 ff. On the other hand, Hesiod's final considerations show how distant the lot of the future mankind is from its initial perfection (ll. 197 ff.).
9 This circumstance compounds the impression that the temporal succession is only a narrative device, with the main function of lining up pictures endowed with a strong paradigmatic value: that is to say, the values implied are more important than the story in which they are "narrated." See Vernant 26 ff., who has clearly focused the structure of the contrast among different epochs (esp. 43 ff. and 52 ff.); see also Kirk 233 ff.
10 See Costa XIX ff. and *passim*, about the importance of the eschatological theme, developed in literary texts especially from Christian authors on. The assumed cyclical conception of the ages in Hesiod's *Erga* is quite problematic. Various commentators (among them Vernant 76 ff.) interpret ll. 174 ff. as the expectation of a new Golden Age; but I think that Gatz's opinion is more persuasive (25): according to him these lines indicate a generic expectation of better times to come, as the text itself does not precisely state what kind of epoch is the one expected by Hesiod (see also ibid. n. 56; Kirk 234).
11 This detail, which, to use Gatz's words (182 ff.) is to be considered as an "äusserst seltene Version," could be seen also in Pind. *Ol.* 2.70 ff.; it surely emerges from the interpolated ll. 173 a[*olim* 169]–e of Hesiod's *Erga* (Gelinne 233).
12 I want to make clear that I am concerned only with a series of important narrative devices, which can almost constantly be found in the various versions of the myth. But in this way I do not mean to reach the deepest level of the myth; I will not try to explain its "meaning." To do that, it would at least be necessary to consider every single variant inside its own context; which would obviously be impossible in this instance.
13 See Novara 723 ff. (esp. 732 ff.). M. Wifstrand Schiebe maintains that Saturn's name is absent, on this occasion, because "the paradisiac period corresponding to Saturn's time is not conceived as a Golden Age" (47 n. 1).
14 That is probably why in this case Virgil did not use mythical "explanations" founded on man's guilt, like Hesiod, who had made Zeus introduce difficulties in order to punish Prometheus' fraud (*Erga* ll. 42 ff.). Virgil rather appreciates the *artes* (an attitude not uncommon in antiquity: see Xenophanes fr. 18 D.K.). About this Virgilian passage see Gatz 162 ff. About the relation between this way of representing human evolution and the Lucretian conception of progress see La Penna 230; Wilkinson 78, 81 ff.; Barchiesi 144 ff.; Johnston, "Saturnia" 48, 70 ff.

15 About Jupiter's curiously providential intervention and the strange conception of such a theodicy, see La Penna 231 ff., 238 ff.
16 La Penna 234 ff. (see also 220 ff.), and Novara (760, 768 ff.), rightly emphasize the links of this passage with the Hesiodic description of the City of the Just (*Erga* ll. 225 ff.), rather than with the description of the *chrúseon ghénos*. Actually, the passage dealing with the City of the Just seems to have the function of showing the *possible* accomplishment of that positive model whose idealized picture represents the remote image of the Golden Age.
17 The same model is later on projected into the future, by the prediction referred to Augustus in *Aen.* 6.792–4: *aurea condet / saecula qui rursus Latio regnata per arua / Saturno quondam* . . . .
18 See Nilsson, *Geschichte* 1.511: "Kronos scheint im Kult keinen festen Platz zu haben, er ist ein Schatten . . . Er ist mythologisch, nicht kultisch."
19 Ancient authors were already aware of the diffusion of this cult: see Cic. *Nat. deor.* 3.17.44, and the passages quoted in the notes *ad loc.* by Pease 2.1061.
20 The identification of the Roman Saturn with the Greek Cronos was ancient and attested in literary texts since the very origins (Liu. Andr. frr. 2 and 14 Morel = 2 and 12 Büchner: see Thulin 219 ff.): cf. Wissowa 428 ff.; Leglay 466 ff., followed by Guittard, "Recherches" 44 ff., who considers the assimilation to Cronos as the last stage of the history of the aboriginal Saturn in Italy: "Cronos n'a jamais effacé Saturne à Rome, mais Saturne lui a plutôt emprunté les éléments qui lui manquaient." According to Guittard ("Recherches" 70 ff.), even the Golden Age theme is to be considered in relation with the hellenization of Roman religion. A summary of the various identifications of Cronos with foreign deities is given by Pohlenz 1998 ff.
21 Pohlenz (1986) supposed that Cronos (traces of whose cult seem to be very ancient) was "ein selbständiger Gott, der ursprünglich mit Zeus garnichts zu tun hat"; and, moreover, that his subsequent importance entirely depended on the story of his sovereignty (see also 1988 ff.). An unlikely interpretation of the opposition Cronos vs Zeus as irrationality vs rationality has been suggested by van der Valk.
22 See Pohlenz 2003 ff., about the link between Cronos and the Titans, and their common lot in Tartarus.
23 About the uncertain presence of this theme in Hesiod's *Erga* at ll. 173 a[*olim* 169]–e, see van der Valk's note (7 ff.); Gatz 31 n. 11, 46 n. 39, 182 ff.; West, *Works* 195 ff.
24 See West, *Theogony* 21 ff., about the cruelty features attributed to the deities corresponding to Cronos in Eastern myths.
25 About the origins of Saturn's cult and of the *Saturnalia* see Nilsson, "Saturnalia" 202; Wissowa 436; Leglay 467 ff. About the gladiatorial games consecrated to Saturn, see Wissowa 438 ff.; Leglay 462 ff. About martyrs sacrificed as "kings of Saturnalia," see Wissowa 440. For instances of human sacrifices related to Saturn see Ovid. *Fast.* 5.621 ff. (cf. Bömer 2.327 ff.); Dion. Hal.

1.38.2 ff.; Macrob. *Sat.* 1.7.31, 1.11.47 ff.
26 That is why *ho epì Krónou bíos* could become a sort of political topos (Aristot. *Ath. Pol.* 16.7 and the note *ad loc.* by Rhodes 217 ff.): see Schwabl, "Weltalter" 822 ff.
27 Brelich 89 puts forward an interesting hypothesis, according to which the *Saturnalia* "costituiscono un'espressione calendariale delle condizioni 'anteriori all'inizio.' " See Leglay 473 ff., about the relations between the feast and the Golden Age theme.
28 Another hint could be found at ll. 173 a–e, which are surely interpolated.
29 It is uncommon to find hints on this subject in ancient texts: see Cratin. fr. 176 Kassel-Austin (= Athen. 6.267 e). The Orphic texts are not more explicit: see fr. 139 Kern, from an Orphic theogony, quoted by Lactant. *Diu. inst.* 1.13.11 (to this theory is probably to be connected Serv. Dan. *Ad Verg. Ecl.* 4.10 = fr. 29 a Kern), and Gatz 52 ff.
30 This is not the only attested version. The fr. 140 and 141 Kern—to give just an example—deal with a cycle of *three* ages: the Golden one under Phanes's rule, the Silver one under Cronos and the *Titanicòn ghénos*, created by Zeus (Gatz 52 ff.). We may say that in ancient texts Cronos-Saturn's royal function is mostly referred to without further specification. Cronos' royal function is particularly emphasized by Vernant 27 ff. in a Dumézil-like perspective.
31 Hints about Cronos's rule are almost always vague and most of the time have apparently to be referred to the godly realm rather than to its actual effects on mankind. We could say that an explicit picture of the god's reign among men is established only from Virgil on.
32 This opposition becomes clearer in versions such as the Platonic one in the *Politicus* 271c ff. (Gatz 57 ff.; Vernant 23, 79). Similar considerations could be applied to Roman Saturn too: see Briquel 144 ff. (esp. 155 ff.).
33 The sovereign of remote times rules in a remote land too: the separation of places is used in place of the sequence of ages in order to outline an oppositional context. About the idealized description of blissful far-off peoples, as well as of remote paradises, see the texts collected and discussed by Lovejoy and Boas 287 ff.; Gernet 144 ff.; West, *Works* 193 ff.; Gelinne, 237 ff.
34 Saturn is enlisted among the kings of Laurentum, as father of Picus in Verg. *Aen.* 7.48 ff. (cf. 177 ff.); Ovid. *Met.* 14.320; Sil. It. 8.439 ff.: see Wissowa 434 ff.; Brelich 89 ff.; Guittard, "Recherches" 48 ff.; Johnston "Vergil's Conception" 57 ff.; Briquel 150 ff.
35 The ancient Latins are sometimes called *Saturni gens* (Verg. *Aen.* 7.202 ff.; Ovid. *Fast.* 1.235 ff.), and the *Saturnia regna* of old are often praised (Verg. *Ecl.* 4.6, *Aen.* 11.252; Calp. Sic. 1.63 ff.). For the name *Saturnia* attributed in various forms to Latium and / or Italy, see Varro *L. l.* 5.42; Verg. *Georg.* 2.173, *Aen.* 1.569 ff., 8.319 ff. (also Serv. Dan. *Ad Aen.* 8.328); Ovid. *Fast.* 5.625 ff. (Rome itself is referred to as *Saturnia* at 6.31); Fest. 430 L.; Colum. 1, praef. 20; Petron. 122, l. 156; Iustin. 43, 1, 3–5; Dion. Hal. 1.34.5; Sil. Ital.

1.70, 3.184, 13.63 and 17.380. The name was originally attributed to the *mons Capitolinus* (called *mons Saturnius*) according to a seemingly traditional story: see Varro *L. l.* 5.42: *Hunc antea montem Saturnium appellatum prodiderunt et ab eo late Saturniam terram, ut etiam Ennius appellat* . . . (cf. also Verg. *Aen.* 8.357 ff.; Fest. 430 L., Dion. Hal. 1.34.4, 2.1.4; Macrob. *Sat.* 1.7.27; Vib. Seq. *Geogr.* 157 Riese (303 Gelsomino); Solin. 1.12 (see Guittard, "Saturnia" 177 n. 3, 184. M. Wifstrand Schiebe (48 ff.) maintains that it was only after Virgil's *Aeneid* that the name *Saturnia* became "commonplace" as referring to Latium and to the *arx* that Saturn would have founded during his reign in Rome. According to M. Wifstrand Schiebe it was Virgil who transferred Saturn's mythical kingdom as well as the Golden Age to Latium, taking as a starting point the traditional data that connected Saturn to Italy. I must confess that I find this hardly convincing because the hypothesis is founded on too many *argumenta ex silentio*: much more interesting is Johnston's proposal to see Virgil as a sort of intermediary between the most ancient traditions about Saturn ("Vergil's Conception" 69).

36 Even Saturn's relation to Ops can be considered in this perspective: see Macrob. 1.10.19 ff. (cf. 1.7.24 ff.); Coarelli 373 ff.; Pouthier. The agricultural character of the Etruscan and of the Sabine deity is stressed by Guittard, "Recherches" 53 ff. (see also 65 ff.), and Leglay 453 ff. The ancient pseudoetymology that derived Saturn's name *a satu* is largely attested: see Varro *L. l.* 5.64; Fest. 202, 432 L., Macrob. *Sat.* 1.10.20.

37 The Euhemeristic version is widely exposed by Lactantius *Diu. inst.* 1.12–14 (esp. 1.14.1 ff.), who follows—as he himself states—Ennius' translation of Euhemerus' *Sacred History* (cf. also Min. Fel. *Oct.* 23.9 ff.). Probably too much importance is attributed to this story by Guittard, "Saturnia" 183: "le mythe d'une Saturnie proprement dite n'a pu se développer qu'après l'assimilation de Saturne à Kronos et comme une conséquence des théories évhéméristes." M. Wifstrand Schiebe, on the contrary, maintains that no legend about Saturn's kingship in Latium subsequent to his kingship among the gods was conceivable in Rome before the *Aeneid* (45).

38 Cultural ("agricultural") elements had already been inserted into Aratus' picture of the Golden Age (ll. 112 ff.): see La Penna 230 ff.; Wilkinson 77 ff.; Johnston "Vergil's Conception" 62 and "Vergil's Agricultural" 16 and 25 ff. See Lovejoy and Boas 36; Gatz 61 ff.; Schwabl, "Weltalter" 795 ff.

39 Probably the same story was already known to Ennius (see Lactant. *Diu. inst.* 1.14.10–12 = Enn., *Euhem.* fr. V V^2): Gatz 124 ff.; Johnston "Vergil's Conception" 63 ff. and "Vergil's Agricultural" 64 ff.

40 Klibansky, Panofsky and Saxl's statement that "the Roman Saturn was originally not ambivalent but definitely good" (135) seems to be exaggerated: cf. Briquel 155 ff. The separation between the two phases of Saturn's history is clear-cut in the Euhemeristic version: traces of it could be seen in Macrobius' distinction (*Sat.* 1.7.18) between an *arcana natura* and another one, *quae aut*

fabulis admixta disseritur aut a physicis in uulgus aperitur. Sometimes a sort of confusion between the two phases emerges: in Ovid. *Her.* 4.131 ff. the *rustica regna* are attributed to the most ancient period of Saturn's story (which apparently contradicts *Am.* 3.8, 35 ff.).

41 On the religious connection between the two figures see Guittard, "Recherches" 63 ff.
42 See Pucci's paper in this volume.
43 The authors who most decidedly stress Saturn's negative features are Serv. (esp. the so-called Serv. Danielinus) *Ad Aen.* 1.23, 3.29, 4.92 (cf. *Ad Aen.* 4.371 and ff.) and Lactantius, while relating Ennius' translation from Euhemerus (see *Diu. inst.* 1.13.2 = Enn. *Euhem.* fr. IX V^2: Saturn and Ops as eaters of human flesh). Cruelty features are also ascribed to Saturn by Myth. Vat. 3.1.1 and, ironically, by Lucian. *Sat.* 5 ff. Saturn's negative side is to be connected with the bad influence of his planet: see Thulin 219; Pohlenz 2011 ff.; Lovejoy and Boas 73 ff.; Wilkinson 83; Johnston, "Saturnia" 81, n. 28 (with bibliography); and, most of all, Klibansky, Panofsky and Saxl 126 ff. (esp. 136 ff.). Strongly negative features are attributed to the African and the Etruscan Saturn respectively by Leglay 460 ff. and Guittard, "Recherches" 50 ff. and 70 ff.
44 Leglay 475 ff. distinguishes the "original" characteristics of the indigenous, agricultural and chthonian Saturn from the acquired features that the deity would get because of his identification with Cronos. These features (among which the qualities connected with the Golden Age theme are to be listed) would make him a character whose name "ne fut plus associée qu'à un thème littéraire." I would think that the merger of Saturn and Cronos was more complex than that, though it did show a constant tendency to put the god's cruel features in the shadow, emphasizing, on the other hand, his beneficent qualities. According to Leglay 477, Saturn's mysterious and "unruly" characteristics had been preserved in the Hellenistic environment, where, around the middle of the second century B.C., the identification of the Carthaginian Ba'al Hammon with Saturn was probably realized.
45 I would agree with Briquel's statements (157), according to which the Greeks conceived of Cronos as a sort of decayed god, banished to Tartarus, who did not influence in any way the world ruled by his son: as far as Rome is concerned, though, "rien n'autorise à croire à un'opposition violente entre Jupiter et Saturne." Even if Saturn lost his sovereignty on the Capitole, even if Latium was not the *Saturnia tellus* of old any more, "rien ne permet de supposer une éviction violente." Both Jupiter and Saturn remained "present" to the Romans, as "Saturne collabore à sa manière à la bonne marche du monde sur lequel règne Jupiter" (see also Johnston, "Vergil's Conception" 58).
46 As far as the Roman religious conception is concerned, however, it is possible to single out Saturn's characteristics, clearly in contrast to Jupiter: Brelich (esp. 89); Guittard, "Recherches" 61 ff.; Pouthier 90 ff.; and Briquel 154 ff.,

about the relation between the cult areas of the two deities. M. Wifstrand Schiebe has tried to solve this ambiguity, maintaining that it was Virgil who, in the *Aeneid*, had transposed the Golden Age from the traditional "Cronian" mythological period to Jupiter's times; subsequent authors would have followed such a story, distorting it more and more, as they tried to "reconcile" it with the traditional tales (44).

47 Briquel 149 notes: "Saturne préside à un âge foncièrement irréductible au monde organisé que nous connaissons"; therefore, "Saturne apparaît comme le dieu du retour périodique à la situation préculturelle, par destruction de l'ordre établi"; he is the "dieu de l'état non ordonné, de l'indistinct, du stade initial de la nature."

48 We could consider Saturn's typical attribute, the scythe, as emblematic of his ambiguity: it is the farm implement and the weapon used to castrate Uranus at the same time (Hild 1084, 1086 and 1088; Wissowa 430 ff.; Leglay 455 ff.; Guittard, "Recherches" 67 ff.). In other words, we can see it as the *hárpen karcharódonta* of Hes., *Theog.* 175 and 179 ff. (see West, *Theogony* 217 ff.) on the one hand, and the *insigne agricolae* as referred to by Fest. 202 and 432 L. on the other (cf. Macrob. *Sat.* 1.7.24; see also 1.8.9 ff., with vague hints to the "dark times" of the god). Furthermore, see Varro apud Aug. *Ciu. D.* 7.19; Ovid. *Fast.* 1.234 (and Bömer 2.31); Plut. *Quaest. Rom.* 42 and Serv. *Ad Georg.* 2.406.

49 Costa 25 ff., maintains that, given the most ancient contradictory connotations of Saturn, it is no wonder that Fazio degli Uberti "dà un'immagine ambivalente di Saturno, additando in lui il padre snaturato ed al tempo stesso l'inventore dell'agricoltura, della moneta, della navigazione: in una parola, il saggio iniziatore della civiltà latina, identificata senz'altro con l'età dell'oro." Even elsewhere Fazio insists on Saturn's civilizing function (*Ditt.* 3.1.7 ff., 3.12.70 ff.).

50 This theme already had authoritative precedents, the most famous of which is certainly Verg. *Aen.* 8.319 ff.: authors like Fazio carried it to extremes.

WORKS CITED

Avalle, D'Arco S. "L'età dell'oro nella 'Commedia' di Dante." *Letture classensi* 4 (1973): 127–143. Rpt. *Modelli semiologici nella Commedia di Dante*. Milano: Bompiani, 1975. 77–95.
Baldry, H.C. "Who Invented the Golden Age?" *Classical Quarterly* n.s. 2 (1952): 83–92.
Brelich, A. "I primi re latini." *Tre variazioni romane sul tema delle origini*. 2nd ed. Roma: Edizioni dell'Ateneo, 1976. 57–103.
Briquel, D."Jupiter, Saturne et le Capitole. Essai de comparaison indo-européenne." *Revue de l'Histoire des Religions* 198 (1981): 131–62.
Cicero, Marcus Tulius. *De natura deorum libri III*. Ed. A.S. Pease. Cambridge: Harvard UP, 1958 (=Darmstadt: Wissenschaftliche Buchgesellschaft, 1968).

Coarelli, F. "Ara Saturni, Mundus, Senaculum. La parte occidentale del Foro in età arcaica." *Dialoghi di archeologia* 9–10 (1976–77): 346–377.
Cocchiara, G. *Il mondo alla rovescia*. Torino: Boringhieri, 1981.
Costa, G. *La leggenda dei secoli d'oro nella letteratura italiana*. Bari: Laterza, 1972.
Dionysius Halicarnassus, *Antiquitatum Romanarum quae supersunt*. Ed. K. Jacoby. Lipsiae: Teubner, 1885–1925 (=Stuttgart 1967).
Ennianae poesis reliquiae. Ed. J. Valhen. 2nd. ed. Leipzig: Teubner, 1903. Rpt. Amsterdam: A.M. Hakkert, 1963.
Gatz, B. *Weltalter, goldene Zeit und sinnverwandte Vorstellungen*. Hildesheim: Olms, 1967.
Gelinne, M. "Les Champs Élysées et les îles des Bienheureux chez Homère, Hésiode et Pindare. Essai de mise au point." *Les Études Classiques* 56 (1988): 225–240.
Gernet, L. "La cité future et le pays des morts." *Revue des Études Grecques* 46 (1933): 293–310. Rpt. *Anthropologie de la Grèce antique*. Paris: Maspero, 1966. 139–153.
Guittard, Ch. "Recherches sur la nature de Saturne des origines à la réforme de 217 avant J. C." *Recherches sur les religions de l'Italie antique*. Ed. R. Bloch. Genève: Droz, 1976. 43–71.
——————. "Saturnia terra: mythe et réalité." *Caesarodunum* XV bis (*Colloque "Histoire et historiographie*. 8–9 Dec. 1978). 1980. 177–186.
Hesiod. *Theogony*. Ed. M.L. West. Oxford: Clarendon, 1966.
——————. *Works and Days*. Ed. M.L. West. Oxford: Clarendon, 1978.
Hild, J.-A. "Saturnus." *Dictionnaire des Antiquités grecques et romaines*. Ed. Ch. Daremberg and E. Saglio. Vol. 4.2. Paris: Hachette, 1911.
Johnston, P.A. "Vergil's Conception of Saturnus." *California Studies in Classical Antiquity* 10 (1977): 57–70.
——————. *Vergil's Agricultural Golden Age. A Study of the Georgics*. Leiden: Brill, 1980.
Kenner, H. *Das Phänomen der verkehrten Welt in der Griechisch-Römischen Antike*. Klagenfurt: Geschichtsverein für Kärnten, 1970.
Kirk, G.S. *Myth. Its Meaning and Functions in Ancient and Other Cultures*. Cambridge: Cambridge UP, 1970.
Klibansky, R., E. Panofsky, and F. Saxl. *Saturn and Melancholy. Studies in the History of Natural Philosophy, Religion, and Art*. London: Nelson, 1964.
Lactantius, Lucius Caecilius Firmianus. *Divinae institutiones*. Paris: Editions du Cerf, 1986.
La Penna, A. "Esiodo nella cultura e nella poesia di Virgilio." *Hésiode et son influence*. Fond. Hardt. *Entr. sur l'Antiquité class.* 7. Genève (1962): 231-70. Rpt. *Esiodo. Letture critiche*. Ed. G. Arrighetti. Milano: Mursia, 1975. 214–41.
Leglay, M. *Saturne Africain. Histoire*. Paris: de Boccard, 1966.

Lovejoy, A.O. and G. Boas. *Primitivism and Related Ideas in Antiquity*. Baltimore: Johns Hopkins UP, 1935 (=New York: Octagon Books, 1965)

Macrobius, Ambrosius A.T. *Saturnalia*. Ed. J.A. Willis. Leipzig: Teubner, 1970.

Nilsson, M.P. "Saturnalia." *Realencylopädie der classischen Altertumswissenschaft*. Ed. A. Pauly and G. Wissowa. Vol. 2 A 1. München: Druckenmüller, 1921. 201–11.

——————. *Geschichte der griechischen Religion*. 3rd ed. München: Beck, 1967.

Novara, A. *Les idées romaines sur le progrès d'après les écrivains de la République. Essai sur le sens latin du progrès*. Paris: "Les Belles Lettres," 1982.

Ovidius, P. Naso. *Amores*. Ed. E.J. Kenney. Oxford: Clarendon, 1961. Rpt. 1984.

——————. *Héroides*. Ed. H. Bornecque. Trans. M. Prévost. 2nd ed. Paris: "Les Belles Lettres," 1961.

——————. *Die Fasten*. Ed. and trans. F. Bömer. Heidelberg: Winter, 1957–58.

——————. *Metamorphoses*. Ed. W.S. Anderson. Leipzig: Teubner, 1977.

——————. *Metamorphosen*. Ed. and trans. F. Bömer. Vol. 1. Heidelberg: Winter, 1969.

Pohlenz, M. "Kronos." *Realencyclopädie der classischen Altertumswissenschaft*. Vol. 9.2. Stuttgart: Druckenmüller, 1922. 1982–2018.

Pouthier, P. *Ops et la conception de l'abondance dans la religion romaine jusqu'à la mort d'Auguste*. Paris: de Boccard, 1981.

Rhodes, P. J. *A Commentary on the Aristotelian "Athenaion Politeia."* Oxford: Clarendon, 1981.

Schwabl, H. "Zum Mythos der Zeitalter in Ovids Metamorphosen." *Latinität und alte Kirche. Festschrift für R. Hanslik zum 70 Geburtstag*. Ed. H. Bannert and J. Divjak. Wien: Böhlau, 1977. 275–85.

——————. "Weltalter." *Realencycoplädie der classischen Altertumswissenschaft*. Suppl. XV. München: Druckenmüller, 1978. 783–850.

Servius. *Servii grammatici quae feruntur in Vergilii carmina commentarii*. Ed. G. Thilo and H. Hagen. Leipzig: Teubner, 1881–89.

Taylor, M.E. "Primitivism in Virgil." *American Journal of Philology* 76 (1955): 261–278.

Thulin, C.O. "Saturnus." *Realencyclopädie der classischen Altertumswissenschaft*. Vol. 2 A 1. München: Druckenmüller, 1921. 218–223.

Tibullus, Albius. *The Elegies*. Ed. K.F. Smith. New York: American Book Company, 1913 (=Darmstadt: Wissenschaftliche Buchgesellschaft, 1971).

Uberti, Fazio degli. *Il Dittamondo e le rime*. Bari: Laterza, 1952.

Valk, M. van der. "On the God Cronus." *Greek Roman and Byzantine Studies* 26.1 (1985): 5–11.

Varro, Marcus Terentius. *De lingua latina quae supersunt*. Ed. G. Goetz and F. Schoell. Leipzig: Teubner, 1929. Rpt. Amsterdam: A.M. Hakkert, 1964.

Vergilius, Publius Maro. *Georgiche*. Ed., trans., and notes by A. Barchiesi, Introd. by G. B. Conte. Milano: Mondadori, 1980.

———. *Opera*. Ed. R.A.B. Mynors. Oxford: Clarendon, 1977.

Vernant, J. P. *Mythe et pensée chez les Grecs. Études de psychologie historique*. 3rd ed. Paris: La Découverte, 1985.

Weinrich, H. *Linguistik der Lüge*. 5th ed. Heidelberg: Lambert Schneider, 1974.

Wifstrand Schiebe, M. "The Saturn of the *Aeneid*. Tradition or Innovation?" *Vergilius* 32 (1986): 43–60.

Wilkinson, L. P. "Virgil's Theodicy." *Classical Quarterly* 13 (1963): 75–84.

Wissowa, G. "Saturnus." *Lexikon der griechischen und römischen Mythologie*. Ed. W.H. Roscher. Leipzig: Teubner, 1909–15 (Hildesheim: Olms, 1965). 427–44.

Xenophanes. *I frammenti: con testo greco a fronte*. Milano: Marcos y Marcos, 1985.

Maurizio Bettini

Iacta alea est: Saturn and the *Saturnalia*

The scene opens and in the middle of the stage lies a sad emperor: it is Caligula. Hidden in his villa on Alba, far from his fellow-citizens' conversation, he is trying to overcome the deep dejection in which his sister Drusilla's death has plunged him. She was the most beloved of his sisters (not exactly loved as a sister, according to Suetonius' insinuations: *Cal.* 24) and Caligula, who has grown a beard and hair, is devastated: he is playing dice. "What a disgrace!" exclaims Seneca (*Ad Pol.* 17.4), who, by the way, hated him, "what a disgrace for the empire! a Roman Prince, in mourning for his sister, who consoles himself playing dice!"

To tell the truth, we are less interested than Seneca in the prince's dignity. Maybe we are so used to Suetonius' *Vitae* and to Tacitus' *Annales* that playing dice in a moment of mourning does not seem to us one of the worst crimes committed by a Roman emperor. Nevertheless, it is odd to see a man struck by death and destiny devoting himself to the dice game. The dice represent something happy and gay. The dice (to get nearer to our subject) are the very symbol of the happiest of all the feasts: the *Saturnalia*. To denote this festal period the poet Martial employs a meaningful periphrasis (2.3). These are the days on which "regnator . . . imperat fritillus," that is to say, the days in which the role of the king is played by that little tower-shaped container (the Latin *fritillus*) they used to throw the dice from. Besides, in the calendar of the year 354 B.C. (the so-called calendar of Philocalos)[1] in which each month is represented by a symbolical scene, December is still depicted as a man playing dice. So let our opening scene close while Caligula continues throwing his enigmatic dice. We shall return to him in a moment. Now, let a second, happier scene open.

It is the evening of December the 17th. The festival has just started; in the streets of Rome companies of men wearing the *pileus* (the "liberty-cap": see Sen. *Ep.* 18.3; Mart. 11.6), are crying out *Io Saturnalia*! the cry that represents the symbol and the signal of this feast (Liv. 22.1; Mart. 11.2; Macr. *Sat.* 1.10.18; Dio Cass. 60.19.3).[2] After a while the wine will start having its effect (Sen. *Ep.* 18.4; Stat. *Sil.* 1.6) — but above all everybody is playing dice (Suet. *Aug.* 71; Mart. 4.14, 11.7, 14.1; Lucian. *Sat.* 2 ff.). During the *Saturnalia*, in fact, the *lex alearia* (the ban on gambling in Rome: see Plaut. *Mil.* 164; Ov. *Tri.* 2.1.472)[3] is lifted, and the *aedilis* cannot punish the players. As Martial says (4.14), *December . . . incertis sonat hinc et hinc fritillis* [in December one hears everywhere the noise of the little dicing boxes]. It is the preoccupation of the season, the very essence of the festival.

But there is an interesting point worth mentioning. During the *Saturnalia* the Romans do not play for money, precious objects or goods, but for innocent nuts (Mart. 4.66, 5.30, 13.1, 14.1; Lucian. *Sat.* 8.18).[4] Lucianus (*Sat.* 8) even amuses himself by inventing a mythical reason for this custom. When asked by the priest, his Saturn explains that this is what people did during the mythical golden age: they played dice, of course, but nuts were the heaviest stake, so that nobody would suffer as a result of losses. Besides, the priest comments, that was the way it should be. In that period men themselves were made of gold: what else could they have staked that was more precious?

Therefore it is not the ambiguous and perverse pleasure caused by one's winning (or by someone else's loss) that pushes the gamblers of the *Saturnalia* to compete against each other. In contrast, many times during the course of history the innocent tinkling of the dice has decided not only the ruin, but also the slavery or the death of the loser. Tacitus (*Germ.* 24) relates that the old Germans "play dice even when they are not drunk, and as if it were a serious occupation: which you will certainly find surprising. And so reckless is their desire to win and lose that, when they have lost everything else, they stake themselves and their own liberty. The loser voluntarily submits to slavery. . . . Such is the obstinacy they show in their perversion: but they call this 'keeping one's faith'. . . ." As a matter of fact, the ethnologist would not hesitate in classing such a form of "keeping one's faith" among the numberless manifestations of that deep cultural pattern whose technical name is "potlach" (Mauss): a system of reciprocal offerings according to which two people try to outbid each other in a competition that will unavoidably lead to the ruin of one of the two competitors, compelled "to keep his faith" to this wicked race. In the opinion of Tacitus, who did not know the culture of "potlach," such a stubborn determinedness *in re prava* was only a blamable madness: but the Germans were perfectly aware of their own culture when they defined their behaviour in terms of "faith." The seriousness with which the old Germans played dice was the manifestation of an abstract form, not of a specific substance: every contract calls for faithfulness — the more ruinous "keeping one's faith" is, the more personal prestige and honour are involved.

Although shorter and less refined, and definitely lacking in the solemn seriousness of the old Germans, the same ceremony was to take place many centuries later on the "ample piazza before the sea" of which the city of Leghorn was so proud. John Evelyn, in the year 1644, tells us that there was a tent "where any idle fellow might stake his liberty against a few crowns, at dice, or other hazard: and, if he lost, he was immediately chained and led to the galleys, where he was to serve a term of years, but from whence they seldom returned . . . " (57). But none of this could happen at the *Saturnalia*, where they played only for nuts. Well, it was the sheer pleasure of playing (but what is the true meaning of the expression "the pleasure of playing"?), it was only the running of the dice on the *tabula lusoria* (the "board") that moved the hands of the *aleatores* ("the gamblers") of the Roman December. The perverse spiral of the "potlach," the romantic madness of the "idle fellows" who crowded old Leghorn, or more simply the gambler's fever described by Dostoevskij from his own experience, had no meaning in the *Saturnalia* dicing. For the same reason, not even the bold interpretation of gambling given by Freud (399 ff.) could help us to understand the real meaning of the December dice. As we know, Freud supposed that in the swift movement of "hands" in the game, in the irresistible temptation, in the pleasure stunning the consciousness that "we are ruining ourselves," one could find traces of old puberal auto-erotic practices: in other words, that childish and dangerous "play" for which the enjoyment of risk would later substitute. Although meaningful, Freud's interpretation was of course greatly influenced by the educational models and bourgeois taboos of his contemporaries.

Thus, on one side we have a mad and desperate prince in full mourning but devoted to dicing: on the other side, a crowd of happy and drunk Romans driving their *fritilli* mad but, note, only in order to exchange little heaps of nuts. What is happening? Well, what was the true "meaning" of this dicing game?

Let us go on. The scene is still the same, with the Romans at the festival of the *Saturnalia*. As a matter of fact, they are not playing with dice only: the whole feast looks like a real *game* played by the whole city. A total, multiple game, ruled by a structural law whose features are as homogenous as they are strong. For in a game, as everybody knows, the *rule* is the main thing: and the *Saturnalia* have one. Let us try to outline a first definition of this rule and call it "the rule of destiny": or rather, "the rule of anti-destiny"—at the *Saturnalia* people pretend that the destiny, the fortune, the personal "lot" of goods and social standing of each and every person do not exist and do not matter. Or rather, they "play" a game in which this happens. But let us see more precisely how this rule acts in the "game" of the *Saturnalia*.

If there is one thing that distinguishes the Romans as a nation, it is their use of the *toga*: that white drape that the citizens of any social condition by day wrapped around their body (according to some complicated technical rules) and by night, at least in ancient times, used as a blanket for their bed (Varro, *De vita pop. Rom.* fr. 44 Riposati). In order to define the Roman nation, the Jupiter of the *Aeneis* (1.282) employs directly the following periphrasis: *Romanos, rerum dominos, gentemque togatam* [the Romans, the owners of the world, people wearing the *toga*].[5] But during the *Saturnalia* the *gens togata* willingly gave up the national dress to wear the *synthesis*: a coloured cloth they used to wear when they went to a banquet (Sen. *Ep.* 18.2; Mart. 6.24).[6] Seneca was shocked by this (*Ep.* 18.2). "What has become of Rome?" he exclaimed. At the *Saturnalia*, he said, we take off our *toga*: so that "what we used to do in case of public misfortune [the reason for taking off the *toga* was to put on mourning dress], we now do merely to enjoy ourselves. . . ." So, on the occasion of the *Saturnalia* it is as if the *cives Romani* in some way gave up their prerogatives. Who really are the Romans at the *Saturnalia*? They are no longer the *gens togata* with which the streets of Rome are peopled in everyday life. They are simply a group of people wearing clothes associated with pleasure and happiness. We can see the reason why Seneca was so scandalized. The Roman citizens left the visible signs of their condition at home, preferring other ostentations.

But this is not all. Let us see now the most characteristic feature of this festival, its oddest prerogative. During the *Saturnalia* any distinction between freemen and slaves is abolished, and the slaves are treated by their masters as if they were equal to them. According to the *libertas Decembris*, the December liberty, as they called it (Hor. *Sat.* 2.7.4; Plut. *Sulla* 18; Lucian. *Sat.* 5; 7; 13), the masters agree also to hear unpleasant truths from their slaves and allow them even to mimic patricians during the feast (Dio Cass. 60.19.3). Furthermore, the banquets are willingly offered by the masters of the slaves: and it may even happen that the masters wait at table, so that roles are completely reversed (Acc. *Ann.* fr. inc. 3 Morel; Iust. 43.1; Sen. *Ep.* 47.14; Lucian. *Sat.* 17; Macr. *Sat.*

1.12). Undoubtedly, the reversal is macroscopic. But if we consider the complex rules of etiquette according to which the places at the table were allocated to each guest in the Roman banquet, another characteristic (less visible than the former ones) will strike the observer's attention: at the banquet the slaves sit in no particular order with their masters (Iust. 43.1); therefore every prerogative or priority is abolished. In the eyes of a free and rich Roman, the banquet at which he was seated during the festival must have seemed very odd.

The masters are no longer masters, the slaves are no longer slaves: it is as if they met half way, on a ground that neutralizes any distinction of roles and social classes. Besides, as we have seen before, in those days the Roman citizens take off the *toga* to put on another dress. Furthermore, in those days people go around wearing the *pileus*, the heavy woollen cap worn in everyday life, by the *liberti*, the slaves who have been set free: everybody wears the *pileus*, masters and slaves—even the emperor Domitianus, the *noster Iuppiter* of poor Martial, wears one (Mart. 14.1). The symbolic meaning could not be more evident. Freemen and slaves tend to get nearer and to merge: and in order to do so they choose to take on the model of the emancipated slave, the social group that lies between the two. The *turba pilleata* invades Rome, the woollen cap triumphs over the social hierarchies.

All that, they say, is thanks to Saturn, the god whose feast is being celebrated. When he reigned all men were perfectly equal, there was no social distinction between the rich and poor, between slaves and their masters (Macr. *Sat.* 1.7.26; Iust. 43.1; Serv. *Aen.* 8.319). Therefore, behind the *Saturnalia* model lies a mythical pattern that every year, at the end of December, surfaces from the festival's depths. Saturn's power calls for the abolition of social hierarchies. Destiny—that more or less equitable *Sors* that wanted some men to be free and other slaves—no longer carries weight: December and the *Saturnalia* have cancelled its effects.

The same deep rule—"anti-destiny," as we called it, the cancelling of the individual *sors*—is able to explain, in my opinion, another typical custom of this festival: the exchange of gifts. Everybody gives and receives, poor and rich alike (Plin. *Ep.* 4.9; Mart. 5.18; 8.41). But here again it is our impression that a mythical pattern, the omnipresent projection of Saturn and the golden age, is called upon to play its role. They say that in that wonderful period there was no such thing as divided property, everything was in common (Verg. *Georg.* 1.126 ff.; Ov. *Am.* 3.8.42). It is therefore improbable that such an increase in mutual reciprocity—the mutual distribution of goods among the people taking part in the festival — should have been unrelated to the mythical model of the golden age when everything belonged to everybody and everything was divided and exchanged by everybody. Even the "destiny" of the goods wobbles dangerously — both dangerously and symbolically, as one might have expected in economic matters. People are warned, in some way, that what they have is not to be possessed but to be given, property is not something fixed that belongs to us but something that circulates. Your *sors* — in the double meaning of "goods" on the one hand and of the "destiny" that allotted these goods on the other[7] — must be divided and redistributed: remember how things were at the height of the golden age, when mankind was happy and peaceful.

Such a troubled and reversed society also had its magistrates: but here again the rule according to which privileges are abolished (the game of "anti-destiny") celebrates its triumph. In the Roman houses, in fact, the slaves held public offices and issued edicts so that, as Seneca says (*Ep.* 47.14), during the *Saturnalia* the *pusilla domus* (the "little house") looked more like a *res publica*. One cannot help but notice, by the way, how strictly related Plautus comedy is to the world of the *Saturnalia*. On his magical stage, very often Plautus' slave poses as a magistrate: he issues edicts, threatens punishment or sanctions, as his slave-fellows must have done — in those fatal days of the *libertas Decembris* — at the homes of patricians. But we have elsewhere had the opportunity of emphasizing the relationships between the world of comedy and the world of the Carnival and *Saturnalia*: here and there happy disorder and comic reversal celebrate their ephemeral triumph over everyday order (Bettini).

So the lowest of the low, the slaves, took on the role and the tone of the magistrates. Not even the *honores* — such a delicate and touchy substance of social life — are immune from the contagion of the game of the *Saturnalia*. These offices formerly assigned according to aristocratic birth and descent, acquired wealth, and individual prestige, are now freely allotted to the lowest among men! Once more, they play the game of destiny: during the *Saturnalia*, the Roman people pretend that individual destiny does not exist — or rather, they "play" a game with their destiny.

The world of the *Saturnalia* was ruled not only by public magistrates (or rather slave-magistrates), but even by a king. Although this king was drawn by dice (Lucian. *Sat.* 4),[8] he had a power that was both funny and absolute: he could order a man to dance naked, another to pick up the flute-girl and carry her three time around the house, another to shout out something disgraceful about himself, and so on. A king just for fun, of course, whose royal destiny was decided by sheer luck, by a lucky cast.[9] It was as if everybody said that anybody could become a king—it was easy, you only had to be lucky when you threw the dice! Hence, a king who received his royal power merely by throwing dice. This is an important detail, worth mentioning because it leads us back to the subject we started from: the *regnator fritillus* of the *Saturnalia*, the current craze for the game that, accompanied by the king of the festival, is finally forced to disclose the whole significance of its role. The dice are the very symbol of this festival, as depicted in the calendar of Philocalos.

The fact of the matter is, the theme of the lot, that is, the "game of chance," appears everywhere in Saturn's festival. In the *Saturnalia* by Macrobius (1.7.2) the learned Praetextatus, exhorted by the guests to explain the origin of the *Saturnalia*, relates that Saturn came to Italy with a fleet, and Ianus who ruled the country, received him as a guest. The grateful Saturn taught him the practice of farming, and Ianus not only wanted him to share his reign, but decided also to show his own gratitude for the future. He had coins made to express his gratitude: "since Saturn had come by sea, he had the effigy of his head engraved on one side of the coin, and a ship on the other. That such was the way the coin had been struck can be deduced from the game children play when they throw the coins in the air and shout "head or ship": so the game witnesses the ancient tradition." In other words, by playing "head or ship" an ancient memory of Saturn was restored—if we admit that Praetextatus was not exaggerating with his admirable scholarship! But if we believe him, the result is that the *alea* of the game and the old divinity of the golden age were strictly linked just like the two faces of one coin: thus we can rightly use this metaphor.

However, the behaviour of the emperor Augustus (fortunately related by Suetonius) confirms the importance of the role played by the lot, the "game of chance," during the festival of the *Saturnalia*. Not only did he casually distribute precious or worthless objects with obscure and ambiguous writings to the guests (we are reminded of the Zodiac plate in Trimalchion's dinner: Suet. *Aug.* 73; Petr. *Sat.* 46.7; M. Grondona 94); but during the banquet, he "also used to sell lotteries with which were drawn things of very different value, or paintings facing the wall: in order to disappoint or to fulfil the buyer's hopes with the incertitude of the lot. The lottery was sold by auction, not to each guest but to each bed, so that the win or the loss was shared by more persons." Here again the lot and the "game of chance" play the main role. The buyer does not know if he will win a precious object or a worthless knick-knack—he does not know if the picture facing the wall is from the hand of a famous artist or is only a useless daub. Besides, the lotteries are sold to groups of three persons (the number a tricliniar bed contained), so that the win or the loss is doubly due to chance: it depends not only on the draw but also on the bed you belong to. So the game plays the role of master in Augustus' banquet too.

Thus the world of the *Saturnalia* is a world marked by the uncertainty, or rather by the reversibility, of the lot. The Roman citizens are no longer Roman citizens, the slaves are no longer slaves, the masters are no longer masters, property is changed into gifts, slaves act as magistrates, the king is drawn by dice, the *alea*, the game of chance, the lottery hovers everywhere. Such is the context in which we have to place the *regnator fritillus* of the *Saturnalia*, the almighty dice game. As a matter of fact, such a triumphant fad reflects, in its clearest and most perfect form, the main rule of the *Saturnalia*: the game of destiny and of its reversibility, that is to say the firm, though ephemeral, belief that man's fate is not immutable but can be changed—that we can re-live the golden age, when everybody was equal and free. Therefore people play at dice for hours on end: and they play not to win money, not to spoil and destroy the partner, but only to exchange little heaps of nuts—people play for the pleasure of seeing a different combination of numbers forming on the *tabula lusoria*; they play to see their own and their opponent's lot changing with marvellous inconstancy, according to chance; they play to exchange the *alternae vices* (as Ausonius called them: *Comm. prof. Burdig* 1.27), the "alternate turns" of winning and losing, to see their own fortune change or remain at each hand. At the *Saturnalia* everything is under discussion, like a cast of dice.

A farther reflection is in order here. The *Saturnalia* are therefore a game, a game ruled by a fixed rule. Like every game, it lasts a definite period of time, after which it is agreed that the game is over: the game is played by people who are aware of doing something different from everyday life and of living with joy and tension. These are exactly the features of the game as described by Johan Huizinga in his famous book, *Homo ludens*. Well, if it is a game we are also likely to meet people who do not want to take part in the game, reluctant people normally referred to as "spoil sports." And we could decidedly not exclude the fact that Seneca and Lucilius had a tendency to be "spoil sports" at the *Saturnalia*. Seneca who was scandalized by the Romans abandoning their *toga*, Seneca who, "knowing Lucilius" (as he himself says), is sure that his friend would prefer to act as an arbitrator rather than join the *turba pilleata* by which the city was invaded; Seneca who finally resolves to participate, because it would not be good to forbear completely from the feast, but intends to do so with many reservations: the wise man, he says, will do what the other people do but not in the same manner (*Ep.* 18.3 ff.). Seneca is reluctant to accept the rule of the game: he does not trust the "rule" of the *Saturnalia*. But towards the game's rules, as Valéry (quoted by Huizinga) knew well, no scepticism is allowed: otherwise playing the game becomes impossible.

But let us go back to our main subject: the *alea*. We have said before that the *Saturnalia* does reflect, in its most perfect and pure form, the "game of destiny." But are we sure that the "dice" and "destiny" are so closely related? We think they are. The dice simulate and represent destiny. Terentius (*Ad.* 739 ff.)[10] says that man's life "is like dicing (*tesserae*): if you throw them and they don't fall (*cadit*) the way you want them to, you have to use your skill to correct what destiny has caused. . . ." So life is a dice game, the lot and destiny rule it according to the casts of *tesserae* — this is somewhat modified by hope in the *ars*, the skill of the player: an optimistic hope leaving the door open for men to act as they like. Although this metaphor is among the most common ones, it is also one of the deepest. Plautus, in his *Rudens* (359 ff.), employs a very significant image in this regard. The slave Trachalio wants to describe the happy outcome the lot has assigned to the vicissitudes of the two girls abducted by the bad pander, Labrax. He had dragged them onto a boat to take them to Sicily and prevent them from being rescued, but they were shipwrecked at sea and now the girls have returned to dry land: they are close to being freed. Trachalio says: "O beloved Neptune, bless you! There is no dice-player better than you. You really made a good cast and spoilt that perjurer. . . ." Destiny struck Labrax and favoured the girls: the sea made a good cast.

Also Lucanus' Caesar gives us a good example. Before the battle of Dyrrachium he could have seized the Greek cities without resistance, but the general disdained such a secure victory. Seized by the love of risk, he wants to enjoy the fatal pleasure of the uncertain lot, by which his own head or his adversary's will be sunk: and *placet alea fati*, Lucanus says, "he prefers destiny's cast of dice" (*Phars.* 6.7). It is difficult, now, not to remember the famous, nay proverbial phrase Caesar is thought to have pronounced when crossing the Rubicon. When the general reached the river (Suet. *Caes.* 31), he stopped a while, meditating on the huge and dreadful enterprise he was about to undertake. Perhaps he was seized by doubt, because he turned towards those around him and said: "we could still turn back. . . ." Then, they say, a vision appeared to him. A man of wonderful size and beauty was seen, sitting nearby and playing the flute.

Many people crowded around to listen to him, shepherds and soldiers, among whom were some buglers. But the man seized the trumpet from one of them and threw himself into the river, playing the battle signal with extraordinary strength. Then he walked towards the other bank. Caesar's mind was made up in a moment: "let's go" he said: *iacta alea est*. . . . A single "cast" marked the destiny of Caesar and that of Rome: here is the hazard, the challenge to the lot. Now they only had to wait for the adversary's cast on the other side of the river. Who would win the game?

A second digression may be offered here. In a similar situation the king of the Heruli — who as a German took the dice very seriously — did not just pronounce a proverbial phrase about dice: he did more. Paulus Diaconus (*Hist. Lang.* 1.20) relates that he was really playing dice while his own people were fighting against the Longobards. This is the same occupation to which the companions of Theodoric, at Quierzy, were devoted in the tent of the king (*Fredegari Chronic.* 4.27). Those Germans were really playing the *alea belli*, the "dicing of the war," as Livius often says (31.35.1; 37.36.9; 42.59.10): but without a metaphor, now.

But these are not only metaphors or proverbial phrases; something more real is involved. The dice *are* the lot, they *are* destiny also because through them the ancient world directly questioned the fates. Among the several ways of divination practised in the Greek and Roman culture, indeed, a pre-eminent place was given to the *kybomantéia*, divination through the dice: as well as to divination through the astragals, a special type of dice with four faces (Halliday 209 ff.; Pease 122). The dice were cast, and their combination acted as a response and a prophecy. The god, "speaking" the language of the cast of the dice, disclosed man's destiny: their fall and their disposition revealed the lot of the applicant. Ancient man was used to linking "dice" and "destiny" together, to feeling that destiny expressed itself through them.

At last, the language itself reveals how deep is the tie with which the notion of "dice" and the notion of "destiny" are joined to each other. The metaphor has become word: both meanings have merged in a mixed expression that can indicate both of them at the same time, because the die, you know, "falls down." This is the crucial and conclusive moment of the game, the moment all the players are anxiously waiting for, the final step by which the win or the loss, fortune or misfortune — with the lofty indifference of the cube that rolls and stops — is decided. *Iudice fortuna cadat alea*, says Petronius (122, v. 174), "let the die fall down in the judgment of fortune." Besides, *cadere*, "to fall down," is the specific verb used to indicate this moment of truth when the die marks the event without appeal.[11] But in Latin such a linguistic use appears very close to the word indicating "chance," "fate": the word *casus*, meaning the "fall" and the "casual happening" of events. The "falling down" of the dice and the "casual happening" that marks man's life seem to have merged in a word that can express both meanings at the same time. The metaphors of Plautus and Terentius, the *alea* thrown by Caesar, the divinatory practice of the *kybomantéia* merge in a word that is both simple and anxiously enigmatic: the *casus*.

Now the scene we opened is closing, the *Saturnalia* are over and the dice-player, as Martial says (5.84), "begs the aedile's pardon:" the liberty of December does not protect him any more from the rigour of the *lex alearia*. After a while a new year will begin and everything will be as before. The dice will be forbidden, the citizens will put on their *togae* again, the slaves will be slaves and the masters will be masters. . . . But at the end of the old year the city of Rome has played the "game of destiny" thanks to the December liberty. While the old year flowed into the new one and created a sort of abuse in real time, a fleeting passage, everybody wanted to flatter himself that personal destiny was not fixed and everything could be thrown time and again, as in the changing turns of dicing. Antiphanes, the Greek author of comedies, said (fr. B 52 Demianczuk): "life cannot be cast again, like a draught." During the *Saturnalia* Roman people dreamed exactly the opposite.

But we were forgetting Caligula — the sad emperor, in full mourning, who played dice hoping to divert his thoughts from the death of his beloved, possibly too beloved sister. Therefore, let the scene open again, finally, on the rich villa on Alba. Perhaps Seneca, at least on this occasion, had been too severe toward Caligula. We cannot exclude the possibility that the emperor, cruelly confronted with fate's ineluctability, threw his dice in order to flatter himself that the lots of men might be "thrown" and changed, as in the game of dicing. Seized by a destiny more powerful than himself, the *princeps*, Caligula might have looked for relief in the very metaphor of changing destiny, as in each hand of the game.

University of Siena

NOTES

1 Cf. Stern. The iconographies illustrating the calendar have been handed down to us through copies of the XIV and XVII centuries, in their turn copies of a IX century copy.

2 On the festival of *Saturnalia* in Rome, see Nilsson 2 A 1: 201 ff.; F. Bömer 2:425 ff.
3 Cf. G. Humbert 1.179 ff. On the lifting of the ban during the *Saturnalia*, cf. Mart. 4.14.7; 5.84.5 ff.; 14.1.3; Aul. Gell. *Noct. att.* 18.13.1. On the play of dicing in Rome, see L. Becq de Fouquetières 302 ff.; for some interesting observations (particularly from the iconographical point of view). see Beschi.
4 See also the interesting fragment of Kratinos 165 Koch = 176 Kassel-Austin.
5 Cf. also Hor. *Carm.* 3.5.10 ff.; Flor. 2.21.3; Plin. *Ep.* 4.11.3.
6 On the *synthesis* Mart. 5./9.14; Suet. *Nero* 51. Cf. Saglio, in Daremberg-Saglio, 4.2.158 ff.
7 Paul.-Fest. 380 L: *sors et patrimonium significat*; compare also the double meaning of the word *fortuna*.
8 Cf. the *Saturnalicius princeps* (the emperor Claudius) in Sen. *Apok.* 8.21 (*contra* Brugnoli): and above all Tac. *Ann.* 13.15: *festis Saturno diebus inter alia aequalium ludicra regnum lusu sortientium evenerat ea sors Neroni*.
9 *Iactus basilicus* ("king's cast") is called a good cast of *tali* in Plaut. *Curc.* 359 (see Lafaye 5:28 ff.).
10 Cf. Plato *Resp.* 604 c; Eur. *Suppl.* 330; Soph. fr. 809 Nauck 2; Alexis fr. 310 Kock.
11 Cf. Ter. *Ad.* 739 ff.; Cic. *Fin.* 3.54; *Thes. ling. Lat.* 3.21.16 ff. and 28.32 ("Archiv. Lat. lex." 3 (1886): 370).

WORKS CITED

Accius, Lucius. *Annales*. In *Fragmenta poetarum latinorum*. Ed. W. Morel. Stuttgart: Teubner, 1963.
Ausonius, D. Magnus. *Commemoratio professorum Burdigalensium*. In *Opuscola*. Ed. S. Prete. Leipzig: Teubner, 1978.
Becq de Fouquetières, L. *Les jeux des anciens, leur description, leur origine, leurs rapports a Paris*. Paris: Didier, 1873.
Beschi, L. "Gli 'Astragalizontes' di Policleto." *Prospettiva* 15 (1978): 4 ff.
Bettini, M. "Un'utopia per burla." *Plauto. Mostellaria e Persa*. Ed. M. Bettini. Milano: Mondadori, 1980.
Bömer, F. "Untersuchungen über die Religion der Sklaven in Griechenland und Rom." Akademie der Wissenschaften und der Literatur in Mainz, Abhandlungen der Geistes- und Sozialwissenschaftlichen Klasse, 7. Wiesbaden: Franz Steiner Verlag, 1957.
Brugnoli, G. "Il carnevale e i *Saturnalia*." *La ricerca folklorica* 10 (1984): 49–54.
Cicero, Marcus Tullius. *De finibus bonorum et malorum*. Ed. H. Rackman. Cambridge, Mass.: Harvard UP, 1961.
——————. *M. Tulli Ciceronis de divinatione libri duo*. Ed. A.S. Pease. Darmstadt: Wissenschaftliche Buchgesellschaft, 1977.
Dio Cassius. *Rhomaikè historia*. With an English trans. by E. Cary. Cambridge, Mass.: Harvard UP, 1961.

Euripides. *Supplices*. Ed. C. Collard. Groningen: Bouma's Boekhuis, 1975.
Evelyn, J. *The Diary of John Evelyn*. London: McMillan, 1908.
Florus Lucius Annaeus. *Epitomae de Tito Livio libri duo*. With an English trans. by J.C. Rohlfe. Cambridge, Mass.: Harvard UP, 1960.
Fredegari et aliorum Chronica. Ed. B. Krusch. *Monumenta Germaniae Historica*, "Scriptores rerum Merovingicarum," II. Hannover: Hahn, 1885.
Freud, S. "Dostojewski und die Vatertötung." *Gesammelte Werke* 14 (1948): 399 ff.
Gellius, Aulus. *Noctes Atticae*. Ed. P.K. Marshall. Oxford: Clarendon, 1968.
Grondona, M. *La religione e la superstizione nella Cena Trimalchionis*. Bruxelles: Latomus, 1980.
Halliday, W.R. *Greek Divination*. Chicago: Argonaut, 1967.
Horatius Flaccus, Quintus. *Opera*. Ed. E.C. Wickham. Oxford: Clarendon, 1963.
Huizinga, J. *Homo ludens*. Boston: Beacon Press, 1962.
Humbert, G. "Alea." *Dictionnaire des antiquités Grecques et Romaines*. Ed. Ch. Daremberg and E. Saglio. Vol. 1. Paris: Hachette, 1877.
Iustinus, M. Iunianus. *Historiae Philippicae*. Ed. O. Seel. Stuttgart: Teubner, 1972.
Lafaye, H. "Tali." *Dictionnaire des antiquités Grecques et Romaines*. Ed. Ch. Daremberg and E. Saglio. Vol. 5. Paris: Hachette, 1919.
Livius, Titus. *Ab urbe condita*. Ed. R.S. Conway. Oxford: Clarendon, 1961-65.
Lucanus, M. Annaeus. *Belli civilis libri decem*. Ed. K. Hosius. Leipzig: Teubner, 1913.
Lucianus Samosatensis. *Opera*. Ed. M.D. McLeod. Oxford: Clarendon, 1972.
Macrobius, Ambrosius A.T. *Saturnalia*. Ed. J.A. Willis. Leipzig: Teubner, 1970.
Martialis, M. Valerius. *Epigrammata*. Ed. W.M. Lindsay. Oxford: Clarendon, 1962.
Mauss, M. "Essai sur le don. Form et raison de l'échange dans les societés archaiques." In *Sociologie et anthropologie*. Paris: Presses Universitaires de France, 1985.
Nilsson, M. "Saturnalia." *Realencyclopädie der classischen Altertumswissenschaft*. Ed. A. Pauly and G. Wissowa. Stuttgart: Druckenmüller, 1894.
Ovidius, P. Naso. *Tristia*. Ed. G. Luck. Heidelberg: Carl Winter Verlag, 1867–1977.
―――――. *Amores*. Ed. J.C. McKeown. Liverpool: Francis Cairnes, 1989.
Paulus Diaconus. *Historia Longobardorum*. Ed. L. Bethmann and G. Waitz. *Monumenta Germaniae Historica*, "Scriptores rerum Longobardicarum et Italicarum, saec. VI–IX." Hannover: Hahn, 1878.
Pease, A.S., ed. *M. Tulli Ciceronis de divinatione libri duo*. Darmstadt: Wissenschaftliche Buchgesellschaft, 1977.
Petronius Arbiter. *Satyricon*. Ed. K. Muller and W. Ehlers. München: Artemis Verlag, 1983.
Plato. *Respublica*. With an English trans. by P. Shorey. Cambridge, Mass.:

Harvard UP, 1969.

Plautus, T. Maccius. *Miles gloriosus; Rudens.* In T. Maccius Plautus, *Comoediae.* Ed. W.M. Lindsay. Oxford: Clarendon, 1904.

Plinius, C. Caecilius Secundus. *Epistularum libri decem.* Ed. R.A.B. Mynors. Oxford: Clarendon, 1963.

Plutarchus. *Sulla.* In *Lives.* Ed. Loeb. Trans. B. Perrin. Cambridge: Harvard UP, 1959-68.

Seneca, Lucius Annaeus. *Consolatio ad Polybium.* In L. Annaei Senecae *Dialogorum libri XII.* Ed. L.D. Reynolds. Oxford: Clarendon, 1977.

_____. *Ad Lucilium Epistulae morales.* Ed. D.L. Reynolds. Oxford: Clarendon, 1965.

_____. *Divi Claudi Apokolokyntosis.* Ed. C.F. Russo. Firenze: Sansoni, 1985.

Servius. *Servii grammatici quae feruntur in Vergilii carmina commentarii.* Ed. G. Thilo and H. Hagen. Leipzig: Teubner, 1881-89.

Statius, Publius Papinius. *Silvae.* Ed. J.S. Phillimore. Oxford: Clarendon, 1905.

Stern, H. *Le caledrier de 354, étude sur le texte et ses illustrations.* Paris: Hachette, 1953.

Suetonius, Caius Tranquillus. *De vita Caesarum libri octo.* Ed. M. Ihm. Leipzig: Teubner, 1908.

Supplementum comicum, comoediae Graecae fragmenta. Ed. J. Demianczuk. Hildesheim: G. Olms, 1967.

Tacitus, Publius Cornelius. *Annales.* Ed. E. Köstermann. Leipzig: Teubner, 1971.

_____. *Germania.* Ed. E. Köstermann. Leipzig: Teubner, 1970.

Terentius, Publius Cornelius. *Adelphoe.* In P. Terentii Afri, *Comoediae.* Ed. R. Kauer and W.M. Lindsay. Oxford: Clarendon, 1926.

Thesaurus Linguae Latinae. Leipzig: Teubner, 1900–.

Varro, Marcus Terentius. *De vita populi Romani.* Ed. Riposati. Milano: Vita e Pensiero, 1939.

Vergilius, Publius Maro. *Aeneis.* Ed. R.A.B. Mynors. Oxford, Clarendon, 1990.

_____. *Georgica.* Ed. R.A.B. Mynors. Oxford: Clarendon, 1969.

Giuseppe Pucci

Roman Saturn: the Shady Side

> Il porte un joli nom, "Saturne," mais c'est un dieu fort inquietant . . .
> G. Brassens

In the fundamental work of Klibansky, Panofsky and Saxl, the personality of the Roman god Saturn is seen as marked by a profound ambiguity (125 ff.). This ambiguity — or perhaps better ambivalence — is, however, principally ascribed to the Greek *Kronos*, with whom Saturn was normally assimilated. According to Klibansky, Panofsky and Saxl, the convergence with the Roman Saturn had the effect of enhancing the positive traits of this divine figure. Indeed, the guardianship of treasury, and weights and measures, and the invention of money itself were attributed to Saturn, not to mention the *Saturnalia*, the festival of joy and license.

The accentuation of the negative traits would have occurred only when the image of the god was associated with the planet which even today bears his name. This identification has its origins in the Hellenistic period through the influence of astrological doctrines extraneous to Greek Olympic religion, and was completed in the Late Empire with the development of astrology as a "religion."

The picture presented to us by Klibansky, Panofsky and Saxl is, in my opinion, not entirely correct. I suspect that one of the reasons for this is that part of the literature that they consulted had a tendency to whitewash the issue.[1] My intention is to demonstrate that the Roman Saturn was, from a very early date, an extremely alarming god, a terrible and awesome figure.

It is a well-known fact that the origins of Saturn were not at all clear to the ancients themselves.[2] Varro, followed by many later authors, derived the name Saturn from *sero/satum* (to sow). However, this etymology is hardly correct, since the quantity of the "a" in *satus* suggests otherwise. Similarly, it is impossible to derive Saturn from *satura* or *saturare*, as suggested by Cicero and others. In this instance too we are dealing with a false etymology, related to the burlesque nature of the *Saturnalia* or to the conception of time and its passing (which presupposes in its turn the assimilation of the Greek *Kronos* with *Chronos*, the god of time).

In reality, the linguistic origins of Saturn are to be found in an Etruscan context. This thesis had been put forward by Scaligerus as early as 1581, and eventually was conclusively demonstrated in 1917 by Herbig (446 ff.), who proved that Saturn was derived from the Etruscan *Satre* (it is one of the many Latin names ending in *-urnus*, *-arnus* and *-erna* that come from the Etruscan, as do *Volturnus*, *Mastarna*, *Saserna*, etc.). The connection between *Satre* and Saturn was facilitated by the discovery, in 1877, of the famous Piacenza bronze liver (see Maggiani 53 ff.), upon which a god named *Satre* appears, placed among the gods of the unfavourable regions. *Satre* was for the Etruscans a chthonian deity, a god of the depths of the earth, with a funereal character.

It is to observe that the astro-mythological conceptions of Martianus Capella,[3] a fifth century A.D. author, resemble closely the scheme displayed by the Piacenza liver. Saturn is to be found in the 14th region, placed between two chthonian regions, the 13th, of the *Manes*, i.e. the Dead, and the 15th, that of *Vejovis*, as a kind of infernal Jupiter.

According to some authorities, the Roman *munera*, the gladiatorial combats originally held to celebrate the funerals of patricians, also derive from the Etruscans (Piganiol; Coarelli 281 ff.). Furthermore, there are many good reasons to relate the *munera* with Saturn. Public *munera* were offered, in the Republican period, by the Quaestors, who drew upon the *aerarium Saturni*. The games took place shortly before the *Saturnalia*, and various sources explicitly connect them with Saturn. Servius considered them a substitute for human sacrifices (3.67). We must accept then the fact that the Roman Saturn was concerned with human sacrifices, which corroborates his chthonian and funereal nature.

It should be noted that *munera* were also offered to other chthonian gods, such as Jupiter Latiar, whom the ancients also called Pluto or Cronos, and therefore related to Saturn. It seems that human victims were still offered to this god even as late as the fourth century A.D. Moreover, in Africa, the execution of prisoners condemned *ad bestias* permitted the legal continuation of human sacrifices to Saturn well into the Imperial period. In the passion of Perpetua, who was martyred at Carthage in 203, it is said that the Christians, before entering the arena, were forced to wear particular costumes: *viri quidem sacerdotum Saturni, feminae vero sacratarum Cereri* (Migne 3:50–51). That is to say, the men, through their costumes, became identified with the faithful devoted to Saturn (which is the meaning the word *sacerdos* has in African inscriptions), whereas the women became identified with the faithful to Ceres, his consort.

We know, of course, that in African provinces, where a strong Punic substratum persisted, Saturn was, in common belief, identified with the great Semitic god *Ba'al Hammon*. The Greeks too identified *Ba'al* with *Kronos*, and to the Punic *Kronos* they attributed the famous bloody sacrifices of babies and adults, which readers of *Salammbo* are sure to recall (cf. Leglay). Some African inscriptions dedicated to Saturn talk of a *mol chomor* (sacrificial lamb), the offering being made — so runs the formula — *anima pro anima, sanguine pro sanguine, vita pro vita*. It is — we can easily guess — a surrogate for human sacrifices.

I think, however, that this identification of Saturn with *Ba'al* is not only a peculiarity of Roman Africa, but can be recognized in Rome itself. *Saturnalia* gives us a clue. It is known that the *Saturnalia* were definitively organized in 217 B.C. The reform included a *lectistermium*, that is, a ritual banquet in which the god himself participated; a *convivium*, or a public feast; and a mass event similar in some respects to our Carnival.[4]

However, why were the *Saturnalia* reformed precisely in the year 217 B.C.? 217 was the year of the battle of Lake Trasimeno, one of the most disastrous Roman defeats of the Second Punic War. This coincidence of dates makes one wonder if, perhaps, the Romans had not turned their attention to Saturn because they were obsessed with the great and fearsome Carthaginian deity, *Ba'al Hammon* himself.

A typical custom in the ancient world was the *evocatio*, a rite by which the enemy's divinity was welcomed into one's own territory in order to induce the god to cease protecting the enemy and to take the side of the new faithful. In this particular instance, it could not have been an *evocatio* in the strict sense of the term, since this could be performed only before an assault upon an enemy city, whereas in this case Rome was enduring a Carthaginian offensive in her own territory. However, there is no reason to exclude the possibility that one of the purposes of the reform of 217 could be to conciliate the god of the enemy.

Significantly, the first coins that bear the image of Saturn upon the reverse appear during the Second Punic War. In the second century they disappear, only to reappear at the end of the century, between 107 and 104, at the time of the Jugurthine War, once again in the face of a threat from Africa. Accordingly, an assimilation of Saturn and *Ba'al* is, in my opinion, beyond doubt. I cannot engage in a comparative study, but I would maintain that there are sufficient elements in archaic Roman religion to explain why Saturn could have been assimilated with the ferocious and blood-thirsty *Ba'al Hammon* (Guittard).

Let us consider at this point the ancient tradition about the origin of the *Saturnalia*. Certain sources connect the festival with the arrival in Italy of the Pelasgians, the mythical pre-Hellenic Aegean people. Macrobius, quoting Varro, tells us that having been forced from their homeland, the Pelasgians received an oracle at Dodona that encouraged them to search for the land of Saturn of the Siccls and Cotyle, the city of the Aborigines, where there was a floating island. After uniting with these people, the oracle said, they were to send a tithe to Phoebus, some heads to the son of Kronos, and a man to his father.

Eventually, after many wanderings, the Pelasgians arrived in Latium, and near Cutiliae they found a lake upon which a curious phenomenon could be observed: in its centre there was a kind of floating island made of shrubs and mud. At this point, they understood that this was the place of which the oracle had spoken, and so here they settled, after driving out the Sicels. The account of Varro and Macrobius concludes in this manner: "conforming to the oracle they consecrated a tithe to Apollo, erected a *sacellum* to Dis and an altar to Saturn, and called the festival *Saturnalia*. For a long time they believed that they were pleasing Dis with human heads and Saturn with human victims, because the oracle had said, offer heads unto Hades and a man to his father" (Macrobius, *Sat.* 1.7.28; cf. Briquel, especially 355 ff.).

Later on, the ferocity of the ritual was to be reduced by Hercules, who, while passing through Italy, told the descendants of the Pelasgians of a way to elude the savage oracle, persuading them to offer to Dis not human heads, but *oscilla*, terracottas artistically made in imitation of the human form;[5] and to Saturn not human victims, but candles. This is the origin of the custom of sending puppets and candles as gifts at the *Saturnalia*. This story is based upon a play on words: *phota* in Greek means man, but it also means torches or candles. Furthermore, Varro aims at setting up a series of correspondences—not only ritual, but also spatial and monumental—between the oracle and the Roman reality. He places Cutiliae in Latium (not in Sabina, which would be more correct), and places the erection of the *sacellum* of Dis and the altar of Saturn in Rome itself. Indeed, the text of Macrobius is essential to the topography of some monuments in the Roman Forum.

The position of the altar of Saturn can be fixed with notable precision. According to some sources it was, as one would expect, in front of the temple of Saturn, at the foot of the Capitoline Hill, between the temple and the *senaculum*. Actually, between the *senaculum* and the temple of Saturn, only separated by a few inches from the former, is a small monument, traditionally identified as the Volcanal. But the Volcanal was a part of the *Comitium*, and ought to be located elsewhere. As Coarelli has recently pointed out, what has up to now been called the Volcanal cannot be the true Volcanal. On the contrary, everything suggests that it is the altar of Saturn itself (161 ff.; 199 ff.).

We know that the altar of Saturn was attached to the *sacellum Ditis*, the shrine of Dis. Now, just one foot to the east of the altar of Saturn there is a circular monument, commonly identified as the *umbilicus urbis*, mentioned by late sources. Coarelli has convincingly argued that this is none other than the *sacellum* of Dis — all the more convincingly in that a *sacellum* was always functionally connected with the altar.

Perhaps more interesting still is that another passage of Macrobius proves beyond a shadow of a doubt that the *sacellum* of Dis was the same thing as the *mundus* (Coarelli 207 ff., 217 ff.). What was the *mundus*? Apparently it was a sort of shaft or subterranean temple of the *Manes* (the spirits of the Dead), which was ritually opened only three times a year. On those days, it was said, *mundus patet*, and it was as if the gates of hell opened and the spirits of the underworld had access to the world of the Living. However, the *mundus* also represented the ideal centre of the city, that is, literally, the *umbilicus urbis*, according to the definition of the late sources. The *umbilicus*, in its turn, was but the Latin translation of the Greek *omphalos* (navel), and both the *omphalos* at Delphi and the one that was probably dedicated to Demeter at Eleusis had a clear chthonian significance.

One point clearly emerges from what we have seen up to now: the reassuring image of Saturn as the pacific god of sowing and harvesting is over-simplified. Saturn is a fertility god because he is a chthonian divinity. Saturn is, in reality, virtually the same thing as *Dis Pater*, with whom he is strictly associated. Saturn is Lord of the Dead. If the two gods came to be considered separately, it is only because of the Greek interpretation, which assimilated Saturn with Kronos, and *Dis Pater* with *Ploutos*, or rather *Hades*. Therefore, if Saturn were to be *Kronos* he could not also be *Hades* (Sabbatucci 346).

So we must now ask: what is the connection between Saturn and the Dead, and how is it possible that this distressing god, who demands human sacrifices, could also be the god of merrymaking and carousing? It is known that the cycle of the *Saturnalia* included at least seven days, from the 17th to the 23rd of December. In addition to the *Saturnalia*, on the 17th, the cycle also comprised the *Opalia* on the 19th, the *Sigillaria* on the

20th, the *Divalia* in honour of Angerona on the 21st, and the *Larentalia*, in honour of Acca Larentia, the mother of the *Lares*, on the 23rd. Following these were *Compitalia*, a movable feast, closely tied to the *Larentalia*, which fell between the end of December and the beginning of January. As one can see, the whole cycle is related to the winter solstice and the end of the year.

We can show that all of the gods involved are infernal deities (Coarelli 257 ff.; Sabbatucci 355 ff.). *Ops*, the wife of Saturn, is almost identified with him as representing the chthonian divinity to whom the "buried" seeds are entrusted whilst awaiting rebirth. *Angerona*, the goddess of the solstice (*angustiae solis*), is mute, and as such she belongs to the underworld, as is well-known to historians of religion. The *Lares* are none other than the souls of the Dead worshipped as gods of the subterranean world; and *Acca Larentia*, their mother, is venerated with the name of *Mania* in the *aediculae compitales*, the shrines of the cross-roads. *Maniae* were also named the grotesque figures, the puppets that were hung on the doors of houses during *Compitalia* to honour the Dead. But Macrobius (*Sat.* 1.7.34) reveals their true significance; he says that in ancient times babies were sacrificed to *Mania*, the mother of the *Lares*. This practice was halted by Brutus, the first Consul, who ordered the substitution of the heads of babies with the heads of poppies. Similarly, during *Compitalia*, figurines would be hung on doors, one for each inhabitant of the house: in that way a doll was offered to redeem a human life. Their nature as surrogate offerings for human sacrifices could hardly be more evident.

The *sigilla* of the festival of *Sigillaria*, as we have seen, had originally the same meaning. They too were ritual offerings magically substituted for a human life. Later they were to become simple toys, frivolities that were exchanged as gifts. There was a fairly active trade in these dolls. It would even seem that the lengthening of the *Saturnalia* was justified, to some degree, by the desire to promote this business. In Rome, the shops that specialized in these goods were at first in the Porticus of Agrippa, in the Campus Martius, and later in the Baths of Trajan on the Oppian Hill. As time passed, not only dolls were exchanged, but an infinite variety of cheap trinkits.[6] A kind of sampler is to be found in Martial's *Xenia* and *Apophoreta*, epigrams that were perhaps written by order for the *Saturnalia* of 84 and 85 A.D. Certainly no one any longer gave any thought to the sinister origin of the custom when exchanging these gifts.

Let us return now to the divinities whose festivals fall within the cycle of the *Saturnalia*. We have said that they are all divinities with a funereal character; but we can be more precise. They are all divinities whose cult is placed, both ideally and physically (Eliade and Lanternari), at critical boundaries, at the frontier between two worlds: between the death and the rebirth of the sun (and therefore of the year); and between the world of the Dead and the world of the Living.

The end of the year is, in short, felt as a passage, and passages — as anthropology tells us — imply crisis. The end of the year, in particular, is a period of cosmic disorder, of danger that must be exorcised. Man lives in fear of seeing the forces that surround him becoming exhausted. He fears, for instance, that the sun might be extinguished forever at winter solstice, or that the corn might fail to be reborn. Vegetation has periods of apparent extinction that are worrisome. Accordingly, the sacred force operating in the agricultural cycle has to be enhanced and regenerated.

Men have to pray to the Dead, because the Dead have under their jurisdiction the buried seeds, as well as the harvest stored in the granaries, the food that will save the Living through the winter. Yet the Dead, just like the seeds, potentially await rebirth. For this reason they come close to the Living, particularly at those moments when the vital tensions of a community reach their maximum. The spirits of the Dead are attracted to what is beginning: the new year, a new explosion of vitality. The Living, with their biological excesses, stimulate the declining energy of the sun and beseech the favour of the underworld, at that fateful moment when the Dead gain access to the world of the Living. Agrarian and funerary rituals combine (Coarelli 277 ff.).

If this is the case, we should expect to find in the *Saturnalia* those elements that confirm, beyond the apparent gaiety, their funereal significance. We have seen that the spirits of the Dead thirst for any biological exuberance and every organic excess, because this overflowing compensates for the poverty of their own substance, making them participate in an impetuous vitality. The *convivium*, the collective banquet of the *Saturnalia*, has just this effect. For during this festival, the Dead return to participate in the fertility rites of the Living. They are hungry, and they have to be satisfied. The exhibition and the immoderate consumption of food tend on one hand to guarantee, through sympathetic magic, the abundance for the following year, and on the other to address the Dead, who become satiated with the sight of the food, and will be therefore satisfied and placated. So we begin to see the *Saturnalia*, despite the aura of gaiety that they create, are a festival for the Dead.

Other elements combine to reinforce the interpretation of the *Saturnalia* as a festival of the Dead and for the Dead, a sort of collective funeral. For example, during the *Saturnalia*, judicial activity was suspended. This was, it is said, because the rite had the function of recreating the primordial state, the age in which Saturn had reigned, when there were no laws because there was still chaos, or because it was the happy age when no one committed any evil actions. In reality, we know that justice was also suspended during public funerals: there was the *iustitium* (from *ius* and *stare*).

Let us now consider the candles. These can be thought of as sympathetic magic, as a means of giving strength to the sun at the critical period of winter solstice (the practice of lighting torches and bonfires at winter solstice is well-known in agrarian societies). But it should not be forgotten that in early Rome private funerals took place at night, by the light of torches and wax candles.

Finally, let us take the role of the game of dice, an essential feature of the *Saturnalia*. It can be demonstrated that the game of dice has an eminently chthonian character (Bachofen). Moreover, it is a cereal symbol, *par excellence*. Herodotus (2.31) tells a story of how an Egyptian king descended into the underworld and played dice with Demeter, the goddess of corn. Another interesting tale in Herodotus (1.94) concerns the invention of dice. He relates that the Lydians invented the game at a time when they were suffering a famine, so that one day they would eat, and the next play dice to distract themselves and to forget their hunger.

In this case, Herodotus has probably trivialized a much more complex symbolic content. According to Bachofen the dice is an expression of the game undertaken by mortals with the powers of the underworld. The seeds are to be considered as the stake, and one plays in the hope of winning a good harvest (Bachofen 141). The peasant who has finished the sowing has no more work to do. In this state of enforced idleness, work inevitably gives way to chance and to the risks of a wager with nature (Sabbatucci 351).

There is also another characteristic element of the folklore of the end of the year, the sexual orgy that accompanies the excessive eating. Indeed in agrarian societies fecundity and fertility, coitus and sowing, tend to become identified with each other. The sexual orgy is an element that forms a part of the disorder; it is the ritualization of the primordial chaos that precedes creation; but it is also the means to restore the vital energies whose explosion has to satisfy the Dead.

In truth, ancient sources do not dwell excessively upon this aspect of the festival of the *Saturnalia*, at least in the fully historical era. However, Lucian invites his reader to dance naked at the *Saturnalia* and to carry a beautiful flautist in one's arms (*Saturnalia* 2); this seems to me sufficiently suggestive. All in all, the *Saturnalia* are not different from those year-end festivals that ethnologists know of from a very great number of agrarian societies. The festival is partly a celebration of the work of sowing and the subsequent rest, and partly a reorganization of the relationships between the Living and the Dead at a liminal time of a sacral crisis that ultimately has to be resolved in favour of the Living. After a period in which the Dead have potentially come into contact with the Living, they have to be convinced to depart. The festival celebrates their leaving.

Why then were the *Saturnalia* principally the festival of slaves (who were served by their master) and children (who were presented with toys)? Because slaves and children are not fully integrated with the society of the Living. From the point of view of social relationships they are in the same position as the Dead to the Living. A festival in their honour is a festival of the Dead, which they represent (Levi-Strauss).

On New Year's Day the Dead bring the threat of chaos among men; they represent the supremely destructive and dangerous moment of the ritual crisis. Therefore, the celebration of the New Year is also a periodic refoundation of the cycle of life, a restoration of cosmic order which is passing through a period of disruption.

The year dies, along with the sun and the seeds. When sowing-season is over there is an absence of work for mankind, but in this period when the sun is weakened there is also an absence of Jupiter, the Olympic god of light and *kosmos*. Saturn, once the supreme god and now the god of the Shades, intervenes as a substitute Jupiter at the moment when the Dead return to the height of their powers. In order to take the place of Jupiter they remove his *compedes*, the strips of wool that bind the feet of the cult statue in the temple of Saturn, and a way of life is instituted that recreates that which myth attributes to the Age of Saturn: a ritualized holiday, the primordial disorder that preceded the advent of any laws. Only thus can time be ritually refounded.[7] Jupiter could not have made the year die, since he plays no role in the dialectic of birth and death. It is Saturn who is in possession of the *orbandi potestas* (Ser., *ad Aen.* 3.139).

We can now begin to understand why this terrifying god demands human sacrifices. The god of the Dead requires new subjects, who are offered in order to ensure the periodic regeneration of the forces of fecundity, and for the regeneration of time. It is true that, with the progress of time, human sacrifices were substituted by other ritual offerings. Cases of the substitution of humans by figurines and candles do not appear to be isolated in Roman archaic history. One of these can be seen, for example, in the aetiological tale told by Ovid in the *Fasti*, concerning the festival of the *Argei* (5.645 ff.). This celebration is also presented as an ancient human sacrifice to Saturn, and once again its origin is attributed to the Pelasgians and to Zeus of Dodona. Here again, as in the case of the *Saturnalia*, the ritual was to be mitigated by Hercules, who advised the substitution of victims (men who were to be thrown into the Tiber) with straw effigies, according to the principle essential to all magical acts: *in sacris simulata pro veris accipiuntur*.

Lactantius also reports the familiar oracle of Dodona and says that, in honour of Saturn, a man was to be sacrificed by being thrown from the Milvian Bridge into the Tiber (*Inst.* 1.21.7). However, since the oracle was ambiguous, and *phota* could equally well mean a man or a torch, the ancients, in order to be sure, threw both a man and a torch. Subsequently, it was Hercules who taught them to offer only manikins. Lactantius seems to have confused several versions, but the substance of the tradition of drowning victims in honour of Saturn remains. We can easily connect with these ancient rites the custom, still surviving in the epoch of Lucianus, of plunging persons head-first into cold water as a facetious punishment for their clumsiness (*Saturnalia* 2). The dive actually simulates a death by drowning; it symbolizes the "passage" into another world.

But the cruel rite in which—according to Timaeus (*FGH* 1.28)—the Sardinians threw into the sea, from high rocks, men over seventy was anything but a joke, although they then burst into laughter (whence the expression "sardonic laughter"). These were real victims, ritually offered to Saturn.

At this point I believe that we should have no difficulty in understanding a passage of Vettius Valens which Klibansky, Panofsky and Saxl quote (133), but do not comment upon, in which, among the forms of death over which Saturn presides, we find death by drowning. The other means are death by hanging, death in chains, and death from dysentery. In my opinion death in chains can be satisfactorily explained by the *compedes* mentioned above. Death by dysentery, I am not so sure about, but it would seem to me that the epithet Sterculius, which Saturn occasionally received, is perhaps significant. As for death by hanging, it is enough to remember the *oscilla*, the ritual substitutes for human figures which were hung to simulate a sacrifice to Saturn. It is no coincidence that we learn from Servius that when someone committed suicide by hanging, and therefore the normal funeral rites (*iusta*) were not applicable, a ceremony was performed *suspensis oscillis, veluti per imitationem mortis* (*ad Aen.* 12.603).

Any discussion about Saturn and human sacrifice cannot be complete without mentioning the execution of the *saturnalicius princeps*. We hear of this practice in the *Acta* of the martyrdom of St. Dasius. The story tells that in 303 A.D. the men of the garrison of Durosturum in Mesia, on the Danube, intended, as usual, to celebrate the *saturnale castrense* by electing by lot one of their fellow-soldiers, who for thirty days would dictate and enforce every sort of licentious behaviour. At the end of this time he would be sacrificed, or would make a sacrifice (the translation is controversial) to Saturn. The man elected that year, the Christian Dasius, refused to yield to vice, and as a consequence was immediately decapitated.[8]

Frazer was firmly convinced that the festival usually concluded with the sacrifice of the *princeps* himself, and that this was perfectly in keeping with the results of his research for *The Golden Bough* (310 ff.). On the other hand, Cumont maintains that the Greek text badly translated a Latin deponent verb, and that therefore the king of the *Saturnalia* neither committed suicide nor was put to death, but only made a sacrifice. The fact remains that folklore offers many parallel cases in which the king of the festival of carousing is symbolically killed (Beduschi 37 ff.). Such a killing put an end to the anarchy that precedes the social foundation of time. In addition, it is the killing of a scapegoat. Before beginning the new year, it is necessary to put to death someone who takes upon himself all blame, all sins (Weinstock 391 ff.). Is it possible that, in the ultimate analysis, this victim is Saturn himself? Frazer thought so, and in many religions a sacrifice of the god of vegetation is performed through the impersonation of the god by a victim.

It is beyond doubt that Roman Saturn, this grievous god whose very name was for Servius a symbol of cruelty,[9] demanded death in order to give back life. Ultimately, as Ambrose Bierce once observed, death is the only side of immortality that man can know.

University of Siena

NOTES

1 See, for instance, Hild's article on Saturn. Although Klibansky, Panofsky and Saxl do not cite it, they certainly used it.
2 Ancient sources concerning Saturn are collected by Wissowa and by Thulin. The etymology is thoroughly discussed by Guittard 43 ff.
3 *De nuptiis Philologiae et Mercurii* 1.58; cf. Guittard 52.

4 On the relationship between the *Saturnalia* and the modern Carnival, see Frazer 306 ff. and more recently Brugnoli 117 ff., republished with substantial changes in Clemente 49 ff.; Tamassia 363 ff. See also Sanga 21 ff.
5 On the *oscilla*, see Picard 47 ff.; Altheim 65 ff.; Ehlers; Metzger 303 ff.
6 Cf. the entries on "Sigillaria" and "Saturnalia" in the *Realencyclopädie*.
7 On Saturn/Kronos and time, see Leach 193 ff.
8 About the execution of the *saturnalicius princeps*, see Cumont, *Les Actes* 5 ff. and *Le tombeau* 369 ff.; Parmentier.
9 Serv., *ad Aen.* 1.23: *Saturni autem nomen quasi ad crudelitatem aptum*.

WORKS CITED

Altheim, F. *Terra mater*. Giessen, 1931.
Bachofen, J. "Sul significato dei dadi e delle mani nei sepolcri." *Annali dell'Istituto archeologico di Roma* 30 (1858); 33 (1861).
Beduschi, L. "La vecchia di mezza Quaresima." *Interpretazioni del carnevale*. Ed. I. Sordi. La Ricerca Folclorica 6 (1982).
Briquel, D. *Les Pélasges en Italie. Recherches sur l'histoire de la légende*. Roma, 1983.
Brugnoli, G. "Il Carnevale e i *Saturnalia*." *Dire e fare Carnevale*. Ed. R. Ferretti. Montepulciano: Il Grifo, 1984. Rpt. in *I frutti del Ramo d'oro*.
Capella, Martianus. *De nuptiis Philologiae et Mercurii*. Leipzig: Teubner, 1983.
Clemente, P., ed. *I frutti del Ramo d'oro. James G. Frazer e le eredità dell'antropologia*. La Ricerca Folklorica 10 (1984).
Coarelli, F. *Il Foro Romano. Periodo arcaico*. Roma: Quasar, 1983.
Cumont, F. *Les Actes de S. Dasius*. Analecta Bollandiana 16 (1897).
―――. *Le tombeau de S. Dasius de Durostorum*. Analecta Bollandiana 28 (1908).
Ehlers, W. "Oscillum." *Realencyclopädie der classischen Altertumswissenschaft*. Ed. A. Pauly and G. Wissowa. Stuttgart: Druckenmüller, 1894.
Eliade, Mircea. *Traité d'histoire des religions*. Paris, 1948.
Frazer, J.G. *The Golden Bough*. London: MacMillan, 1913.
Guittard, Ch. "Recherches sur la nature de Saturne des origines à la réforme de 217 avant J.C." *Recherches sur les religions de l'Italie antique*. Genève: Droz, 1976.
Herbig, G. "Satre-Saturnus." *Philologus* 74 (1917).
Hild, J.A. "Saturnus." *Dictionnaire des antiquités grecques et romaines*. Ed. Ch. Daremberg and E. Saglio. Vol. 4. Paris: Hachette, 1909.
Klibansky, R., E. Panofsky and F. Saxl. *Saturn and Melancholy*. London: Thomas Nelson, 1964. Ital. trans. Torino: Einaudi, 1983.
Lactantius, Lucius Caecilius Firmianus. *Divinae institutiones*. Paris: Editions du Cerf, 1986.
Lanternari, V. *La grande festa. Vita rituale e sistemi di produzione nelle società tradizionali*. Bari, 1976.

Leach, E.R. "Kronos and Chronos." In *Rethinking Anthropology*. London, 1973. Ital. trans. *Nuove vie dell'antropologia*. Milano, 1973.

Leglay, M. *Saturne africain. Histoire*. Paris: Ed. du C.N.R.S., 1966.

Levi-Strauss, C. "Père Noël supplicié." *Les Temps modernes*. 1952. Ital. trans. *Razza e storia e altri studi di antropologia*. Torino: Einaudi, 1967.

Lucianus, Samosatensis. *Opera*. Ed. M.D. McLeod. Oxford: Clarendon, 1972.

Macrobius, Ambrosius A.T. *Saturnalia*. Ed. J.A. Willis. Leipzig: Teubner, 1970.

Maggiani, M. *Studi Etruschi* 50 (1982).

Meuggi, H. *Mélanges offerts à P. Collart*. Lausanne: De Boccard, 1976.

Migne, J.-P. *Patrologia latina.*. Paris: Garnier, 1878 ff.

Nilsson, M. "Saturnalia." *Realencyclopädie der classischen Altertumswissenschaft*. Ed. A. Pauly and G. Wissowa. Stuttgart: Druckenmüller, 1894.

Ovidius, P. Naso. *Fasti*. Ed. J.G. Frazer. Cambridge: Harvard UP, 1959.

Parmentier, L. "Le roi des Saturnales." *Revue Philologique* 21 (1897).

Picard, C. *Revue Archéologique* 38 (1928).

Piganiol, A. *Recherches sur les jeux romains*. Strasbourg-Paris: Stra, 1923.

Sabbatucci, D. *La religione di Roma antica. Dal calendario festivo all'ordine cosmico*. Milano: Il Saggiatore, 1988.

Sanga, G. "Personata libido." *Interpretazioni del carnevale*. Ed. I. Sordi. *La Ricerca Folklorica* 6 (1982).

Servius. *Servii grammatici quae feruntur in Vergilii carmina commentarii*. Ed. G. Thilo and H. Hagen. Leipzig: Teubner, 1981-89.

Tamassia, R. "Saturno e il carnevale." *Annali della facoltà di Lettere e Filosofia dell'Università di Siena* 5 (1984).

Thulin, C. "Saturnus." *Realencyclopädie der classischen Altertumswissenschaft*. Ed. A. Pauly and G. Wissowa. Stuttgart: Druckenmüller, 1894.

Weinstock, S. "Saturnalia und Neujahrfest in der Martyrenakten." *Festschrift Th. Klauser*. Munster: Aschendorffsche Verlagsbuchhandlung, 1964.

Wissowa, G. "Saturnus." *Ausführliches Lexikon der griechischen und römischen Mythologie*. Ed. W. H. Roscher. Leipzig: Teubner, 1884–1937.

Amilcare A. Iannucci

Saturn in Dante

Dante distinguishes between Saturn the god and Saturn the planet, both of whom he represents positively.[1] The first clearly derives from classical literary sources, primarily Virgil's *Aeneid* (8.319–25) and Ovid's *Metamorphoses* (1.89-112). He is the King of Crete (*Inf.* 14.94–96) and Lord of the Golden Age, the first in a succession of ages during which "the world . . . lived chastely" (*Inf.* 14.96) and justice prevailed (cf. *Purg.* 22.148–150; *Purg.* 28.139–40; *Par.* 21.26–7).

Especially present in Dante's mind are Virgil's famous verses in the fourth *Eclogue*, commonly taken in the Middle Ages to prophesy the coming of Christ (Comparetti 96–103):

> magnus ab integro saeclorum nascitur ordo.
> iam redit et Virgo, redeunt Saturnia regna;
> iam nova progenies caelo demittitur alto.
> (*Eclog.* 4.5–7)

> [The great line of the centuries begins anew.
> Now the Virgin returns, the reign of Saturn
> returns; now a new generation descends from
> heaven on high.]

These verses Dante quotes directly in the *Monarchia* (1.11.1), paraphrases in the *Commedia* (*Purg.* 22.70–72), and alludes to in *Epistle* 7.6 in order to celebrate Henry VII of Luxembourg and the new golden age he was to inaugurate. In the passage from the *Commedia*, Dante has Statius claim Virgil's "prophetic" text as the origin of his conversion to Christianity:

> ' . . . Secol si rinova;
> torna giustizia e primo tempo umano,
> e progenie scende da ciel nova.'
> Per te poeta fui, per te cristiano.
> (*Purg.* 22.70–73)

> [' ... The ages are renewed;
> justice and man's first time on earth return;
> from Heaven a new progeny descends.'
> Through you I was a poet and, through you,
> a Christian.]

Here Dante replaces the "Virgo" of the original with "giustizia" and "Saturnia regna" with "primo tempo umano." He explains in the *Monarchia*:

> Itam redit et Virgo, redeunt Saturnia regna.

"Virgo" namque vocabatur Iustitia, quam etiam Astream vocabant; "Saturnia regna" dicebant optima tempora, que etiam "aurea" nuncupabant. (*Mon.* 1.11.1)

> ["Iam redit et Virgo, redeunt Saturnia regna."

By "Virgin" he meant Justice, who was also called Astraea. By "Saturnian kingdoms" he meant the best ages, which were also called the golden.]²

In the Earthly Paradise, the "virgin" Matilda—who at one level of Dante's elaborate theological allegory is a figure of Astraea—associates the pagan myth of the golden age with the Christian truth of Eden, as described in *Genesis*:

> Quelli ch'anticamente poetaro
> l'età de l'oro e suo stato felice,
> forse in Parnaso esto loco sognaro.
> Qui fu innocente l'umana radice;
> qui primavera sempre e ogne frutto;
> nettare è questo di che ciascun dice.
> (*Purg.* 28.139–44)

> [Those ancients who in poetry presented
> the golden age, who sang its happy state,
> perhaps, in their Parnassus, dreamt this place.
> Here, mankind's root was innocent; and here
> were every fruit and never-ending spring;
> these streams—the nectar of which poets sing.]

These words may be taken as a final tribute to Virgil (and Statius), in whose presence they are uttered (*Purg.* 28.145–47). But they also represent the culmination of a process whereby pagan Saturn and Astraea and the age they stand for are drawn into Dante's Christian world-view, through an appropriation typical of his typological mode of signifying.

More specifically, they become part of a dichotomy which is at the very heart of Dante's Christian epic of conversion, namely the contrast—often evoked—between an ideal past and present corruption. The promise of future redemption involves the recreation of that remote, innocent past. In this teological scheme, the darker side of pagan Saturn has no place. The cruel tale of Saturn devouring his children, known to Dante through Ovid (*Fasti* 4.197–214), is hinted at in *Inferno* 14.100–102 but is clearly suppressed. There are no further allusions to the deed in the poem.

The other Saturn—the planetary ruler—is based on descriptions in astrological texts of Saturn and his influence. However, in this case, too, the negative aspects of Saturn are all but completely purged from Dante's depiction of the planet-god. In this literature, as Klibansky, Panofsky, and Saxl have amply documented in *Saturn and Melancholy* (see esp. 140–50, 178–95), Saturn was generally seen to be a sinister if not downright malignant force. Saturn—coldest, driest, and slowest of planets—was associated with abject poverty, old age, and death, as well as many other negative elements—violence, cruelty, solitude, sadness, desolation. Those born under his influence were gloomy and melancholic, and occupied the lowest levels of society—cripples, beggars, criminals, grave diggers and the poorest of peasants. In the *Trésor* Brunetto Latini calls Saturn "crudele e fellone, fredda natura" (342) [cruel and traitorous, a cold nature]. A Florentine astrological text of the second half of the thirteenth century states that "Saturno significa tristitia et malenconia, fatica et male" (*Tractato del corso della Luna* 111) [Saturn stands for sadness and melancholy, toil and evil]. Moreover, "La proprietà di Saturno è costringimento e riceptaculo significatore di tutti i mali et iniquità et pericoli et morte" (113) [The property of Saturn is constraint: he is the receptacle and instigator of all evil, wickedness, dangers, and death]. Little or none of this appears in Dante's portrait of Saturn.

In the *Convivio* (2.13), Dante, following an established tradition,[3] associates each of the planets with one of the seven liberal arts. Saturn is coupled with astrology—i.e. astronomy—which is a "high and noble" science. The analogy is suggested to Dante because Saturn is the slowest and highest (furthest away) of the planets. The noble science of astronomy requires much study and great patience to master. Thus Saturn's "slowest" is turned into a virtue.

In the *Paradiso*, much of Saturn's malignant character is mitigated by the fact that the planet is "in exile" in the sign of Leo, i.e. in the sign opposite Saturn's regular domicile.[4] When this happens, the planet's characteristics are modified:

> Noi sem levati al settimo splendore,
> che sotto 'l petto del Leone ardente
> raggia mo misto già del suo valore.
> (*Par.* 21.13-15)
>
> [We now are in the seventh splendor; this,
> beneath the burning Lion's breast, transmits
> to earth its rays, with which his force is mixed.]

Jacopo della Lana, one of Dante's early commentators, obviously attuned to the astrological lore of his time, explains: "Nota come la influenzia venne mista alla terra dalla natura de' corpi celesti: Leone si è caldo e secco, come è detto, Saturno è freddo e secco. Or mischia queste due complessioni, averai eccellente secco" (3:320) [Note how the influence arrives on earth filtered by the nature of the two celestial bodies: Leo is hot and dry as stated, Saturn is cold and dry. Now mix these two constitutions, and you produce an excellent dry]. This celestial coincidence favours the recovery of a positive aspect of Saturn: Saturn as the patron and protector of philosophical and religious contemplation, a view which has its roots in ancient and medieval Neoplatonism (Klibansky *et al* 151–59). Thus, Dante makes the seventh sphere host the contemplative souls. However, this particular stellar alignment permits Dante to present us with contemplatives who, like St. Peter Damian and St. Benedict, combine the meditative and mystical temperament with the zeal of the reformer. This is possible because, whereas Saturn's cold nature is conducive to meditation, Leo's hot nature lends itself to action. The mixture of the two influences results in an alternation between contemplative ecstasy and a compulsion to act (Capasso 185). This idea is perhaps best expressed in Tommaseo's elegant gloss on this passage: "La freddezza di Saturno si contempera col calore del Leone, a simboleggiare che nell'anima de' solitarii buoni è pur calore d'affetto" (3:300) [The heat of Leo tempers the coldness of Saturn to symbolize that in the soul of the good solitary spirits there is also the passion of love].

In the seventh sphere of the *Paradiso*, the two Saturns—the ruler of the Golden Age and the planetary protector of the wise—seem to fuse:

> Dentro al cristallo che 'l vocabol porta,
> cerchiando il mondo, del suo caro duce
> sotto cui giacque ogne malizia morta,
>   di color d'oro in che raggio traluce
> vid' io uno scaleo eretto in suso
> tanto, che nol seguiva la mia luce.
> (*Par.* 21.25–30)

[Within the crystal that—as it revolves
around the earth—bears as its name the name
of that dear king whose rule undid all evil,
   I saw a ladder rising up so high
that it could not be followed by my sight:
its color, gold when gold is struck by sunlight.]

The union of the benign image ("*caro duce*") of the "Roman" Saturn of Virgilian and Ovidian extraction and the Neoplatonic view of the exalted planetary god who presides over philosophical meditation is reinforced by the imagery of the seventh sphere. The ladder which soars into the sky is an obvious emblem of contemplation. It recalls Jacob's ladder in *Genesis* (28.12), referred to explicitly in the following canto (*Par.* 22.70–77), and may also allude to the ladder which adorns the gown of Lady Philosophy in the *Consolation of Philosophy* (1.1). However, the ladder's colour—golden—was probably suggested to Dante by the Golden Age over which the mythical god reigned.

    Dante's representation of Saturn in the *Paradiso* is even more extraordinary if one bears in mind that the two Saturns—the mythical figure and the planetary ruler—were usually kept quite separate in medieval literary texts, as Klibansky, Panofsky, and Saxl point out (192–94), citing the *Romance of the Rose*, Lydgate, Gower, and Chaucer as examples. Moreover, the image of the planetary ruler that prevailed in this literature was that of a cold, dark, and destructive force. In *L'Acerba*, Cecco d'Ascoli calls Saturn "quella trista stella,/ Tarda di corso e di virtù nemica,/ Che mai suo raggio non fè cosa bella" (1.1.19–21) [that sad star, slow in motion and enemy of virtue, whose rays never produced anything beautiful]. Not even residency in the sign of Leo can mitigate his negative influence in Chaucer, who has the old Saturn say of himself in *The Knight's Tale*, "I do vengeance and pleyn correccioun, / Whil I dwelle in the signe of the leoun" (2461–62) [And I do vengeance, I send punishment, . . . when I am in Leo . . .]. Dante seems to depart quite consciously from this pattern. He blurs the distinction between the two Saturns (in the *Paradiso* at least, if not elsewhere) and retrieves the positive Neoplatonic portrait of the cold star, largely shunned by his literary contemporaries and near-contemporaries. Through a felicitous double conjunction—literary and astronomical—his Saturn becomes "a friend of virtue" and produces "beautiful thoughts"—thoughts of rising to God through contemplation.

There may, however, be another less flattering allusion to Saturn in the *Commedia*, which no one to my knowledge has noticed before. It occurs in Dante's celebrated response in *Inferno* 15 to Brunetto Latini's prophecy concerning his imminent exile from Florence:

> Ciò che narrate di mio corso scrivo,
> e serbolo a chiosar con altro testo
> a donna che saprà, s'a lei arrivo.
> Tanto vogl' io che vi sia manifesto,
> pur che mia cosci̇enza non mi garra,
> ch'a la Fortuna, come vuol, son presto.
> Non à nuova a li orecchi miei tal arra:
> però giri Fortuna la sua rota
> come le piace, e 'l villan la sua marra.
>
> (*Inf.* 15.88–96)

> [What you have told me of my course, I write;
> I keep it with another text, for comment
> by one who'll understand, if I may reach her.
> One thing alone I'd have you plainly see:
> so long as I am not rebuked by conscience,
> I stand prepared for Fortune, come what may.
> My ears find no new pledge in that prediction;
> therefore, let Fortune turn her wheel as she
> may please, and let the peasant turn his mattock.]

The commentators are somewhat perplexed by the last two verses ("giri Fortuna la sua rota/ come le piace, e 'l villan la sua marra") and usually gloss them by stating that they sound like a proverb whose meaning is now lost. Singleton's gloss is typical in this regard and I cite it as the sole example: "The peasant (*villano*) idly whirling his mattock is juxtaposed, in a defiant, challenging tone, to Fortune turning her wheel. The phrase, 'e 'l villan [giri] la sua marra' seems to echo some unknown proverb" (268). Elsewhere I have studied the rich commentary tradition on this obscure passage in an effort to shed light on Dante's treatment of the theme of exile in the *Commedia* (Iannucci 115–43). I should now like to return to this passage and consider it strictly from the perspective of Dante's representation of Saturn.

The image of Fortune turning her wheel in verse 95 evokes the traditional medieval personification of the goddess and is in complete harmony with Dante's earlier, more detailed discussion in *Inferno* 7.67–96 (Patch; Pagliaro 161-84; Tollemache; Bommarito). If there is a difference in Dante's two evocations, it is in tone rather than significance. In the Brunetto canto the accent falls on a personal note — Dante's "misfortune" — while in *Inferno* 7 the discourse is all theoretical, aimed at bringing the Boethian pagan goddess into a Christian orbit. What is important from our point of view is that the medieval personification of Fortune is intimately bound with the representation of Time — Time understood as *Kairos*. This connection, studied by Patch, Panofsky, and others,[5] will eventually lead us to Dante's "peasant" (*villano*) and Saturn.

In Greek, *Kairos* means Time, conceived of as "the brief, decisive moment which marks a turning-point in the life of human beings or in the development of the universe" (Panofsky 71; cf. Kermode 47). In ancient art this concept of Time was personified in the figure of Opportunity, illustrated as a man with wings at both shoulders and heels. He carried a pair of scales balanced on the edge of a straight razor, and later, on one or two wheels. His bald head sported a single lock of hair, the forelock by which one seizes Opportunity. By the eleventh century, this allegorical notion of *Kairos* as Opportunity had begun to merge with the related but separate image of Fortune. The eventual assimilation of the two concepts was probably facilitated by the fact that the Latin word for *Kairos*, that is, *Occasio*, was of the same gender as *Fortuna* (Panofsky 72; cf. Patch 115–17). Dante's conception of Fortune in *Inferno* 15 clearly betrays its history. Exile, caused by the "blows of Fortune," marks a critical moment, the turning-point in Dante's life.

This brings us to the image of the peasant tilling the soil with a hoe (verse 96), which Dante juxtaposes, not by chance, with that of Fortune turning her wheel. As it turns out, this image too is linked with Time — Time conceived in this case not as *Kairos* but as *Chronos*, i.e. chronological, sequential Time. The two images, therefore, belong to the same order of ideas. The relationship between the image of the peasant and Chronos is complex, and involves the mediation of Kronos or Saturn, as Panofsky has illustrated in his seminal essay on "Father Time" in *Studies in Iconology* (69–93), to which I appeal in reconstructing briefly the evolution of this relationship to Dante's time. The Greek word *Chronos* sounds very much like the name of the god, Kronos, known to the Romans as Saturn. Because of his association with agriculture and rural life in general, he was often depicted carrying a sickle. The fact that Chronos and Kronos were virtual homonyms was used to justify the identification of the concepts they represented, which indeed shared some characteristics. Thus Saturn's sickle, appropriate originally because of his role as patron of agriculture, was soon viewed as a symbol of the continuous flux of time. The myth that Saturn devoured his own children was allegorized, because of the Chronos-Kronos link, to mean that time devours what he creates.

In the course of time, the Kronos-Saturn figure lost much of his majesty. A dignified if somewhat morose figure, he was depicted in classical art with a sickle in his hand and a veil covering his face. By the Middle Ages, he was represented in less flattering terms. This was due to a large extent, as we have already noted, to his identification with a planet whose influence was generally felt to be sinister and malignant. Astrological imagery emphasized the dark side of Saturn's character, including the more negative aspects of his connection with rural life. Restoro d'Arezzo, for instance, calls Saturn "the King of peasants" who "first made man work the land with a hoe" [che 'l primo fo lavoratore colla zappa] and because of this "he signifies toil, tribulation, anguish and lamentation" (2.2.1) [avarà a significare fatica, tribulazione, angustia, lamentazione]. Saturn himself took on these characteristics. He was depicted mostly as a sick and gloomy old man, often in the garb of a peasant. In place of his original sickle he now carried a spade or mattock. Even this was later replaced by a staff or crutch as Saturn's role as patron of agriculture was subsumed by images suggesting the decrepitude of old age.[6] However, this final transformation of the Kronos-Saturn figure seems to have occurred largely after Dante's death. During his lifetime the image of "Father Time," i.e. the iconography of Kronos-Saturn, had evolved to the stage where he appeared as a peasant turning the soil with a hoe.

To bring this fact into focus, let us take the great fresco cycle in the Salone of the Palazzo della Ragione of Padova, conceived—it would appear—by the Paduan astrologer and philosopher Pietro d'Abano and executed by Giotto and his students during the first two decades of the 14th century (Barzon; Saxl 280–86; Grossato; Ivanoff). In these frescoes, there are two different representations of Saturn and numerous scenes illustrating his qualities. In one of them we see him as a king; he is, however, poorly dressed. He is biting one hand, while with the other he holds a stick with the letter "S" (Saturn) on top (fig. 1). In the other, instead, he is represented as an old man, almost naked, leaning on a hoe (fig. 2). Alone, in the deserted countryside, he looks into a mirror, "quasi a contemplare la sua vecchiaia e miseria" (Barzon 96) [as if contemplating his decrepitude and misery]. There are other scenes which illustrate Saturn's role as patron of agriculture. In two of these we find a peasant who works the fields with a hoe. Finally, another of Saturn's children, a beggar, is represented as an old man who walks with a crutch. This last image suggests an evolution of the iconography of Time (already in progress) which will see Saturn himself represented as an old peasant carrying not a sickle or a hoe, but a crutch.[7]

I have singled out the frescoes of Palazzo della Ragione not because I believe them to be a "source" for Dante in the strict sense of the word, but simply to offer an example of a typical contemporary representation of Saturn.[8] In Dante's time, the iconography of Time had evolved to the point where Saturn was represented as a peasant turning the soil with a hoe. In this light I suggest that Dante's *villano* in *Inferno* 15 is a figure of Kronos-Saturn, i.e. of Time. If this is the case, the exact meaning of verses 95–96 would be "let Fortune turn her wheel as she pleases and let Time continue its relentless course."

But there is more: Saturn was the protector not only of peasants but also of hidden treasures. For example, in the frescoes of the Palazzo della Ragione this quality of Saturn was represented by the figure of an old man kneeling on the ground and hiding something in a dark place.[9] Seen from this perspective, a passage in the *Convivio* acquires new meaning and helps elucidate the significance of verses 95–96 of *Inferno* 15:

Veramente io vidi lo luogo, ne le coste d'un monte che si chiama Falterona, in Toscana, dove lo più vile villano di tutta la contrada, zappando, più d'uno staio di santalene d'argento finissimo vi trovò, che forse più di dumilia anni l'aveano aspettato. (*Conv.* 4.11.8)[10]

[Indeed I once saw the place, on the side of a mountain named Falterona, in Tuscany, where the basest peasant of the entire region found, while digging about, more than a bushel of Santelenas of the finest silver which had been waiting for him for perhaps 2000 years or more.]

It is important to note that this passage is part of a larger discourse on "fortune": indeed, it is an example of the first of the three ways riches may be acquired: ". . . da pura fortuna, sì come quando sanza intenzione o speranza vegnono per invenzione alcuna non pensata" (*Conv.* 4.11.7) [. . . by chance, as for example when they are acquired without design or unexpectedly by virtue of some unplanned event]. Commentators have assumed that Dante is recounting a fact from his own experience in order to exemplify how little merit has to do with the acquisition of wealth (Pagliaro 176). They have also tried to identify the exact place where "il villano da Falterona" discovered the fabulous treasure (Bassermann 606).

In reality, in this passage Dante takes up and renders concrete the example Boethius gives at the end of the first prose section in Book 5 of the *Consolation of Philosophy* of the unpredictable operation of fortune.[11]

Fortune is the unexpected intersection in time of two independent lines of causality, as when one man buries a treasure to hide it, and another digs it up, not because he is looking for it, but because he is tilling a field. Unfortunately, Boethius uses the term *"cultor agri"* rather than the low Latin *"villanus."* However, there is little doubt that we are dealing with the same figure that we find in the *Convivio*, where Dante's specification of the *villano*—da Falterona—has the effect of veiling the figure of Saturn, the protector of peasants and hidden treasures. The coupling of fortune with a peasant already occurs, therefore, in the *Convivio* and the association goes back at least to Boethius. However, in Dante's concise formulation in *Inferno 15*, the pairing takes on—as has been noticed—the proverbial ring of a popular expression. Moreover, in the infernal context the example is transformed into a metaphor. The peasant becomes Time itself. As the peasant's hoe can unearth gold or stones, silver or rocks, so the passage of Time can bring fortune or misfortune, prosperity or exile.

On the heels of Boethius, Dante in both the *Convivio* and the *Commedia* links fortune with a peasant, but often the image of the peasant yields to the concept which it personifies, i.e. Time. As far as I can tell, Dante never brings the two concepts—Fortune and Time—together in a single syntactical unit. However, in *Paradiso* 17 he does, referring to his exile, speak alternately of the "blows of Fortune" and "the blows of Time," which would indicate that in his mind the two concepts were connected:

> dette mi fuor di mia vita futura
> parole gravi, avvegna ch'io mi senta
> ben tetragono ai *colpi di ventura*.
> (*Par.* 17.22-24)

[. . . what I heard
about my future life were grievous words—
although, against the blows of chance I feel
myself as firmly planted as a cube.]

> Ben veggio, padre mio, sì come sprona
> lo *tempo* verso me, per *colpo* darmi
> tal, ch'è più grave a chi più s'abbandona.
> (*Par.* 17.106-108)

[. . . "I clearly see, my father,
. . .how time is hurrying toward me in order
to deal me such a blow as would be most
grievous for him who is not set for it."]

The pairing of Fortune and Time was, however, relatively common in the Middle Ages and the Renaissance, as Patch has demonstrated (115–17). Of the many examples he gives, I shall cite only one, from the *Orlando Furioso*: "per colpa di Tempo e di Fortuna" (34.73) [by fault of Time and Fortune]. Ariosto's verse glosses Dante's difficult passage in *Inferno 15* more accurately and elegantly than any learned commentary could ever hope to do. What is lacking in Ariosto is the defiant, challenging tone which animates Dante's expression, giving it a proverbial ring.

It is impossible to determine conclusively whether Dante was fully aware that behind his peasant lurked the menacing figure of Saturn, although the evidence seems to suggest that he was. However, he certainly was aware that the image of the peasant turning the soil with a hoe must somehow be connected with Time, and that Fortune and Time belonged to the same order of phenomena. The expression should not, therefore, be taken simply as an emotional response to Brunetto's prophecy, but rather as a precise testimony to the fact that Dante realizes that Time — *Chronos* — is moving relentlessly towards exile, and that this event will mark a dramatic turning-point in his life — a *Kairos*. It will be the task of Cacciaguida (and not Beatrice, as it turns out) to delineate clearly to him what exile will bring:

> Tu lascerai ogne cosa diletta
> più caramente; e questo è quello strale
> che l'arco de lo essilio pria saetta.
> Tu proverai sì come sa di sale
> lo pane altrui, e come è duro calle
> lo scendere e 'l salir per l'altrui scale.
>
> (*Par.* 17.55-60)

> [You shall leave everything you love most dearly:
> this is the arrow that the bow of exile
> shoots first. You are to know the bitter taste
> of others' bread, how salt it is, and know
> how hard a path it is for one who goes
> descending and ascending others' stairs.]

So Cacciaguida, speaking from the perspective of eternity (*Par.* 17.17–18), finally glosses "il parlar nemico" [the hostile words] of Farinata, Brunetto, and others who in Hell and Purgatory had alluded to Dante's exile. In fine, before Dante's ultimate redemption — the theme of exile is resolved at the anagogical, not the historical plane — he must suffer much from the blows of fortune and time: "colpi di ventura e di tempo."

Dante's portrait of Saturn in *Inferno* 15 clearly differs from the one which emerges in other parts of the *Commedia* where his positive traits are featured. He is identified with the "Saturnia regna," the mythic Golden Age when virtue and justice prevailed: "il caro duce/ sotto cui giacque ogne malizia morta" (*Par.* 21.26–27). Moreover, as planetary ruler, he is presented in the best possible light. A fortunate conjunction of the planet with Leo allows Dante to retrieve the Neoplatonic tradition of Saturn as overseer of the contemplative life. It is worth noting, however, that in the sphere of Saturn, in contrast to the rest of Paradise, Beatrice does not smile and the blessed do not sing (*Par.* 21.4-12, 58–63). The reason given is that if this were to happen, Dante would be completely overwhelmed since his faculties are still not ready for such an occurrence. This detail may, however, betray a trace of Saturn's negative reputation. Those born under his influence may be wise but they are not happy. The darker side of his character emerges more forcefully in *Inferno* 15, where he is depicted as a lowly peasant working the land. Despite his decrepit state, he still exerts a powerful negative influence over the course of man's destiny. In Dante's case, it leads to exile.

University of Toronto

NOTES

1 For a brief account of Dante's representation of Saturn, see the entry in the *Enciclopedia dantesca*, which is divided into three parts: the first, by Padoan, deals with the mythological figure ("Saturno"), the second, by Poulle, with Saturn the planet ("Il Pianeta"), and the third, by Aurigemma, with the souls in the sphere of Saturn ("Cielo di Saturno"). See also the short entry on "Saturnia regna" by Pastore Stocchi.
2 Cf. Singleton, *Purgatorio 2. Commentary* 528. For the myth of Astraea in the *Commedia*, see Singleton, *Journey to Beatrice* 184–203.
3 See, for example, Restoro d'Arezzo, *La composizione del mondo* 2.8.6. See also Busnelli and Vandelli 188–89.
4 Saturn's principal house is Aquarius, his secondary one Capricorn. See *La composizione del mondo* 2.2.1; Barzon 4.
5 The following section, which traces the iconographical depiction of *Kairos* and *Chronos* to Dante's time, is indebted principally to Panofsky's essay on "Father Time," and Klibansky *et al.* 125–214. Also useful: Patch, *The Goddess Fortuna in Medieval Literature*; Wittkower; Chew 1–69; Macey 1–66.
6 For this evolution, see Panofsky, figures 35–68, and figures 39 and 40 in Klibansky *et al.*

7 For a description of all the illustrations relating to Saturn, see Barzon 95–100; especially pertinent to our discussion are figures 91C, 92C, 94B, 102B, and 104B. For a more recent and general treatment (with illustrations) of the Palazzo della Ragione, see the essays in *Il Palazzo della Ragione di Padova*.
8 Dante probably never had occasion to see Giotto's work. It is also unlikely that he had direct knowledge of Pietro d'Abano's works, on which the great Paduan fresco cycle is generally assumed (Barzon 187–205; Saxl 280–86; Ivanoff) to be based. However, for a comparison of some of Dante's opinions with the astrological doctrines of Pietro d'Abano, see Nardi 43–65.
9 See Barzon 97–98 and figure 102C.
10 This passage has been related to *Inferno* 15.95–96 by at least two commentators: Pagliaro 176–77 notes the similar phrasing but makes little of the connection; on the other hand, Pézard 401–405 deals more extensively with the possible relationship between the two passages, but links them in an abstruse and fanciful manner. See Iannucci 120–22.
11 The commentators, including Busnelli and Vandelli, seem to have overlooked the Boethian source of Dante's passage. I would like to thank A. Wingell of the University of Toronto for having suggested it to me. I quote the passage (5.1.38–53) in its entirety: "Quotiens . . . aliquid cuiuspiam rei gratia geritur aliudque quibusdam de causis quam quod intendebatur obtingit, casus uocatur, ut si quis colendi agri causa fodiens humum defossi auri pondus inueniat. Hoc igitur fortuito quidem creditur accidisse, uerum non de nihilo est; nam proprias causas habet quarum inprouisus inopinatusque concursus casum uidetur operatus. Nam nisi cultor agri humum foderet, nisi eo loci pecuniam suam depositor obruisset, aurum non esset inuentum. Haec sunt igitur fortuiti causa compendii, quod ex obuiis sibi et confluentibus causis, non ex gerentis intentione prouenit. Neque enim uel qui aurum obruit uel qui agrum exercuit ut ea pecunia reperiretur intendit; sed uti dixi, quo ille obruit hunc fodisse conuenit atque concurrit." [When . . . anything is done for some certain cause, and some other thing happeneth for other reasons than that which was intended, this is called chance; as if one digging his ground with intention to till it, findeth an hidden treasure. This is thought to have fallen thus out by fortune, but it is not of nothing, for it hath peculiar causes whose unexpected and not foreseen concourse seemeth to have brought forth a chance. For unless the husbandman had digged up his ground, and unless the other had hidden his money in that place, the treasure had not been found. These are therefore the causes of this fortunate accident, which proceedeth from the meeting and concourse of causes, and not from the intention of the doer. For neither he that hid the gold nor he that tilled his ground had any intention that the money should be found, but, as I said, it followed and concurred that this man should dig in the place where the other hid.]

WORKS CITED

Alighieri, Dante. *La Commedia secondo l'antica vulgata*. 4 voll. A cura di G. Petrocchi. Milano: Mondadori, 1966–67.
————. *Commedia*. 3 voll. Con ragionamenti e note di N. Tommaseo. Milano: Francesco Pagnoni, Tipografo Editore, 1869.
————. *The Divine Comedy*. Trans. A. Mandelbaum. 3 vols. New York: Bantam Books, 1986.
————. *The Divine Comedy*. 6 vols. Translated, with a commentary, by C.S. Singleton. Princeton: Princeton University Press, 1970-75.
————. *Convivio*. Commentato da G. Busnelli e G. Vandelli. In *Opere di Dante*. Vol. 5. Parte 2. 2a ed. Firenze: Le Monnier, 1964.
————. *Dante's Il Convivio (The Banquet)*. Trans. R.H. Lansing. New York: Garland Publishing, 1990.
————. *Le opere di Dante*. 2a ed. Firenze: Nella Sede della Societ Dantesca, 1960.
Aurigemma, M. "Cielo di Saturno." *Enciclopedia dantesca*. A cura di U. Bosco et al. 5 voll. e appendice. Vol. 5. 1976. Roma: Istituto dell'Enciclopedia Italiana, 1970–78. 42–43.
Barzon, A. *I cieli e la loro influenza negli affreschi del Salone in Padova*. Padova: Tipografia Seminario, 1924.
Bassermann, A. *Orme di Dante*. Bologna: Zanichelli, 1902.
Boethius. *Theological Tractates* and *The Consolation of Philosophy*. Trans. H.F. Stewart and E.K. Rand. Cambridge, Mass.: Harvard University Press, 1918.
Bommarito, D. "Boezio e la fortuna di Dante in *Inf.* VII, 61–96." *L'Alighieri* 20.1 (1979): 42–56.
Capasso, I. *L'astronomia nella Divina Commedia*. Pisa: Domus Galilaeanna, 1967.
Cecco d'Ascoli. *L'Acerba*. A cura di A. Crespi. Ascoli Piceno: Casa Editrice di Giuseppe Cesari, 1927.
Chaucer, Geoffrey. *Works*. 2a ed. Ed. F.N. Robinson. Boston: Houghton Mifflin Co., 1961.
Chew, C. *The Pilgrimage of Life*. New Haven: Yale University Press, 1962.
Comparetti, D. *Vergil in the Middle Ages*. Trans. E.F.M. Benecke. 1908. Hamden, Conn.: Archon Books, 1966.
Grossato, L. "La decorazione pittorica del Salone." In *Il Palazzo della Ragione di Padova*. Venezia: Neri Pozza, 1964. 45–67.
Ivanoff, N. "Il problema iconografico degli affreschi." In *Il Palazzo della Ragione di Padova*. Venezia: Neri Pozza, 1964. 69–84.
Kermode, F. *The Sense of an Ending*. London: Oxford University Press, 1970.
Klibansky, R., E. Panofsky and F. Saxl. *Saturn and Melancholy*. London: Thomas Nelson and Sons, 1964.
Lana, Jacopo della. *Commento alla Comedia di Dante degli Allagherii*. A cura di L. Scarabelli. 3 voll. Bologna: Tipografia Regia, 1866.
Latini, Brunetto. *Il Tesoro*. Volgarizzato da Bono Giamboni. A cura di P. Chabaille.

Vol. 1. Bologna: Presso Gaetano Romagnoli, 1878.
Macey, S.L. *Patriarchs of Time*. Athens and London: The University of Georgia Press, 1987.
Nardi, B. *Saggi di filosofia dantesca*. Milano: Società Anonima Editrice Dante Alighieri, 1930.
Ovid. *Fasti*. Trans. J.G. Frazer. Cambridge, Mass.: Harvard University Press, 1959.
_____. *Metamorphoses*. 2 vols. Trans. F.J. Miller. London: William Heinemann, 1916.
Padoan, G. "Saturno." *Enciclopedia dantesca*. Vol. 5. Roma: Istituto dell'Enciclopedia Italiana, 1976. 41.
Pagliaro, A. *Ulisse: ricerche semantiche sulla Divina Commedia*. Vol. 1. Messina-Firenze: Casa Editrice G. D'Anna, 1967.
Il Palazzo della Ragione di Padova. Venezia: Neri Pozza, 1964.
Panofsky, E. *Studies in Iconology*. New York: Harper and Row, 1972.
Pastore Stocchi, M. "Saturnia regna." *Enciclopedia dantesca*. Vol. 5. Roma: Istituto dell'Enciclopedia Italiana, 1976. 41.
Patch, H.R. "The Goddess Fortuna in the *Divine Comedy*." *The Thirty-Third Annual Report of the Dante Society of America*. Cambridge, Massachusetts (1914):13–28.
_____. *The Goddess Fortuna in Medieval Literature*. 1927. New York: Octagon Books, 1967.
Pézard, A. *Dante sous la pluie de feu (Enfer, Chant XV)*. Paris: J. Vrin, 1950.
Poulle, E. "Saturno: Il Pianeta." *Enciclopedia dantesca*. Vol. 5. Roma: Istituto dell'Enciclopedia Italiana, 1976. 42.
Restoro d'Arezzo. *La composizione del mondo*. A cura di A. Morino. Firenze: Presso L'Accademia della Crusca, 1976.
Saxl, F. *La fede negli astri*. A cura di A. Settis. Torino: Boringhieri, 1985.
Singleton, C.S. *Dante Studies 2: Journey to Beatrice*. Cambridge, Mass.: Harvard University Press, 1958.
Tollemache, F. "Fortuna." *Enciclopedia dantesca*. Vol. 2. Roma: Istituto dell'Enciclopedia Italiana, 1970. 983–86.
Tractato del corso della Luna. In Pezzella, S. *Astronomia ed Astrologia nel Medioevo da un manoscritto inedito (Sec. XIII) della città di Firenze*. Firenze: Editrice La Giuntina, 1982.
Virgil. *Aeneid*. 2 vols. Trans H.R. Fairclough. Cambridge, Mass.: Harvard University Press, 1974.
_____. *Eclogues*. Trans. H.R. Fairclough. Cambridge, Mass.: Harvard University Press, 1974.
Wittkower, R. "Chance, Time and Virtue." *Journal of the Warburg Institute* 1 (1937–38):313–21.

FIG. 1: **Saturn as King.** Salone, Palazzo della Ragione, Padova.

FIG. 2: **Saturn with hoe.** Salone, Palazzo della Ragione, Padova.

James F. Burke

The Polarities of Desire: Saturn in the *Libro de buen amor*

The two traditional opposing views of the nature of Saturn are well represented in Spain of the thirteenth century in works having to do with Alfonso the Wise. The *Setenario*, a composition which recounts the accomplishments of Alfonso's father Ferdinand III, is negative in its assessment of the god and planet. "Et la ssu propriedat quel dauan era pereza e tristeza e duelos. . . . Et de los metales le dauan el plomo porque es negro e huele mal e non ffazen dél color que paresca ffermoso. . . . Et aoráuanle derechamente contra trasmontana, donde viene el frio" (62-63). [And the propriety which they gave to him was slowness and sadness and sorrows. . . . And of metals they assigned to him lead because it is black and has a bad smell and one cannot derive from it a beautiful colour . . . and they worshipped him oriented in the direction of the north wind which brings the cold.]

In the *General Estoria* Alfonso's corps of writers present Saturn in a positive light. Alfonso, like most ambitious medieval rulers, had money problems and this is, perhaps, the reason why Saturn's description is given almost entirely in commercial terms. "Saturno . . . e fue princep derechero, e começo muchos derechos en la tierra: vender las cosas a medida e a peso, et fazer por los buenos logares mercados pregonados e coteados, a que se acogiessen los omnes a vender e a comprar, et mando tomar metales en precio de las otras cosas segund valiessen, et fazie las yentes sin toda contienda e a cada uno en lo suyo, e tenie la tierra en paz, en justicia e abondada" (1.156). [Saturn . . . and he was a prince who rendered justice according to the law, and he established many just practices in the land: the selling of things by measure and by weight, and the establishing of well-known and legally regulated markets in good places to which people might go to buy and sell. And he ordered that metals be accepted as payment for other things in line with what they were worth, and he made people live together without problems, each person with his own, and he thus caused the land to exist in peace and justice and with abundance.] If the composers of the *General Estoria* were aware of Saturn's patronage of artistic creativity and learning, they do not show it, but I think that we can assume that they would have been aware that the Saturnian golden age would have encompassed more than peace and commerce. The modern Spanish scholar J.E. Cirlot in his *Dictionary of Symbols* has noted that when Saturn is merged with Cronos, even in his positive aspect, another variety of difficulty appears. The slow, implacable dynamism of realization and communication, the progress in things temporal are countered by the restlessness and insufficiency which emerge in the individual haunted by the passage of time and his knowledge of the fact that he will eventually cease to exist, as it were, devoured by Saturn (265–266). It also was characteristic of the medieval explanation of human psychology to believe that the individual particularly blessed by Saturn in the first area would be more prone also to the sufferings in the second by the *melancolia nigra* (Klibansky).

In any discussion of progress and passion in the Middle Ages and Renaissance, the subject of love is always important and it is not surprising that writers and thinkers would have been interested in how Saturn, and those aspects associated with him, would have affected the lover. In the *Roman de la Rose*, in Lydgate, Gower and in Chaucer's *Knight's Tale*, to cite only a few examples, the theme of Saturnine influences is entwined with ruminations on the subject of love and and how the individual is affected by amorous passions.

In addition to those connected directly with the figure of Saturn, there were also themes having to do with the idea of the *Saturnalia* and all its associated symbols. The Romans probably named their lively winter festival of renewal after Saturn because of the association of this god with ideas of progress and positive change (York; Bermejo Barrera 27). But again in these ceremonies the positive aspects of renovation and replenishment are countered by negative themes such as sacrifice and an emphasis on momentary destruction so that eventual recreation can occur.

In Spain in the early fourteenth century it is clear that writers understood the connection between such common Saturnian themes as the world upside down, inversions in the political sphere and the like, and the ultimate well-being of the political order.[1] Juan Manuel in his *Conde Lucanor* uses the story of the ruler who is allowed absolute sway for a year and then is removed at the end, in his *exemplum* 49. In fact, the first *exemplum*, as well as the last three, in some manner treat or imply the idea of inversion and role reversal as coupled to the political context (Burke,

Frame). But nowhere in the *Conde Lucanor* is there reference to Saturn or to the *Saturnalia*.

The *Libro de buen amor*, which was composed roughly in the same period as the *Conde Lucanor*, does combine on the other hand reference to the old god with allusions to activities which resemble those of the *Saturnalia*. Here the central problem, as is obvious in the title, relates to the individual who is attempting to deal with passion and desire. What is *buen amor* and what is *loco amor* and how does the individual know the difference between them? The duality present in the Saturnian tradition offers an excellent backdrop against which to present the individual struggling with a definition of love and its attendant circumstances.

Some years ago I studied the Golden Age drama *La estrella de Sevilla* in which I attempted to demonstrate that the beautiful and desirable heroine Estrella, whom the play teasingly associates with Venus, is really a black Saturnine star (Burke, "The Estrella"). Eventually the principal male character, the King, who is at first blinded by lust for Estrella and thereby compelled to evil deeds, will come to understand his duty and will finally proceed to establish the kind of just kingdom spoken of by the writers of Alfonso the Wise. In *La estrella de Sevilla*, the King, having experienced the turmoil of the play and having learned from it, and deeply affected by the positive influence of Saturn, will effect a restoration of justice and concord. In *La estrella de Sevilla* the playwright relates the passion of the individual to the well-being of the state—all in a context of symbols and ideas traditionally associated with Saturn. Such an association is readily understandable considering the ancient belief that Saturn and the *Saturnalia* relate in some fashion to the well-being of the political sphere.[2]

The *Libro de buen amor* is also concerned with concepts of order and harmony. Resolution here is not implied or achieved within the body of the work. If such occurs (and it is not at all clear that such is implied), it must be through, and in accord with, a series of systems outside the text. Thus, although there appears to be no direct involvement of the *corpus politicum* as in the *Conde Lucanor* or *La estrella de Sevilla*, such could very well be understood depending upon how far one extends the series of parallel systems.

Judson Allen has shown that the medieval writer usually does not incorporate all the important threads relevant to his or her work into the composition itself. Rather the work is "assimilated to" or placed in parallel with other systems which the medieval world considered important. In a literary work after the Renaissance such as *La estrella de Sevilla*, all important themes will be adequately displayed and dealt with within the text itself. Thus in this work ideas of love, Saturn, and political order all find resolution before the play closes.

There is no sense of closure in the modern sense of the word in Juan Ruiz's poem. Its themes are in interplay with those of numerous other systems outside the text and the end of the poem arrives when the poet decides to continue no longer his recounting of this interplay.[3] In accord with another widespread medieval tradition he, in fact, invites others to "gloss" his text so that in effect the interplay of parallel systems might be understood as practically endless.

At the level of what medieval commentators called the *forma tractatus* (Allen 117–178), the apparent surface structure of the work, the *Libro de buen amor* is a series of poetic compositions knit together loosely by the figure of the archpriest-poet himself and by various interlaced themes. His avowed purpose is to teach about the "buen amor" of Christ and the Virgin, while presenting simultaneously a rowdy rendition of the various aspects of the "loco amor de este mundo." Nowhere in the text is there a direct association of the hero-poet with Saturn, but Peter Dunn has demonstrated that such is doubtless present.[4]

Near the beginning of the work the poet reasons that his constant desire for women can only come from a strong influence of Venus in his life:

> muchos nasçen en Venus, que lo más de su vida
> es amar las mugeres, nunca se les olvida;
> trabajan e afanan muy mucho, sin medida,
> e los más non recabdan la cosa más querida.
>
> En este signo atal creo que yo nascí:
> sienpre puné en servir dueñas que conoscí;
> el bien que me feçieron non lo desgradesçí:
> a muchas serví mucho, que nada acabesçí.
> (*Libro* 152–153)

[Many are born under the sign of Venus and most of their life
has to do with loving women, they never forget this;
they struggle and toil a great deal, without measure,
but the majority never achieve their object.

I think that I was born under this sign:
I always exerted myself to serve the women that I knew;
I was not ungrateful for the good that they did me:
I served many a great deal but I never achieved success.]

Thus the poet is never really successful in any of his amorous escapades and he is later forced to ask himself: "¡quál fue la razón negra por que non recabdé?" (*Libro* 577). Toward the end of the book, while attempting to seduce a nun for the hero, his go-between Trotaconventos gives a long description of the poet. Using ancient and medieval tracts concerned with physiognomy, Dunn demonstrates that this description shows that the poet bore the physical markings of Saturn. The good love of the individual born under Venus will be as impossible for him as it would be for Estrella in *La estrella de Sevilla*.

The *Libro de buen amor* comes down to us in two manuscript versions, both of which are much later than the time of the supposed composition of the work (Deyermond). The second manuscript reflects what seem to be changes and additions to an original. This manuscript begins with ten stanzas in which the archpriest begs to have release from some variety of prison—whether real or metaphysical. This version thus is headed with a section in which the poet finds himself in a situation traditionally associated with Saturn.[5] Coming, as it does, at the beginning of the book, before the poet recounts his amorous adventures, there is the implication that the desire expressed here for liberation means escape from the process of time which is, of course, expressed textually with the amorous adventures.

> Señor Dios, que a los jodíos, pueblo de perdiçion,
> saqueste de cabtivo, del poder de Faraón,
> a Daniel saqueste del poço babilón:
> saca a mí d'esta mala presión.
>
> (*Libro* 1)

[Lord God, who delivered the Jews, a lost people,
from the power of Pharoah,
Who brought Daniel forth from the lions's den in Babylon:
Deliver me from this evil prison.]

Now the adventures of love of the poet divide roughly into two parts in the book. The first occur atemporally. They are not related particularly to time or to its passage. The second main group of adventures is closely connected sequentially to calendar events, those of the liturgical year and behind them those of traditional folklore.

The sequence begins in the month of March when the poet tells us that he is visited by an old woman who scolds him for a lack of vigor in pursuing his amorous quests. Next on March 3, the feast of St. Emeterius, he starts out across the still snowy mountains on a pilgrimage to Segovia.

Both on the way there and on his return he is attacked and ravished by hideous wild women who are the opposites of the lovely ladies whom he has been so ardently desiring. After his return home to safety, there is a long description of the battle between Doña Cuaresma and Don Carnal with her initial victory. On Holy Saturday Don Carnal re-enters Toledo in savage splendour to be followed the next day, Easter Sunday, by Don Amor.

On Low Sunday, the traditional day for weddings after Easter, the Archpriest finds himself again enamoured and sends for his old retainer Trotaconventos to continue his chase of love. On St. Mark's Day, April 25, he sees a beautiful woman praying devoutly before a statue of Christ. He attempts to set up an assignation with her, as usual, without success. This episode is the last one in the calendar sequence which runs from March 3 through April 25. If one accepts that the trip to Segovia is in some fashion metaphorically parallel to Carnival, as several critics have (Beltrán and de Lope), then the sequence is one from Carnival up to the time of the May ceremonies. The themes of Carnival and in fact of many of the "rites of spring" have been traditionally associated with the Roman *Saturnalia* (Caro Baroja; Burke, "Juan").

Modern students of these kinds of practices and ceremonies having to do with change and renewal which began in December and continued as long as June have understood these rites as ones related to the rebirth of the year. Ancient communities developed an elaborate ceremonial which not only celebrated the increasing light as well as the anticipation and arrival of spring, but which was also understood as playing an important role in ensuring that renewal did take place.

In the *Libro de buen amor* the old woman who scolds the poet can be seen as illustrative of these principles. Such a figure was often used as a representation of the vanishing winter (Burke, "Juan"). The mountain girls who attack the hero en route to Segovia demonstrate the inversion of roles so frequently encountered in such rites. The battle between Doña Cuaresma and Don Carnal has been understood by ethnologists as related to and perhaps even ultimately deriving from a primitive ludic battle between winter and spring staged as a drama. The entry of Don Carnal on Holy Saturday into Toledo followed by the elaborate *adventus* of Don Amor on Easter Sunday is an assimilation of these two figures into the legitimate liturgical sequence of the moment, which is absolutely related to themes of renewal and resurrection.

In the *Libro de buen amor* the next event takes place on Low Sunday. In Rome the Saturday before Low Sunday was the date of the *Cornomania*, a feast still recorded in the eleventh century, whose description demonstrates its place among the rites of spring (Boiteux). And finally St. Mark's Day, the 25th of April, corresponds to the Roman *Robigalia*, the moment at which certain practices were performed to protect the sprouting wheat against rust.

Students of such rites have noticed that they express and are always concerned not only with the positive aspects of renewal but also with certain problematic features. The Spanish anthropologist Josefina Roma Riu has pointed out that in these rites, largely ignored by official religion, there survives the ancient worry and preoccupation with ancestors. At the beginning of these cycles, it was believed that the dead return and that they must be assured a passage across the earth and a return to the other world lest they exercise a negative and destructive influence upon the longed-for revival of nature.

The French ethnologist Jacques Bril, in his study of the function of the mask in such ceremonies, relates these coverings to the figure of the primordial father figure or to socio-psychic avatars of him such as supposed spirits of ancestors, legendary heroes, and the like. This father figure is a metaphor for the organizing principles which give form and structure to a culture. Such structures are obviously basic and necessary to the existence of a community but they must be examined, altered, and renewed if the group is to survive. The rites of spring then are concerned on one plane with the structures which organize the cosmos and the natural world, while on another they deal with those which coordinate human society. Always accompanying the rites of joyous celebration are the fear and suspicion that the process will not succeed and that the community will have to endure the unpleasant consequences.

In the *Libro de buen amor* the archpriest-hero suffers from Saturnian influences. The dualities traditionally associated with Saturn find expression in him as they do in *La estrella de Sevilla* in terms of love. For him the question of love has been ordered and decided by a system (the ecclesiastical one) which requires him to suppress the physical aspects of it or sublimate it into acceptable expressions of fraternal and human feeling. He is unable to do this and what results is a merging of his personal difficulties concerning this important problem of human order with the greater framework having to do with the community and the cosmos. The liturgical year and the folkloric practices having to do with renewal and the return of spring constitute this framework. As the year moves through its cycle, so the hero also undergoes experiences which are parallel. Love and desire are constantly revived in him just as yearnings for the order and harmony of a lost Golden Age haunt the imaginations of political thinkers. Saturn presides over progress in things temporal but he is also symbolic of the insufficiency of the order of existence within the plane of the temporal. The processes of renewal must take place annually but they will never achieve the perfection of the lost Golden Age. The poet's problems of love will never be resolved within the bounds of this earthly precinct. The introductory stanzas with the pleas of the poet for release provide the only answer for final and definitive resolution. Ultimately the only perfect and final renewal, the resolution of all disharmonies, will take place for the poet, as they do for Troilus in Chaucer's *Troilus and Criseyde*, not on this earth but in another realm.

University of Toronto

NOTES

1 Such themes are also common to Carnival. In the Renaissance and afterwards it was commonly held that there was some variety of connection between this period of excess and release and the *Saturnalia*, although such is difficult to establish (Caro Baroja, *passim*).
2 As far as I am aware, no one has been able to explain adequately why and how this nexus of themes came to be related. Thus it is impossible to say whether practices common to Carnival and to the *Saturnalia* really imply that the former derives from the latter — although, certainly writers from the Renaissance forward have thought so (Caro Baroja, *passim*).
3 See Hult for an excellent study of systems of closure in medieval works.
4 Luce López-Baralt also discusses Juan Ruiz and his astrological sign. She thinks that he might have been born under Venus in aspect with Saturn, with Mars in opposition.
5 For example the famous line in Chaucer's *The Knight's Tale*: "Mine is the prison in the derke cote" (2457). See also Klibansky, *passim*.

WORKS CITED

Arcipreste de Hita. *Libro de buen amor*. Ed. Jacques Joset. 2 vols. Madrid: Espasa-Calpe, 1974 (Clásicos Castellanos 14, 17).
Alfonso X. *General Estoria*. I. Ed. A.G. Solalinde. Madrid, 1930.
———. *Setenario*. Ed. Kenneth H. Vanderford. Buenos Aires: Instituto de Filología, 1945.
Allen, J.B. *The Ethical Poetic of the Later Middle Ages: A Decorum of Convenient Distinction*. Toronto: U of Toronto P, 1982.

Beltrán, L. *Razones de buen amor: oposiciones y convergencias en el libro del Arcipreste de Hita*. Madrid: Castalia, 1947.

Bermejo Barrera, J.C. *Mitología y mitos de la Hispania prerromana*. Madrid: Akal, 1982.

Boiteux, M. "Cornomania et carnaval romain medieval." *Le Carnaval, la fête et la communication: Actes des premières rencontres internationales. Nice, 8 au 10 mars 1984*. Nice: Editions Serre, 1985. 111–125.

Bril, J. *Le Masque ou le père ambigu*. Paris: Payot, 1983.

Burke, J.F. "'The Estrella de Sevilla and the Tradition of Saturnine Melancholy." *BHS* 51 (1974): 137–156.

———. "Juan Ruiz, the Serranas, and the Rites of Spring." *JMRS* 5 (1975): 13–35.

———. "Frame and Structure in El Conde Lucanor." *RCEH* 8 (1984): 263–273.

Caro Baroja, J. *El Carnaval: análisis histórico-cultural*. Madrid: 1965.

Chaucer, G. *The Works of Geoffrey Chaucer*. Ed. F.N. Robinson. 2nd ed. Boston: 1957.

Cirlot, J.E. *A Dictionary of Symbols*. Trans. Jack Sage. New York: Philosophical Library, 1962.

De Lope, M. *Traditions populaires et textualité dans le "Libro de Buen Amor."* Montpellier: C.E.R.S., n.d.

Deyermond, A.D. *Historia de la literatura española: la edad media*. Trans. Luis Alonso López. Barcelona: Ariel, 1974.

Dunn, P. "De las figuras del arçipreste." *Libro de buen amor Studies*. Ed. G.B. Gybbon-Monypenny. London: Tamesis, 1970. 79–93.

Hult, D. *Self-fulfilling Prophecies: Readership and Authority in the First Roman de la Rose*. Cambridge: CUP, 1986.

Klibansky, R., E. Panofsky and F. Saxl. *Saturn and Melancholy: Studies in the History of Natural Philosophy*. London: Nelson, 1964.

López-Baralt, L. "Sobre el signo astológico del Arcipreste de Hita." *Huellas del Islam en la literatura española*. Madrid: Hiperion, 1985. 43–58.

Roma Riu, J. *Aragón y el carnaval*. Zaragoza: Guara, n.d.

York, M. *The Roman Festival Calendar of Numa Pompilius*. New York: Peter Lang, 1986.

Donald A. Beecher

From Myth to Narrative: Saturn in Lefevre and Caxton

That the various fragments of myth associated with the name of Saturn and implicitly his Greek counterpart Kronos persisted in the mythological writings of the Christian West is, in a theoretical sense, remarkable. Since scholars in that age were no longer in touch with the occult significance of these fragments relating to the fertility cults of the ancient Mediterranean world,[1] it was not particularly obvious to them what to do with a brutal protagonist remembered for consuming and disgorging his own children, and for having his genitals cut off by his son and cast into the sea. Yet certain of those pieces of an assumed story about this pagan *cosmocrator* not only survived, but managed to preserve their narrative integrity in spite of internal contradictions, and in spite of centuries of adaptation, glossing, moralizing and allegorizing—through which manipulation alone the Christian mythographers could justify their interest in this pagan lore. The tortuous route by which the Saturn group of narrative parts made its way from the already remotely remembered versions of the late Roman compilers Fulgentius, Macrobius, Servius and Martianus Capella through the early Christianizing of Lactantius, the encyclopedic entries of Isadore of Seville and Vincent of Beauvais, down through the moral glossing of Bersuire and the cataloguing of Albricus, to the first signs of a humanist recovery from original sources in Boccaccio's *Genealogy of the Gods*, I leave to the description of such scholars as Jean Seznec in his *The Survival of the Pagan Gods*, and to Klibansky, Panofsky and Saxl in their monumental *Saturn and Melancholy*. What becomes clear is that while the matter of Saturn had staying power, it also contained a heterogeneous complement of elements that brought the same challenge to each redactor of the myth: how to recover the story of Saturn without doing violence to the diverse components of the Saturn tradition. What follows is an analysis of the formula through which a late fifteenth-century court poet met that challenge and thereby produced what was arguably the best known and most widely received version of the Saturn myth in the French and English speaking worlds throughout the Renaissance.

For this writer, the task was not merely how to gather up all the parts, but how to make them cohere in a single narrative account of Saturn and his deeds that possessed an acceptable degree, by fifteenth-century standards, both of historical and of psychological verisimilitude. Perhaps once that course of redaction had suggested itself to him, many of the answers would have become apparent, but it cannot be discounted that all the jarring parts of the tradition remained to be dealt with, parts, in fact, so discordant that only a writer of considerable inventiveness could hope to bring them together. Klibansky, Saxl and Panofsky offer a resumé of the sources for the Saturn tradition from Hesiod and Homer to Macrobius and Lactantius that, together, produce a composite personality marked by contradiction and ambivalence (134–135). According to the surviving episodes of his story, he was at once the god of the golden age, a benefactor and inventor, the ruler over a realm of happy primitive men, and a man tormented by the oracles and doomed to devour his own children in order to avert the prophecy that he would be overthrown by his own son. He was associated with the sickle which was both a symbol of the harvest, and the instrument by which he was mutilated. By Homer's account, he was exiled to the nether world and there held a prisoner; by Lactantius' account, he was a wanderer and fugitive. How could the ruler over a state of innocence and prosperity remain identified with a being who practiced infanticide and who waged war against members of his own family? Add to the complications inherent in the mythological tradition the iconographical accounts stemming from Fulgentius of a Saturn with covered head bearing his scythe, and the astrological tradition of Saturn as a planetary deity who presided over old age, melancholy, hopelessness and physical decay — the Saturn who continued to make his malefic influence felt through the astral influences upon terrestrial beings — and we have all the ingredients that together defied the syncretist impulses of the humanist compilers.

Boccaccio's *Genealogy of the Gods* contains one of the earliest manifestations of discontent with the didacticism and the uncritical methods of the medieval compilers. Boccaccio acknowledged the need to return to the sources, to collate and compare, to separate the authentic and true from the spurious. Throughout the last 25 years of his life, he sifted through a massive body of materials, guided by this critical spirit, and produced a work that Seznec describes as "the chief link between the mythology of the Renaissance and that of the Middle Ages" (220). But as Seznec is equally willing to point out, Boccaccio did not have the analytical means to resolve the narrative confusion imposed by his divergent sources, and hence he was unable to rediscover, beneath the multiple versions, the primitive core of ancient myth — the authentic story of each personality. Seznec translates a few lines of apology from Boccaccio's "Dedicatory Epistle" that testify to his own sense of failure: "If these things and others are erroneous, it is not my intention to disprove them, nor to correct them in any way, should they not lend themselves to some kind of orderly redaction. I shall be content with reporting what I have found, and shall leave philosophical controversies aside" (223). That lack of an orderly redaction is particularly apparent in his handling of the chapter on Saturn opening his Bk. 8. He could do no more in following his scholarly integrity, than to include an account of the iconographical lore, together with a medley of half-digested observations from Macrobius, Lactantius and Mythographus 3, and a profile of the planetary force drawn from Albumazar.[2] To his credit, as the authors of *Saturn and Melancholy* point out, "as far as we know, Boccaccio was the first mythographer to declare that the astrological statements were worthy to be placed beside mythological statements concerning Saturn" (175). But his honesty as an historian could only compound the task of the mythological narrator who sought to tell the "story" of the god. Given that Boccaccio considered all of his sources equally reliable, their diversity could only pose obstacles to the creation of a unified narrative. Boccaccio's greatest failing for the later mythographers such as Lilio Gregorio Giraldi was his imperfect handling of sources,[3] but for the non-erudite reader, it was that he could not reconcile his scholarly obligations with his narrative impulses. For that reason his work could well become the most consulted of source books during the Renaissance on matters pertaining to the pagan gods, but it could never fulfil the popular need for a unified narrative account.

The late medieval writer who, in a sense, resolved the Saturn "perplex" through amplification of the materials found in the mythographers according to the narrative conventions of historical romance, was in all likelihood not seeking, as his major preoccupation, to overcome the Boccaccian impasse. Raoul Lefevre (or Le Fèvre), as a cleric attached to the Burgundian court during the reign of Philip the Good, was under commission to furnish the court with a monumental account of the fall of Troy, to be written in French prose and, implicitly, in accordance with all the favoured conventions of realism and rhetoric that characterized the romance literature of the age.[4] Undoubtedly his attention was fixed on the matter concerning Saturn as a result of his historical interest in retracing the founding of Troy to the earliest ages of Greek history. Taking Saturn, in euhemeristic fashion, as one of the earliest rulers of the Kingdom of Crete, he set about the creation of his introit to the story of Troy by reconstructing the reign of Saturn as a series of historical events, simultaneously making as much as he could of the surviving fragments of mythological narrative. In the image of these events, he created his characters, furnishing them with the desires and wills necessary to account for those events in human causal terms.

Taking Boccaccio for his source, Lefevre rationalizes the order of events by arranging them in sequence, and by furnishing each episode with causal circumstances that arise from preceding events. He begins with the conflict between Saturn and his elder brother Titan over the succession to the throne, and moves through a series of crises from the confrontation with Cybele, Saturn's sister and wife, over the destiny of their children, to the war with Titan, the return of Jupiter and on to the final struggle between father and son that results in the fulfilment of Apollo's dreaded prophecy that Saturn's rule would be forcefully usurped by his own offspring. That was work for a competent court clerk and *raconteur*. What will prove remarkable about Lefevre's adaptation of Boccaccio's materials is that he does not reject the astrological Saturn in the process, but in fact succeeds in his narrative reorganization largely by tracing the series of doleful calamities that constitute Saturn's life to his own brooding, melancholy and fateful personality. Probably more by accident than by design at the outset, Lefevre, in the process of disciplining myth through the application of historiographical method, rediscovered the characterological force in the Saturnine Saturn for organizing and motivating the historical narrative, and thereby managed to reconcile the two conflicting traditions.

Lefevre honours his obligation to the established details of the mythographers, but always as an historian looking for naturalistic interpretations that would conform to the level of verisimilitude established by the historical narrative. He therefore accepts the hint from Lactantius, as recorded by Boccaccio, that certain men in ancient times were called gods "after theyr folyssh and derke custome" because they had performed something of great profit for the commonwealth (10). In this manner, Lefevre carries the euhemeristic mode to its ultimate expression. Saturn is entirely desacramentalized and appears simply as a ruler near the beginning of time when the world was of gold, when men were steadfast and solid as mountains and rude as beasts, in the age just following the repopulation of the earth by the children of Noah. His father Uranus was, admittedly, the founder of the religion of the pagan gods and son of Demogorgon, but these two personalities he represented merely as earthly rulers. The process is at its most transparent when Lefevre deals with the castration myth. Since the act is so graphically specific, it surpassed Lefevre's powers to assign to it a counterpart action at a lower mimetic level; it is one of the few instances when Lefevre is driven to symbolic treatment. Since Jupiter began his reign by distributing his father's treasures to the Arcadians, the poets had reason to claim that "Iupiter geldyd his fader and caste his genytoyrs in to the see / of whom was engendryd venus / That is to saye that he castyd the tresours of hys fader in to the belyes of his men / whereof engendryd alle delectation whyche is comparyd and lykenyd unto venus &c" (102). Despite the clumsiness of the solution, it clearly illustrates the force of the displacement of myth towards the lower mimetic form of romance which, in Northrop Frye's scheme of genres, falls half-way between myth and realistic fiction because of the remote memory of the mythic patterns apparent in the action, the more realistic circumstances, and the more identifiably human causal explanations (136–137). That displacement towards a fictive realism remained consistent with Lefevre's purposes as an historian. It is, in fact, by dint of the fictive realism that his mythic narrative could begin to take on the concreteness of historical event.

A good deal has been written about the qualities which create the impression of realism in late medieval romance — realism in a relative sense, at any rate, by comparison with the more bare and schematic story-telling conventions of preceding centuries. Seldom did such realism entail the lavish descriptions of places or persons, of customs, gestures and facial expressions.[5] These were offered only where they were essential to an understanding of the action, though exceptions were made for such matter as battle scenes where arms, chariots, the advance and retreat of troops, the blows and wounds were described in great rhetorical detail, whether in deference to convention or to popular taste. Lefevre's detailed accounts of the wars involving Saturn are true to common practice. Rather, the sense of realism is most apparent in the increased sensitivity, on the part of the omniscient narrator, to the relationships between human will, destiny and the unfolding of events, and this is revealed through the rhetorical amplification of key episodes in order to explore in far greater detail, motives, feelings and reactions, and to underscore by the weight of the prose the relative significance of each contributing episode.

Finally, there is the search for logically causal and consequential order in the narrative. Boccaccio tells us only that Saturn made a pact with his brother Titan that he would devour his own children. Lefevre seizes upon that detail and surrounds it with realistic circumstances. We are made to understand, by way of fuller explanation, that Titan was deformed and disfavoured, and therefore compelled to cede his rights to the throne to the younger but more clever and popular Saturn upon the condition that Saturn would slay his offspring as assurance that none would succeed him to the throne. Saturn no longer devours his children, but he will drink their ashes mixed with wine as proof of their deaths. We may pause at the improbability of the scenario, but Lefevre finds the means for maintaining the substance of myth while gaining the suspension of disbelief at the level of romance fiction—at the level of the possible if not the probable, which makes for the level of adventure and wonder desired for the genre. It is a delicate balance. The repercussions of that initial pact manage to take on a degree of political and psychological importance, and serve in turn to drive the action forward with the logic of a plot to be resolved, through Saturn's passionate conflict with his wife Cybele over the destiny of their offspring, through the secret collusion of the women to spare the children and to deceive the king with false evidence of their deaths, through the eventual discovery of their survival by Titan and the refusal of the women to reveal their whereabouts, to the declaration of war by Titan and the final release of the vanquished and imprisoned Saturn by his son Jupiter. The destiny inherent in that pact, elaborated upon in each successive episode, serves to create an economy of fable that satisfies the demands for a refined degree of mimetic action. In brief, the order of plot is imposed upon the disorder of the mythic fragments through rhetorical amplification and through a cogent adjustment of action to character at a level in keeping with the habits and conventions of late medieval narrative practice.

Equally significant is the fact that such rhetorical amplification also includes dramatic treatment of the moments of crisis and decision. Literary conventions come even more to bear as the inner thoughts of the protagonists are revealed through pensive monologues and combative dialogues — where the shaping ideas and values of history are polarized in the course of the arguments among the family members. It is during these exchanges that we see most clearly how personalities are at once shaped by and attempt to alter destiny. Faithful to a common medieval theme, Saturn, cursed to a life without heirs by the conditions of his oath, and at the same time mortally fearful of each new birth of a child lest that child survive to carry out the prophecy of the oracle, laments the heavy blows of fortune and imposes upon himself a personal exile in brooding melancholy, sensing only too clearly that he must collaborate against his will in shaping the destiny that he struggles to avoid. Lefevre dramatizes the impasse with destiny in the form of a series of personal lamentations, and even more poignantly through a series of passionate confrontations with his wife, who takes a mother's stand in defence of her children. The dynastic chronicle takes on overtones of a domestic tragedy. As the moment of Jupiter's birth draws nigh, Saturn again commands his wife to destroy the child and send him evidence of the murder, even while he agonizes over the unnaturalness of the deed. Cybele raises her voice in prolonged protest against the heinous crime of infanticide which is contrary to honour, reason, pity, equity and justice, a sin against nature and an intolerable act by a man who should be the mirror and example of his people. Saturn's determination to have his children slain results in a contest between paternal cruelty and maternal pity. Cybele's determination to spare the child, the laughing Jupiter who mocks the knife which the womenfolk hold against his throat, is an equally powerful force from which arise the conditions that lead to trickery, the birth legend of Jupiter (which Lefevre makes a long detour to amplify in the same narrative manner) and the eventual war between father and son that replaces the titanomachy of Greek myth.[6] By repressing the recondite and supernatural through the cultivation of the workaday realism of Burgundian romance conventions, and by investing his characters with feelings and temperaments revealed through dialogue and monologue, Lefevre was clearly in possession of the right formula for reconstituting the legends of the pagan gods in a way that would make them palatable and attractive to the readers of town and court in Artois, Picardy, Dijon and Bruges.

We cannot protest that his adaptation of the mythic materials represents a further corruption of a primitive mythological core, and certainly not in terms of the presentation of those materials in contemporary sources. The euhemerizing process had, in ancient times, already obscured the origins in cult and religious belief, and those who followed could only look to the diverse literary traditions with a scholar's eye and attempt to collect them, or set about to recreate a selection of those materials in the image of another age. As a storyteller, Lefevre moved in the only direction open to a late medieval writer, namely to recast his materials in a contemporary form and setting through the application of contemporary literary techniques. In the process of that transformation, Lefevre sheds the accumulated layers of allegorical interpretation and didactic gloss. That, in itself, is a kind of return. With the removal of that moralizing crust, he might have been tempted to restructure the rise and fall of Saturn as a political *exemplum*, replete with warnings against irrational and tyrannous kings and promises of divine retributive justice. But the striking feature about Lefevre's historicized myth is that he avoids the ready-made formulae for shaping history into a lesson for magistrates, or a lesson on the fall of princes in the wheel of fortune, or the *de casibus* traditions. This is not to say that the work lacks meaning or intimations of theme, but these he allows to emerge by implication through the strength of the characterizations and the situational irony. Thus while it was the instincts of the historian that rescued the myth of Saturn from the confusions of the humanist compilers, it was the intuition of the *romancier* and tragedian that rescued that history from the didacticism of the moralist tradition.

What Lefevre undoubtedly began as a genealogical preamble took him over 100 quarto pages to complete, with the concluding episodes of the exiled Saturn's voyage to Troy and his pursuit by Jupiter spilling over into the following sections. Lefevre had clearly found something in the matter of Saturn that sustained his interest beyond the simple chronicling of events. To be sure, it required some effort to work up to a degree of historical verisimilitude the series of events built around the broken oath, the fatal prophecy, and the war of the gods now made men that brings the various motifs of the plot to resolution. But more than this, Lefevre became interested in dramatizing the personality of a protagonist driven by his melancholy temperament. With each adversity, Saturn is revealed as a man sinking more deeply into brooding and despair. Astutely, Lefevre avoids letting him lapse into total madness, but he allows that the series of bitter personal defeats leads to the shaking and gradual disintegration of a great spirit.

With the eventual defeat of Titan through the might of Jupiter and his allies, the narrative comes to a moment of repose. Jupiter marries his sister Juno amidst great rejoicing and all the land is at peace. Lefevre emphasizes the irony that Saturn could have ended his days in tranquillity had not the old fears of the usurpation of his throne not suddenly returned to darken his mind yet again. The oracle is now completely internalized as a paranoid fixation, devoid of all provocation; it is the cause that drives him to war with his son. That was Lefevre's own inspired interpretation of the events, to which he adds a dimension of jealous hatred as the aging king looks upon the youth heaped with favour and honour as the tormented Saul looked upon the giant-slaying David. What follows is the agonizing drama of an innocent and noble son besieged in war by a half-crazed father whose every move confirms his unfitness to rule in the eyes of his advisors and soldiers. The more he attempted to force their collaboration in a cause they deemed unjust, the more the people resisted his tyranny and longed for the change of power he was so intent upon avoiding. Lefevre underscores the tragic irony in relating the inevitability of events to the demon of Saturn's own melancholy insecurity. Some of his men defected to other lands; others fought half-heartedly and died in vain. The drama of rhetorical confrontation poignantly returns, this time as father and son meet on the battlefield, as Jupiter exercises all his forensic powers to dissuade his father, and as the irrational old man turns a deaf ear. The ensuing battle is long and bloody, in the end "the dede bodyes laye oon vpon an other beheded and smyten in pecys." Saturn is driven into exile with a remnant of his men, lamented at home at the same time that Jupiter is crowned in his place amidst general acclaim. In this sequence of events, Lefevre allows his amplification of word and event to generate a necessary action, but he shapes that history according to a tragic vision, not of the fall of an overreacher, but of a stubborn and tortured mind whose inclinations to melancholy suffering tend to exacerbate the circumstances that cause his grief. Saturn becomes a study in the political incapacitation and the mental disintegration of a once protean personality. Lefevre makes clear that melancholy in relation to events is a two-way avenue insofar as the man who is melancholy because he perceives himself as fortune's foe is simultaneously inclined to contribute to the adversities attributed to fortune. This was no by-product of an accidental arrangement of events. From myth to historical narrative, guided by the conventions of romance realism, Lefevre discovers the substance of a tragedy of character. Trusting to the events and characters themselves to yield up their meanings, he nevertheless arranges them in a way that enhances the ironies of situation, including that of a melancholy ruler whose misery coincides with the golden age of peace and prosperity. Lefevre could never ultimately reconcile these conflicting elements, but he could juxtapose them through a relation of irony so that even the contradictions of the mythological tradition find a place together in his literary vision.

The success of that vision is not easy to demonstrate today. In all likelihood we must accept that Lefevre's achievement was rather more for an age than for all time. He was a writer for the Burgundian court, and in that role catered to their tastes for elaborate feudal histories, epic wars and long rhetorical confrontations. But a timely application of his skills, together with the powers of the printing press raised Lefevre to popularity throughout the Renaissance. It was that power of the press that carried his work from the court to the city, and undoubtedly, it is the record of those early editions that will remain the strongest testimony we have today that Lefevre's formula for the handling of the matter of Saturn and of Troy was perfectly adjusted to the tastes of his age. No fewer than twelve manuscripts survive, and there is clear record that between the first edition, published by Caxton and Mansion in Bruges in 1469, and the last French edition in 1544 there appeared some twelve editions of the *Recueil des Troyennes Ystoires*.[7]

The importance of the work in the English-speaking world is even greater, since William Caxton, under commission by the Duchess Margaret of Burgundy, set about to translate the work into English. His version was completed on December 19, 1471, and by 1474 the work had passed through his press in Bruges, making it the first printed book in English.[8] It was to be many years before the *Recuyell of the Historyes of Troye* would fall from popularity in England. Wynkyn de Worde reissued it in 1503, and it reappeared ten times thereafter down to 1684. The editions of 1596, 1607 and 1617 are assurances that it was in demand during one of the most accomplished periods in English literature. Given this evidence of wide popularity and circulation, it would seem prudent to assume that while the myth of Saturn was variously fragmented and redeployed by court poets in celebrating their patrons through flattering associations with the golden age of Saturn and the return of Astraea,[9] by neoplatonic philosophers as the basis for a doctrine of poetic fury and intellectual inspiration, or by astrologers and physicians as the basis for a codification of the melancholy temperament, that in fact, for the common reader, the central mythological tradition of an historical Saturn as a god-man ruler at the beginning of time still held. At the least, through the widely disseminated medievalized version of Lefevre and Caxton, the patrons of the book industry remained familiar with a Saturn whose dynastic struggles belonged remotely to the story of Troy; they knew him as a ruler whose power was circumscribed by the destiny of a fatal oath to a brother and a foreboding warning by Apollo; and they knew him as a melancholy protagonist who would bring on his own demise through his irrational attack upon Jupiter. For the common reader in the northern Renaissance, Saturn had been rescued from the obscurity of the encyclopedists and medieval mythographers by a recasting of his myth according to the conventions of Burgundian historical romance.

Carleton University

NOTES

1 For a study of the earliest religious significance of Kronos, see Guthrie: "The scanty remains of the actual cult of Kronos which have lingered on into historical times . . . suggest that he had been a god of the harvest" (53). The Titanomachy that brings his reign to an end is, possibly, a symbolic representation of natural forces in conflict, of storm and darkness against light. It may also reflect the defeat of the fertility religions by the war and sky gods of the invading Greeks. There are, nevertheless, traces of a dance cult in the name of Zeus, son of Kronos, showing signs of an amalgamation of the resident with the invading gods in a family structure, advanced in explanation of established rites. See also Eliade 248 ff., who provides a concise account of the various levels, traditions, and early transformations of the myth.

2 I have consulted Boccaccio in the facsimile of the French translation, *De la genealogie des dieux* fols. 135r–138v.

3 In the Dedication to Ercole d'Este and throughout the work Giraldi makes references to the failures of his predecessors, and to Boccaccio's in particular.

4 For further information on Raoul Lefevre and the authorship question of *Le Recueil des Troyennes Ystoires* see the Introduction by H. Oskar Sommer to the typographical reproduction of the first edition of *The Recuyell of the Historyes of Troye* 47–81. Hardly anything is known of his life. "According to the majority of mss. of 'Le Recueil,' the printed editions, and the English translations, he was a priest and chaplain of the Duke Philip the Good of Burgundy, and compiled as such, at the command of his lord and master, the trilogy of Troye . . . " (71). All quotations of the text are from this edition.

5 For two such studies see Muscatine, esp. "Realism and Romance" 41 ff. and "The Realistic Style of the Bourgeois Tradition" 59 ff.; and Stevens.

6 The birth of Zeus or Jupiter has all the characteristics of a birth of the hero narrative. Rank offers a generic profile of the phenomenon. The child has distinguished parents. Often there is a prophecy "cautioning against his birth, and usually threatening danger to the father . . . " He is saved by animals or people of low station, grows to power and rediscovers his parents in some dramatic fashion. "He takes revenge on his father, on the one hand, and is acknowledged, on the other" (161). At last he comes to power and honours. Saturn's role is, to a degree, to serve as progenitor and victim of the heroic son. Lefevre, in effect, structurally and causally integrates the two stories, and at the same time offers an interpretation which is the by-product of his elaboration upon both characterological and narrative content.

7 For a summary of the French editions see Woledge 129–130.

8 For a summary of the English editions see the Introduction by H. O. Sommer, *Recuyell of the Historyes of Troye*, 82–119.

9 Among the standard works on the adaptation of the Saturn myth to Renaissance court poetry are those by Levin, Samaras, and Yates.

WORKS CITED

Boccaccio, G. *De la genealogie des dieux*. Paris: Phelippe le Noir, 1531. New York and London: Garland Publishing, 1976.

Eliade, M. *From the Stone Age to the Eleusinian Mysteries*. Vol. 1. *A History of Religious Ideas*. Chicago: U of Chicago P, 1978.

Frye, N. *Anatomy of Criticism*. New York: Atheneum, 1967.

Giraldi, L.G. *De deis gentium libri sive syntagmata XVII*. Lugduni: apud haeredes Jacobi Junctae, 1565.

Guthrie, W.K.C. *The Greeks and Their Gods*. Boston: Beacon Press, 1950.

Klibansky, R., E. Panofsky and F. Saxl. *Saturn and Melancholy: Studies in the History of Natural Philosophy, Religion, and Art*. London: Thomas Nelson, 1964.

Lefevre, R. *The Recuyell of the Historyes of Troye*. Trans. William Caxton. Bruges: Caxton and Mansion, ca. 1474. Intro. to the facsimile of the first edition by H. Oskar Sommer. London: David Nutt, 1894.

Levin, H. *The Myth of the Golden Age in the Renaissance*. New York: Oxford University Press, 1969.

Muscatine, C. *Chaucer and the French Tradition*. Berkeley: University of California Press, 1964.

Rank, O. *The Myth of the Birth of the Hero*. New York: Robert Brunnen, 1952.

Samaras, Z. *Le Règne de Cronos dans la littérature française du XVIe siècle*. Paris: A.-G. Nizet, 1983.

Seznec, J. *The Survival of the Pagan Gods: The Mythological tradition and its Place in Renaissance Humanism and Art*. Trans. Barbara F. Sessions. New York: Harper and Row, 1961.

Stevens, J. *Medieval Romance: Themes and Approaches*. New York: W.W. Norton, 1974.

Woledge, B. *Bibliographie des Romans et Nouvelles en prose Française antérieurs à 1500, Société de Publications Romanes et Françaises*. 42. Genève: Librairie Droz, 1954.

Yates, F.A. *Astraea: The Imperial Theme in the Sixteenth Century*. London and Boston: Routledge and Kegan Paul, 1975.

Roberto Guerrini

Saturn at Città di Castello

Palazzo Vitelli alla Cannoniera is one of the residences that the illustrious Vitelli family owned in Città di Castello where, for a long period of time, it exercised its power. The Palazzo is an important museum boasting works by Raphael (one of his first, the celebrated *Gonfalone della Trinità*), Signorelli and other Italian and foreign artists.[1] In addition to the paintings, there are, in the staircase and in the rooms on the first floor, sixteenth-century frescoes—decorations that only recently have begun to be studied adequately. The Palazzo Vitelli alla Cannoniera is proving to be a rich new source of information for Renaissance iconography. Images and subjects that appear include ancient history, in the Salone and Room IX, mythology, astronomy, sibyls, prophets, muses, emperors, celebrated lovers from antiquity, graffiti and grotesques.

Various artists worked on the construction of the Palazzo and decoration of its interiors, especially during the years 1520–40. These include Vasari, Gherardi (il Doceno), Cola dell'Amatrice and pupils, among whom the mysterious Battista di Città di Castello. Much information on the Palazzo is provided by Vasari himself in his *Vita di Cristofano Gherardi e di Cola dell'Amatrice*. Although the frescoes were well known to scholars before, until recently the meaning of their themes and iconology remained obscure. For example, it was thought that in the Salone, battles of the Vitelli family were represented. However, as I demonstrate in the catalogue, they deal with episodes of antiquity illustrating in chronological succession the deeds of Hannibal, Scipio, Caesar and Alexander. I arrived at this conclusion by means of a study of antique literary sources, chiefly by historians such as Livy, Plutarch, Caesar and Diodorus Siculus, and from the examination of other pictorial cycles such as those of the Farnesina, Fontainebleau, the Paolina Rooms of Castel Sant'Angelo, the Frieze of Scipio in the Throne Room, Palazzo dei Conservatori in Rome, and so forth.

With specific reference to the staircase, the work of Ronen has only recently permitted the identification of various composite elements. As a consequence, the *Saturn of Città di Castello*, which is quite significant and expresses better than any other example the Renaissance conception of this figure, was not only left out of *Saturn and Melancholy*, but also numerous other articles Saxl dedicated to the subject, as well as other works, including the essay by Chastel.

Before examining the image of Saturn, I think it opportune to explain briefly its setting and context. The owners, Alessandro Vitelli and his wife, Paola dei Rossi of Parma, are quite apparent at the entrance of the Salone. At the top of the second flight of stairs, after the celebrated lovers from antiquity, a Latin inscription appears: "Paola di Parma and her husband for their own tranquillity and that of their parents had these works carried out so that the family virtue would not go lost." One notes the particular importance that Paola of Parma assumes. The inscription refers to her husband only indirectly. The true inspiration for the program, at least regarding the staircase, would seem to be Paola, a fact until now disregarded, and one that we will return to later on. For the moment let us look at the figure of Alessandro Vitelli, whose personality emerges much more from the frescoes of the inner rooms.

According to family tradition, still alive in the 16th century, Alessandro Vitelli was a mercenary captain, when the Vitelli, already Signori of Città di Castello, continued to fight in the service of this or that party during the wars that rocked Italy during this period. Alessandro fought on the side of the Medici, the Farnese and Charles V, from whom he obtained in 1537 the title of Prince of Amatrice. Alessandro's contact with Cola dell'Amatrice, the painter who with his workshop worked on the decoration of the Palazzo, probably dates from this period.

Alessandro collaborated in the repression of the Florentine Republic, carrying out a dark and ambiguous role in the events that led to the advent of the Florentine princedom with the assassination of Duke Alessandro de' Medici by his cousin Lorenzino. He also contributed to the dissolution of the Sienese Republic. "Where there was liberty to stifle, there was Alessandro Vitelli," wrote a nineteenth-century biographer. A sort of Prince *alla Machiavelli*, he was, also according to family tradition, cruel, violent and pitiless. At the same time, however, Alessandro was cultured, refined and a lover of art. Profiting by the Florentine situation and acting as a protector for artists and literati, he procured many works of art and created around himself a court of notable importance. It is this type of personality that, as I said, can be found in the frescoes of the Salone and Room IX.

As I showed for the first time in the catalogue of the Palazzo, on the south wall of the Salone there are illustrated episodes from the life of Hannibal according to the account by Livy, and other ancient authors, such as Silius Italicus: *Hannibal's Oath and the Capture of Saguntum*; *The Crossing of Rodanus*; *The Battle in the Alps*; *Overcoming the Mountains*; *The Battle of Ticinus*; *The Battle of Trebia*; *The Naval Battle of Lilybreum*. The episodes continue on the west wall with *The Battle of Trasimeno* and *The Battle of Cannae*. On the same wall there follow stories about Scipio: *Appointment to Proconsul*; *The War in Spain*; *The War in Africa*; *Triumphal Entrance into Rome*. On the north wall appear the stories of Caesar, dealing with the famous battles of *Pharsalus*, *Zela*, *Thapsus* and *Munda*, and *The Death of Pompey*. On the east wall are yet more episodes from Caesar's wars, this time focusing on the conquest of Gaul. Here is represented, among other things, an episode not found elsewhere and indicative of the personality of Alessandro: *Caesar Has the Uxellodunum Rebel's Hands Cut Off*.[2] The east wall also represents stories from the life of Alexander the Great, a character who, because of the correspondence of names, seems particularly close to Alessandro Vitelli. Again we see battles, such as that of *Issus*, but we also see *The Meeting with Diogenes*. The theme extends to Room IX, where the decoration was entirely dedicated to Alexander the Great. Here it is possible to discern the following episodes: *Bucephalus in the Form of a Unicorn is Tamed*; *The Siege of Halixarnassus* (?); another version of *The Battle of Issus*; *The Siege of Tyre*; *The Generosity toward Darius whose Body is Covered with a Cape*; *The War against Porus*; *The Generosity toward the King*; and perhaps *The Story of Roxane* in a form not found in any other cycle.

We have a repertory of battles, clashes, and scenes of violence, but also acts inspired by chivalrous sensitivity, kindness of soul, and love. Some of the subjects are present in other cycles, while others are rare and unusual. In these frescoes, therefore, there is a complex mixture of antique and modern literary sources, themes, cultural and figurative traditions of great importance, not yet fully appreciated, because it is here for the first time that they are presented.

Let us now turn to the staircase, where, as I said, we find especially the imprint of Paola dei Rossi's personality. Her descent from Parma suggests the possibility of influence of the rich and stimulating world of Emilian mannerism. Evidence for this idea may be found in the frescoes of the *Stufetta*, the bathroom on the ground floor whose decorations have yet to be completely uncovered. One of the visible figures, a nymph splashing water, recalls the myth of Atteone as it appears in the decoration of Fontanellato in the fortress of Sanvitale.

On the first landing, philosophers, prophets and sibyls appear with their respective scroll ornaments in the style of Peruzzi, Pinturicchio and Perugino, but also Parmigianino and his school. Of particular interest is the episode of *Diogenes and the Platonic Philosopher*. Further along the first flight are presented the muses around Apollo, illustrating various myths. For the muses the author of the program seems inspired by literary sources such as Martianus Capella and, on the figurative level, by the *Tarocchi of Mantegna*. To every muse, in fact, is attributed a particular musical instrument, as in the series of famous engravings. After the grotesques and emperors in the second landing one arrives at the celebrated lovers of the third landing, with the *Triumph of Love* theme, for example, *Hercules and Omphale*, and on the second flight one sees medallions in which more celebrated lovers are pictured, including *Pompey and Cornelia*, and *Ovid and Corinna*.

The ceiling at the end of the third flight bears the images of the planets. In the triangular compartment at the base of the vault hangs the figure of *Saturnus-Cronos*, who assumes a fundamental importance in the set of planets. Saturn is represented with all the characteristics of humanistic iconography. He is an old man holding a scythe, who is eating one of his children (this detail, absent from ancient representations, appears in the late medieval period, as we know from Panofsky). The dragon of time twines around one of his legs. At the sides are his zodiac signs, the houses of Aquarius and Capricorn, the beginning and the end of the year (figs. 1 and 2).

The other planets appear inside hexagons with blue backgrounds: *Iuppiter* with his houses, Pisces and Sagittarius; *Mars* with Aries and traces of Scorpio; *Apollo*, the Sun with his sign Leo and the mythological raven below; *Venus* accompanied by Cupid with her sign Taurus, while below Libra can be seen; and, then, *Mercury* between Gemini and Virgo with the unicorn. The famous symbolic animal, as we have seen, makes his appearance also in the histories of Alexander. The unicorn belongs to a rich cultural and figurative tradition, and it perhaps constitutes a kind of homage to Paul III and the Farnese, who made it one of their preferred emblems. The cycle concludes with *Luna*, the Moon, represented in the image of Diana, who crowns a bull; in the background is the sign of Cancer. It is not clear what ceremony the goddess's gesture is meant to evoke, but in any case it seems to suggest a rendering of homage to the Vitelli family.

On the lunette underneath Saturn, dim traces of an allegoric representation may be seen: a nude woman bearing emblems of power, a papal tiara, a cardinal's hat and a baronial crown. The state of conservation does not permit a well-determined reading, and the precise sense of this image is unclear.

The presence of the planets in a context inspired by an encyclopedic ideal, and according to a medieval and Renaissance tradition, may come as no surprise, especially on the literary and figurative levels. Martianus Capella provides an example of the canonical coupling of the muses and the planets. The pertinent references that can be established are in fact very numerous, from the Palazzo Trinci of Foligno and the Templo Malatestiano of Rimini, to the Collegio del Cambio in Perugia, where sacred and profane history, astronomy and the liberal arts are linked. However, a second look proves that there is something new and unusual in Cola's cycle compared to previous or contemporary models. For example, on the ceiling of the Cambio, frescoed by Perugino, which together with Foligno provides the most immediate comparison on Umbrian soil, *Apollo the Sun* is at the centre, while the other planets, Saturn included, are arranged around this figure.

Different also is the case of the Chigi Chapel in Santa Maria del Popolo, conceived by Raphael, where the planets assume a circular movement. All rotate around the figure of God the Father, which is placed in the oculo of the vault. In Città di Castello, the insertion of Saturn in the triangular compartment of the vault assigns to this planet a predominant role. It seems necessary to infer alchemical or magical significance, but the present state of the research on the subject does not permit us to make definitive conclusions. The context, the order, and the presentation of the planets pose certain problems in relation to classical culture as well as the medieval and Renaissance tradition that go beyond the perspective of this paper.

It is possible, however, to examine more carefully the figure of Saturn. The various elements of which it is composed may be traced on a literary plane to numerous sources, from Fulgentius, to the Vatican mythographers, to the *Genealogiae* of Boccaccio, to the *Libellus de imaginibus deorum*, without it being possible to specify any precise or unique source. The figure of Saturn seems to constitute a union of various literary traditions.

On the figurative plane, however, the constituent elements are quite unusual for this date. The hexagon model with a blue background recalls the Roman cycles of Peruzzi in the Farnesina, and of Pinturicchio in the Borgia Apartments in the Vatican. But in these works the iconography of Saturn is different. The Peruzzi Saturn is a solemn, decorous old man adorned with wheat, a real Saturn (not Cronos) who, according to the horoscope of Agostino Chigi, is found in the sign of Pisces, suggested by Venus according to a rather rare myth.

Another representation with a differing iconography is found in the *Room of the Sibyls* (Borgia Apartment) by Pinturicchio who uses the well-known iconographic model of the "Children of the Planets." The god is placed above in a cart pulled by dragons, and below are various figures of human beings indicating astral influences. The monstrous act of eating a baby does not even appear in other cycles, such as that of the Cambio. In the Tempio Malatestiano or in the Campanile di Giotto this element is only suggested, not realistically represented. The image of Saturnus-Cronos who eats his children is not unusual in the Renaissance, as Panofsky has shown, but its antecedents are found mostly in mythological illustrations such as those of the *Ovide Moralisé*. For the transfer of the motif to the representation of the planets, the same scholar cites Nordic and Flemish examples. A parallel situation is offered in this case too by the *Tarocchi of Mantegna*, where Saturn appears both as a planet and as a spirit of time, even if there are notable differences in the figure of Saturn (in one there is a repellent old man, in the other a sort of king).

Finally, there is a manneristic phase with explosive, isolated representations of the theme (often in the form of a drawing), and with details that are more or less realistic and repulsive. This tendency culminated in the disquieting work of Goya. From the beginning of the 16th century various examples can be summoned forth. In addition to Rosso Fiorentino, who we know worked in Città di Castello, we can recall some Emilian artists because of the stylistic similarities with which they express the theme: Primaticcio, Ugo da Carpi and Parmigianino, in whose work are present the zodiac signs, the same as those of the Palazzo Vitelli.[3] This is yet another sign of the ties that seem to exist between the decorations and the suggestion of the "manierismo padano."[4]

I have tried to shed some light on our understanding of the Vitelli Saturn, bringing forth evidence of various kinds. Some new elements of his design have (albeit dimly) emerged. Many aspects remain problematic and beg for further study. I think, however, that the importance of the Saturn at Città di Castello has been established with sufficient clarity. In many ways it is one of the most interesting representations of its type in the Renaissance.

University of Siena

NOTES

1 A complete catalogue of this museum was recently published by Electa of Milano (see below *Pinacoteca Comunale di Città di Castello*), and presented with great acclaim by Federico Zeri. I myself collaborated on the iconographic section.
2 Even among the historians the episode is handed down only by Hirtius and Orosius.
3 For the drawings of Saturn eating his children, see Parmigianino, Paris, Louvre 6405; Ugo da Carpi (?), Rotterdam, Museum Boymans van Beunings 112.9; Primaticcio, Paris, Louvre 8515.
4 The influence of Paola Rossi on the program of the staircase remains obscure, but perhaps the traces of "manierismo padano" are connected to her presence.

WORKS CITED

Chastel, A. "Le mythe de Saturne dans la Renaissance Italienne." *Phoebus* 1 (1946): 125–34.

Fabretti, A. *Biografia dei capitani avventurieri dell'Umbria*. 4. Montepulciano, 1846.

Hind, A.M. *Early Italian Engraving*. 1. London, 1938.

Klibansky, R., E. Panofsky and F. Saxl. *Saturn and Melancholy: Studies in the History of Natural Philosophy, Religion, and Art*. London: Thomas Nelson, 1964.

Pinacoteca Comunale di Città di Castello. Ed. F.F. Mancini. Milano, 1987.

Raffaello giovane a Città di Castello. Catalogo della mostra. Città di Castello, 1983.

Ronen, A. "Palazzo Vitelli alla Cannoniera: The Decoration of the Staircase." *Commentarii* 26 (1975): 56–89.

Saxl, F. *La fede negli astri*. Torino: Settis, 1985.

Seznec, J. *The Survival of the Pagan Gods: The Mythological Tradition and its Place in Renaissance Humanism and Art*. Trans. B.F. Sessions. New York: Harper and Row, 1961.

Shepard, O. *La leggenda dell'unicorno*. Firenze, 1984.

FIG. 1: **Saturn.** Palazzo Vitelli alla Cannoniera, Città di Castello.

FIG. 2: *detail*, **Saturn** figure.

Leatrice Mendelsohn

Saturnian Allusions in Bronzino's London *Allegory*[1]

The only undisputed personification in Bronzino's so-called *Allegory of Love* in London (fig. 1), the only name on which all scholars agree, is that of Time.[2] Paradoxically, Time is conspicuously absent from Vasari's description of the painting which names six of the seven figures represented. The passage in Vasari is the only known contemporary reference to the painting:

Fece un quadro di singolare bellezza, che fu mandato in Francia al re Francesco; dentro il quale era una Venere ignuda con Cupido che la baciava, ed il Piacere da un lato e il Giuoco con altri Amori; e dall'altro la Fraude, la Gelosia ed altre passioni d'amore. (Vasari, *Vite* 7.598)[3]

[He made a panel of singular beauty which was sent to France to King Francis in which there was a nude Venus with a Cupid who was kissing her, and on one side Pleasure and Jest with other Loves; and on the other side Fraud, Jealousy and other torments of love.]

This paper will confront two problems not dealt with in previous studies devoted to the *Allegory*. First, the identity and role of the figure known as Time, and second, the function of the painting, questions which are interdependent.

Usually identified as the glowering, bald-headed grey-beard in the upper-right hand corner of the painting (fig. 2), Time's attributes, an hour-glass and wings, might seem to render his identification obvious but this would hardly explain Vasari's omission. The likelihood of the painting's absence from Florence by at least 1547 may account for this *lapsus*. Vasari's silence about the painting's patron and function and his vagueness regarding the number and identities of the figures suggest that it was not readily available to him.[4] At the same time, he must have seen it since he mentions specific personifications who appear in no other work

101

by Bronzino. I will, therefore, continue to use Vasari's names for the six other figures while reconsidering the identity of "Time."

Vasari tells us the recipient was Francis I, whose death provides a *terminus ante quem* of 1547 for the painting. Although there is no document stating that the painting was originally intended for Francis I, thematic and compositional affinities with works already in his collection reinforce Vasari's statement.[5] It is usually assumed that the patron was Cosimo I de' Medici, because of the "royal" nature of the gift (Smith, "Jealousy" 256), yet during the same period other important works sent by wealthy Italian patrons, not Medici, found their way to the French court.[6] In this paper I will propose some new literary sources for the painting that support connections with both France and Venice.

The first iconographic analysis of the painting appeared in Panofsky's essay tracing the origins of "Father Time"[7] in the Greek figure Chronos. Originally split into a transient form, Kairos or Opportunity, and a more permanent form, Aion, these aspects of Time were fused with the Roman Kronos (the god who usurped the throne of his father, devoured his own children, and was in turn supplanted by Jupiter). In this way the qualities of the Roman planetary god Saturn were appended to those of Time (Panofsky 73 ff.). According to Panofsky, it was in the Renaissance that harmless Time was first invested with destructive powers. While he observed that in the London *Allegory* the upper left figure exhibits "a feminine disgust which parallels the masculine wrath of old Chronos," Panofsky did not comment further on the saturnine aspects of this image of Time (Panofsky 90).

One possible reason for Panofsky's neglect of this aspect of the figure was the premise on which he based his discussion: that informing the allegory was the popular theme of "Time revealing Truth and Falsehood."[8] Here, instead, he saw illustrated a variation or twist: "Truth and Time revealing Falsehood." In a later version of the essay, Panofsky altered his original identification of the upper left hand figure from "Truth companion of Time" who reveals, to "Night" who conceals, in this way underlining the figure's inherent ambiguity. Despite the loss of the original emblematic idea and of Truth herself, Panofsky's reading of the *Allegory* as the "exposure of vice" in the form of "Luxury surrounded by personifications and symbols of treacherous pleasures and manifest evils" remained unchanged (Panofsky 90).[9] Time's purpose, now impeded by Night, was to "unmask falsehood and bring Truth to light," but Panofsky did not indicate where Truth could be found now that she was no longer depicted. If the representation of vice is in itself sufficient to signify the simultaneous "unmasking" of falsehood and revelation of Truth, we must ask how this is accomplished. The method depends on a covenant between artist and viewer that assumes a familiarity with Cinquecento allegorical method and the didactic function of images.[10]

Ideally the riddle of the painting should not—cannot—be solved by dissecting each figure separately as recent scholars have done, but by analyzing the relationships among the interacting elements, just as one would with a literary allegory. By necessity, however, the focus of this paper will be on the relationship between Time-Saturn, his female counterpart in the upper left zone and their function with respect to the surrounding personifications. The interpretation proposed here assumes that all the figures are participants in a consistent, unifying, allegorical conceit.[11] The absence of a document or commentary explaining the painting's function or indicating its provenance has, until now, made interpretation of the painting difficult and necessarily speculative. Our modern difficulty in interpreting this enigmatic work is not unrelated to the problems of the Cinquecento viewer, who was aware that certain subjects were acceptable in public only if disguised, i.e. hidden "sotto alcun velame" (Castelvetro 1.134). In his commentary on Aristotle's *Poetics*, Castelvetro connects this technique to the presentation of lascivious subjects in comic theatre.[12] In the painting the relationship of image to message is neither direct, nor parallel; instead, one serves as a cover for the other.

If one views our painting seriously, as most scholars have done, it appears chillingly, even embarassingly, sensual. But if approached from a different angle, the exaggerated postures and the artificial embrace appear ridiculous, almost comic. Correspondances between figures depicted in the painting and a contemporary description of carnival personifications in a previously known but untapped manuscript now make it possible to connect this painting with popular festival entertainment.

Description[13]

Using only seven figures and a minimum of background, Bronzino presents the spectator with a close-up of three full-length classical nude figures: an adolescent male (Cupid), an adult female (Venus), and a child (*Giuoco*). These are placed against a drape that acts as backcloth, drawn curtain, and floor covering beneath Venus which unites the separate figures against a blue field.[14] It is held by two figures, male and female, who appear to exercise some control over the scene presented below and before them.[15] Cut off behind the ear, the head of the female is covered by a small clump of curls and a stream of diaphanous fabric (fig. 3). The puttolike figure of *Giuoco* (fig. 4), attending the central pair, tosses roses. A bracelet of bells circles his left ankle while his right foot is pierced by a branch of thorns that draw blood (fig. 5). On a recessed plane and in shadow are two contrasting, rather un-classical figures. On the left side, a livid creature (*Gelosia*), tears its hair (fig. 6). On the right, the face of a pretty young girl is attached to a reptilian body with leonine haunches (*Piacere*: fig. 5). She profers with her left hand a honey comb while her right hand, twisted behind her, hides a poisonous scorpion's sting. Venus, Cupid, and *Giuoco* thus form a triad while the other four personifications provide background and frame. Subsidiary objects offer additional clues to the painting's subject: two doves beneath the foot of Cupid correspond compositionally to three masks (one bearded) partially hidden behind the right foot of Venus (fig. 7). Laurel fronds cover the upper background; myrtle is found near Cupid. Like the masks and the doves, the foliage carries a variety of possible meanings, the most common of which is matrimony. Time is given a wing and hourglass to identify him. Cupid kneels on a red satin pillow and carries a quiver from which one arrow projects, hidden by a sprig of myrtle. Venus holds a golden apple in her left hand and withdraws an arrow from Cupid's quiver with her right. Posed to sensuously reveal the rear view of his body, Cupid is kissing Venus.[16] He touches her breast with his right hand and grasps her crown with the left. The crown is ornamented with a miniature, gilded figure who, kneeling, seems to comb her hair with a shell; alluding to the Venus Anadyomene, it may also represent a Siren (fig. 8). In the absence of a single, agreed upon, allegorical theme, however, these attributes may be construed as support for a diversity of interpretations. Only when the central allegorical conceit is properly identified can their individual meanings be ascertained.

The figures are displayed on a relief-like, enamelled, surface with the foreground figures compressed into a shallow airless space. The remaining heads, hands, and attributes entirely fill the unused area like jigsaw parts fitted into a rectangular grid. The effect is of a space too small to contain all the forms and thus makes logical their apparent immobility; indeed they appear *unable* to move. While the kiss is explicit in detail, it does not constitute a completed action. There is, in fact, no narrative action. The composition resembles an *emblema* in which a series of symbols are combined with an epigrammatic message and a motto. It exhibits the quality of conciseness attached both to emblems and hieroglyphs, that quality recommended by Aristotle in the *Rhetorica* (3.11.8) to create vividness and more effectively transmit didactic meaning.[17] If it originally had an accompanying text, it is no longer known and we are left to decifer the painting's message on purely visual grounds. The paucity of clues has increased in reverse proportion the numerous, often diametrically opposed, interpretations since Panofsky's. Levey (30–33), for example, asserted that the painting was not an allegory of Lechery or Luxury but a "Triumph" of Venus and her erotic power. This change of title from the "Exposure of Luxury" to the "Triumph of Venus"[18] was the first of several reactions against Panofsky's moralistic view of the representation which took the form of a "defense" of Venus and the power of love and beauty.

The work's ability to engender antithetical reactions points up the ambiguity of its effect on the viewer. Freedberg (435) justly observes that the painting "pretends a moral demonstration of which its actual content is the reverse: the exposition of a sexuality so knowing as to be perverse, and so refined as to be at once explicit and oblique." This statement underscores the deliberate ambivalence of the work: erotic but at the same time forbidding. The immobility of pose, and the *un*fleshlike, marble-like tone of the body-surfaces idealize the central figures into exemplars of adolescent and female beauty.[19]

While at first these seven figures seem disparate, they can all be shown to signify deception and thus are thematically related. Despite his external attributes, which associate him with the later composite Time, Bronzino's figure more closely resembles the archetypal Roman Kronos, the god Saturn. A negative reading of Time is found in contemporary and medieval sources. As soon as one identifies the figure dominating the upper zone of the painting as saturnian, his "influence" becomes a key to unlocking the allegorical meaning. Saturn's presence, combined with the actions of Venus, Cupid and *Giuoco*, and the ambivalent natures of the subsidiary figures would have signaled to the sixteenth-century viewer that, like Venus herself, the work was not to be taken at face value and should be considered false, both as an image of beauty and a guide to behaviour.

Time / Kronos / Saturn

The revelation of the painting as a falsehood is accomplished by Saturn whose negative planetary aspect dominates. As the deposed King of the Golden Age and father of *Venus Volgare* (Voluptuousness),[20] he is said to preside over: "blindness, corruption, hatred, guile, craftiness, fraud, disloyalty and harmfulness."[21] Thus Saturn masterminds and exposes the deception below enacted by Venus and her son, who engage in mutually deceptive acts. Cupid, seduced and seducing, is being disarmed, while his mother, whose body and crown are within his grasp, appears oblivious to her own entrapment. Sensual, corporeal and expressly illicit love is explicitly depicted: the pose of Cupid alludes to sodomy.[22] The double duplicity of Mother and Son renders neither triumphant as neither seems fully cognizant of the other's trickery while the privileged viewer sees all. All the surrounding personifications emanating from the center are generated by the act of seduction. *Gelosia*, *Piacere* and *Giuoco*, each refer to ambivalent aspects of love.

Saturn's dual aspect — he was originally two-faced like Janus — is consistent with the mutability of the other personifications depicted in the *Allegory*. As "god of opposites" (Klibansky 134), he manipulates and controls the figures below. In ancient literature, Venus and Cupid were traditionally given more than one form, signifying their multi-valenced natures.[23] *Giuoco* (more aptly translated Jest or Trickery than Folly), *Gelosia* (Jealousy), and *Piacere* (Pleasure), are similarly characterized by duplicity or "two-facedness." In the case of *Giuoco* and *Piacere*, this duality is made manifest through disguise.[24] The theme is signaled by the three masks placed at the foot of Venus, while *pentimenti* reveal another mask originally placed near or under Cupid's foot (Gould 42).[25] *Gelosia* (sometimes interchangeable with *Invidia* or Envy) is often seen as the opposite of the virtue of Love and is described as such in the *Vocabolario degli Accademici della Crusca*, where the model quotation reads: "Invidia è contradio vizio della virtù dell'amore, ed è in due maniere: l'una è a dolersi del bene altrui, l'altra a rallegrarsi dei mali altrui" (*Vocabolario* 2.906)[26] [Envy is the vice contrary to the virtue of Love and exists in two forms: one is to bemoan the good fortune of others, the other to rejoice in their bad luck].

The image of the planetary Saturn appears early in Florence, in the Campanile reliefs and on the Porta della Mandorla of S. Maria del Fiore.[27] His ubiquitousness in Medici imagery is well documented in studies by Chastel, Cox-Rearick (1984), Richelson and Rousseau. Saturn also appears in the decorations for the Medici villas of Castello and Careggi,[28] and in important rooms of the Palazzo Vecchio begun in the 1550's: the Sala dell'Udienza, the Sala degli Elementi (1555), and the Sala di Opi (1555–9), as well as the later Terrace of Saturn (1560–6).[29] Shown in combination with the zodiacal sign of Capricorn, Saturn indicates Cosimo's adoption of the horoscope of Augustus.[30] Though authoritarian, this Medici Saturn presents an essentially positive image of astrological rule.[31]

In contrast, there exists another image, that of the sinister Saturn. Alain de Lille's medieval *Anticlaudianus* characterizes the reign of Saturn with a list of negative qualities: "Hic dolor et gemitus, lacrimae, discordia, terror, tristities, pallor, planctus, iniuria regnant . . ." (4.8).[32] It expresses the opposite of Virgil's vision of Saturn's Golden Age: "Redeunt Saturnia regna . . ." (*Eclogae* 4.4–10), the official view which prevailed during the reign of Cosimo I when he assumed the guise of Saturn as a ruler.[33] While it is true that Cartari in his manual of symbolic images of the Gods (based on ancient and medieval sources) began his treatment of Saturn with Virgil: "Il primo fu Saturno . . . " [First there was Saturn . . .] (Cartari 23), the present is described negatively, *in contrast to* and not as a re-evocation of the Golden Age: "che coreva la età d'oro, la verità fu aperta, & manifesta a tutti; non nascosta, come fu dapoi sotto tante menzogne, & tanti inganni" (Cartari 26) [during the Golden Age, truth was apparent and revealed to all; not hidden as it has been since under many lies and deceptions].

This present age of chaos and crime resembles the world described by Alain de Lille, in his *De planctu naturae*, in which "the nocturnal chaos of Fraud is everywhere" (Sheridan 167). De Lille belongs to a long French-Latin tradition of satirical prose-poetry, popular and influential in sixteenth century Italy. The Italy described by the *poligrafo* Anton Francesco Doni (*I Mondi* 50v)[34] mirrors de Lille's image of a negative state. Neither the Medici villa decorations, now known only through drawings and descriptions, nor the later paintings in the Palazzo Vecchio, represent Saturn's negative influence. Yet it is surely an age of lies and deceptions over which Bronzino's Time-Saturn reigns and not the happy Golden Age revived by Cosimo I.

The visual transformation of Time into a negative saturnine figure corresponds closely to images found in Doni's writings.[35] Castigating the Gods in *I Mondi* (102), Doni calls Saturn and Mars "i maltrovati," and the others "falsi & buggiardi" [fakes and liars].[36] Gods and Men, Man and the Gods, are compared and the pagan Gods appear as mere aggrandizements of man's weaknesses. Inspired by Lucian's *Satires*,[37] their world is a parody of the Paduan Academy and its members, examples not to be imitated. Early in this collection of dialogues, Time is described allegorically (*I Mondi* 16) as "a large man beyond measure in majesty" with a middle aged forehead and eyes, youthful cheeks and mouth, and an old beard,[38] who, alongside Fate, "ruled the world, the heavens and everything." In another of his works, *Le Pitture. . .* , Doni incorporates the negative aspects of Saturn into the image of a "Time, capable of every deceit and every fraud."[39] This grotesque, satirical figure of Time travels above the earth "walking on air without moving his feet," commenting upon the human foibles and vices observed below.[40] But it is in one of his own *burlesque* poems that Bronzino describes a personage who, though unnamed, most resembles the figure in the painting. In a Capitolo called *Il Piato*[41] Bronzino employs the medieval literary device of a dream sequence in which a series of distortions and contraries ("contrarie larve e vision confuse / m'appaion tosto e modi torti e strani...") are enumerated; among them is the following image:

> Ecco intanto apparir per l'aria un vecchio
> con due grand'ale, una nera, una bianca,
> e del sol si facea misura e specchio.
> Giunto alla pura con la mano stanca
> le squarciò 'l velo e con l'altra la piglia
> dicendo: "Io son venuto a farti franca.
> Qui non aresti luogo, o vera figlia,
> e meno altrove in terra: alzianci al cielo,
> ove l'ordine tuo non si scompiglia."
> Ma come il lume apparse e cadde il velo
> delle celesti membra, agl'empi scorse
> per gl'occhi un pauroso, invido gelo.
>
> (Bronzino, *Il Piato* 17.4.205–16)[42]

[Just then, there appeared in the air an old man with two great wings, one black and one white, who was the measure and mirror of the sun. Reaching into the atmosphere with a tired hand he tore the curtain and with the other drew it, saying: "I have come to set you free. Here you have no place, o my true daughter and less so elsewhere on earth. Come up here to heaven where your order won't be disturbed." But like the light the curtain rose and fell from the celestial body and a frightful, envious chill flowed from his eyes toward the wicked.]

In Bronzino's *rima* as in the visual allegory, the personification takes the form of a divine being, but—although abstractions—these figures behave like men, are morally weak and, ultimately, comic. Although specific lines by Bronzino seem nearly identical to passages from Doni's *I Mondi*, it is primarily in their satirical tone that they most correspond.[43] Written in the style of popular carnival songs, the words and incidents usually, if not always, refer to sexual practices, parodying not only academic literary genres but church and state as well.

Doni also provides physical descriptions of Time-Saturn. In *I Marmi*, the interlocutor, the sculptor Tribolo, describes *Il Tempo* as "a big, beautiful man with a great beard, a real character [*figurone*] resembling Michelangelo's *Moses* on the tomb of Julius II in Rome." Bronzino's Time, like Michelangelo's *Moses*, depends on an antique type which emphasizes the god's Titanic nature (Bober and Rubenstein 101). In light of the belief that one of the *River Gods* on the Capitoline represented Saturn (as documented in the early guide book *Mirabilia urbis Romae*), the head of the Vatican *Tiber*, probably by Michelangelo himself and thus resembling the *Moses*, is another likely visual prototype.

Bronzino's god takes his appearance from mythographic descriptions of Saturn's planetary aspect, for example that in the *Theologia Mythologica*, published in 1532. There under "De Simulacro Saturni" we read a description from Ptolemy stressing the importance of Saturn's eyes, the most pronounced feature of Bronzino's figure.[44] It is particularly through his glance that Saturn, the "wicked old man,"[45] rather than the wise creator, is connected to his co-conspirator, whom I will here call Fraud (fig. 3: head of Fraud).[46] Ultimately the appearance which Bronzino gives Time-Saturn may allude to Cosimo himself. The eyes of Saturn are similar to those bulging eyes of Cosimo as represented, for example, in the bust by Cellini which the patron-model did not appreciate.[47] Prominent eyes, however, appear in other portraits by Bronzino such as his own and those identified as Gelli and Giambullari in his *Descent from Limbo* (Gaston 41, 48). It is possible to see resemblances between the engraved portrait by Enea Vico of Giambattista Gelli in *Le Medaglie del Doni* (*Giorgio Vasari, cat.*: fig. 350) and a likely representation of the same person in Bronzino's tapestry representing *Joseph in Prison and the Banquet of Pharoah* (Rome, Quirinale, c. 1545), a scene which may allude to Cosimo and other members of his court (Adelson, *The Tapestry* 373, n. 38). We might, therefore, alternatively read the figure of Saturn as a malevolent author-artist who unveils the protagonists of a play just as Gelli in his *Circe* satirically revealed the Medici's followers.

On a contemporary historical plane, possible allusions to Cosimo's family are suggested by the resemblance of other figures in the painting to known portraits by Bronzino. Not only does the pretty head of *Piacere* resemble Bronzino's portrait of Bia, Cosimo's illegitimate daughter,[48] but Cupid and Folly bear faint resemblances to portraits of Cosimo's other children.[49] Nor should we exclude the possibility that in a satirical context Venus might allude to Cosimo's wife Eleonora of Toledo. The motto on her portrait in the Wallace Collection (inv. 555) reads FALLAX. GRATIA. ET VANA EST. PULCHRITUDO., a motto equivalent to the emblematic moral message of the *Allegory*. But instead of a negative *Pulchritudo* in the form of Venus we have in the portrait (and those from which it derives) the positive example of Eleonora portrayed as Juno, goddess of marriage.[50] One cannot always be certain of the meaning of these allusions but it is clear that they exist. It is necessary now to establish the context in which they operate and their function within the allegory.

Such resemblances to specific individuals, hardly accidental, may reflect the actual participation of the court in carnival spectacles such as *intermezzi*, *carri*, *mascherate* and the *bufolate*.[51] The themes of the *bufole*, in general, treated lightly, are similar to the moralizing yet pagan subject of the Bronzino painting.[52] In these theatricals the parts were played by masked nobles. Similar parodies existed in literary form as well, for example Machiavelli's verse version of the *Golden Ass* of Apuleius, in which the friends of the Medici are satirized in disguised form, and Giambattista Gelli's *Circe*, in which various animals resembled recognizable Medici followers.[53] As god of opposites and of secrets, Saturn's presence alerts us to the fact that the figures presented are disguised in ways that reveal their true nature.

A masque presented as part of the festivities for *Carnevale*, March 10, 1546 (S.F.), represented "One Hundred Arts" (BNF Capponi, 91.69v).[54] The theme, elaborated in the text of the carnival songs, was "the world and its madness." Six *bufolate* were presented. The most important of these for our argument was the 5th: "La quinta bufola fu' del Duca, che veniva a guisa di . . . con maschere di Morte con una falce in mano coperti tutti fin a terra in bianco" [the fifth bufola was the Duke's, who came in the guise of . . . with masks of Death with a sickle in hand, covered entirely in white, down to the ground].[55] Beyond this mention of the Duke's participation in 1546, we have another description in the Diary of a *bufola* enacted for the feast of San Giovanni the previous year (June 24, 1545), which documents the close relationship between the personifications included in these spectacles and the figures represented in Bronzino's London *Allegory*. These are described as "sei bellissime figure alla Bronzina, tutte fatte de mani d'uno scultore, domandato il Tribolo" (BNF Capponi 91.60r–v)[56] [six beautiful figures "alla Bronzina," all made by the hand of a sculptor named Tribolo].

Among these personifications were: "*Crudeltà . . . Disperazione* con la bocca aperta" and *L'Inganno*, whose description is particularly important for our painting: "L'Inganno, in questa maniera le porgeva con una mano un fiore, dall'altra minacciando la morte con un pugnale in mano" (Capponi 91.60 r–f.)[57] [Deception, in this manner holds out with one hand a flower, while in the other threatens death with a knife in hand].

L'Inganno or Fraud and *Disperazione* or Despair closely resemble Bronzino's *Piacere* and *Gelosia*, to apply Vasari's labels. Other personifications listed in this *bufola* include *La Malinconia* (Melancholy), *La Carestia* (Famine), and *La Povertà* (Poverty). The setting is allegorical, the Temple of Discord, each figure standing before a portal.

We can, I believe, reasonably assume that the same type of, if not the identical, allegorical text lies behind both the festival decorations cited above and Bronzino's painting. The allegories in our painting, therefore, do not necessarily antedate Tribolo's sculpted decorations.[58] The dates given for these two Medici festivals correspond roughly to the two years during which Vasari says Bronzino worked on carnival decorations for the Palace. Vasari wrote: "Fece anco in palazzo, quasi ne' medesimi tempi [i. e. while decorating the chapel of Eleonora of Toledo] due anni alla fila per carnevale, due scene e prospettive per comedie, che furono tenute bellissime. Fece un quadro di singolare bellezza, che fu mandato in Francia . . ." (Vasari, *Vite* 6.598). This notice is inserted between Vasari's mention of Bronzino's work on the chapel of Eleonora of Toledo and his description of the painting. These *scene* and *prospettive* (scenic backdrops) made by Bronzino two years in a row and considered "very beautiful" are described almost in the same breath as the description which follows of the *Allegory*. While this is not absolute proof that the painting formed part of carnival decorations (the citation seems a separate one), we should consider the likelihood that it formed part of some theatrical or decorative complex. This is supported by its very large size and the fact that thematically it would appear to belong to a series. At the very least the *Allegory*, painted on the heels of, or contemporaneously with the stage designs would have shared their stylistic qualities. We know that Bronzino worked in the theater. Vasari records that in 1533 he assisted Bronzino on the "prospettive" for a *commedia* performed by the Compagnia dei Negromanti in the Casa Antinori (Frey 2.852, ricordo 58). Bronzino also worked on the "apparati" for the wedding of Cosimo I (Vasari, *Vite* 6.87), with Aristotile da Sangallo on theatre "prospettive" (6.443–7), and later on the "apparato" for the wedding of Francesco I, Cosimo's son (8.618).

Below the "curtain raisers" Time and Fraud, the painted allegorical figures are frozen as if in a *tableau vivant*, not unlike those employed during Cinquecento *intermezzi*.[59] The visual effect of the work is, in fact, in keeping with the tone of *intermezzi* included in all Renaissance performances of Roman satires and their imitations.[60] Shearman's remarks on *intermezzi* (104 ff.) are relevant to Bronzino's style in this painting:

Intermezzi were *tableau vivants*, dependent upon novelty but paradoxically highly schematized. Above all it was the relation of these *tableaux* to the spectator that was different and characteristic of Mannerism . . . emotionally detached, [the spectator] is invited to admire the performance and its style.

Our admiration of its artifice similarly conditions our response to Bronzino's painted *tableau*. In its satirical tone and emblematic form it compares not only with *intermezzi* but with other mimetic formulas used for masques and *bufolate*. It also shares with epithalamic paintings, such as the *Venus and Cupid* by Lotto in the Metropolitan Museum, not only a punning wit[61] and theatrical qualities but standard attributes such as the blue cloth, myrtle and roses, and a possible portrait reference. *Intermezzi* were also popular as wedding entertainments, for example those composed by Pierfrancesco Giambullari for the celebrations connected to the wedding of Cosimo I and Eleonora in 1539 (Minor-Mitchell; Giambullari; Vasari 6.86–89). The Bronzino *Allegory* draws upon a common literary background utilized for these celebrations, especially the repertoire of personifications found in the epithalamic visual tradition. Like these decorations, our painting belongs to the satiric genre in which the "humor of inversion" is employed to achieve an entertaining effect which nevertheless carried a moralizing message (Eco), the same tradition from which Bronzino's burlesque rhymes derive. The use of the blue cloth here is not merely an esthetic device but may signal an earlier and more classical expression of those comic-satirical inversions deriving from popular and classical "wisdom" that appear in art somewhat later, in the North. I propose that the work formed part of some kind of theatrical decoration used during a carnival or other celebration such as those described above, and was subsequently incorporated into a decorative scheme for a ceiling or palace interior. This happened on other occasions, for example in the case of Vasari's designs for *La Talanta* in Venice.[62]

Fraud

Having established Time as a negative persona, imbued with Saturn's powers, we can now consider his relationship to the figure in the upper left who shares the heavenly zone and the task of manipulating the cloth. We see in action a Saturn who exercises control over secrets, "knows of every dark occasion," and exerts "a decisive influence on the fate of men and the course of all earthly events . . ." (Klibansky 130, taken from Abu Ma'sar). The "fraudulent" eye of Saturn is fixed on this figure. Together they form a *cornice* which corresponds to a dramatic prologue.[63] Like a pair of Victories, or the "coulisse" figures on a Roman sarcophagus, they define and frame the limits of the picture.[64] Variously named Truth, Night, Fraud, Oblivion and Chastity, her identity must be checked against her open-mouthed, bare-headed, mask-like appearance characterized by sightless eyes. Her head is covered by a small patch of carefully formed curls placed at the crown and a curve of billowing fabric (fig. 3).[65] In the absence of a more compelling suggestion and because the other names proposed by Vasari, in my opinion, can convincingly be attached to the other personifications, I consider this figure to be the one he calls *Fraude*.[66]

Although a fully satisfactory literary description has not yet been proposed (which accounts in part for the variety of names put forth) we come very close with a description of Fraud in Alain de Lille's *De planctu naturae* prefaced by: "Fraud no longer seeks the cloak of pretence nor does the noisome stench of crime seek for itself the fragrant balsam of virtue so as to supply a cloak for its evil smell. Thus does the nettle hide its impoverishment of beauty with roses. . . ."

> Opposite stood Falsehood, hostile to Truth, and very watchful. Her countenance was clouded with the soot of dishonor, and confessed none of Nature's gifts, for old age had subjected it to hollow creases and drawn it all together in folds. Her head was seen to be unclothed with covering hair. Nor did she compensate for the baldness by an enveloping robe; but an infinity of little patches, joined by a great number of threads, had composed a cloak for her. Secretly spying on the pictures of Truth, she rudely marred whatever Truth harmoniously formed. (Sheridan, prose 9.167)

The *De planctu naturae* or *Complaint of Nature* used a series of personifications loosely linked to a narrative to moralize upon and parody human weakness. Known to Dante, the text belongs to a tradition of personification continually transformed and re-moralized up through the Renaissance. While it could have been known to Bronzino in its original Latin (a manuscript is recorded in the Medici Library at San Marco in the inventory of 1545 which probably corresponds to a manuscript now in the Laurenziana),[67] more likely Bronzino would have known the text in a transformed vernacular version (Moffit 92). There are many stylistic affinities between the medieval text and the mannerist allegory.[68] The author combines a dream motif with a mirror image[69] and employs exaggerated rhetorical language as a metaphor for excess in human behaviour. Deliberate rhetorical virtuosity is a vice comparable to sexual licentiousness, sodomy in particular. In the *De planctu naturae* sodomy is equated with Chaos, opposed to social order or government and to Nature. Though Bronzino's Fraud is not old and seeks "the cloak of pretense" hiding behind a mask of apparent beauty, she is similarly characterized by her baldness. The distorting power of fraud with respect to truth is alluded to in her mask-like face without eyes. If there isn't a one-to-one correspondance between Alain's description and our personification, the role she plays in the medieval allegory is nevertheless comparable to her function in the painting. Fraud is viewed by Alain as the antithesis of Truth and represents the chaos and degenerateness of the world under the sway of a "monstrous Venus" who temporarily assumes the procreative duties of Nature. Fraud makes her appearance in a context of contraries which demonstrate the negative effects of the opposite of heavenly love or *Caritas*, i. e. cupidity or *voluptas*.[70] She participates in an inversion of the usual hymn to the celestial Venus. In de Lille's *Complaint* we have a literary antecedent of Bronzino's painting which shows us a positive image reversed to its negative, that is, falsified as if reflected in a distorting mirror.[71] In Bronzino's *Allegory*, Fraud, transforming Truth by obscuring it, provides a counterpoint to the figure of Time in his revelatory function.

We can see in the painting traces of the unnamed "Vecchio," from Bronzino's dream poem, who rends the curtain. A deceptive, consuming, saturnine Time finds an accomplice in Fraud. Time and Fraud, like Time and Death or Time and Fortune, act jointly to produce contrary results: Time exposing, Fraud—like Panofsky's Night—obscuring. Therefore, Fraud's gesture of holding the veil (or cloak) need not be seen in opposition to that of Time.[72] Instead the two can be read as a couple who, in combination, express duality.[73] Time exposes an act of deception and in doing so, demonstrates the presence of falsehood. If a truth is exposed, however, it is a negative truth exuding a negative influence. But in this picture we are never shown "Truth," or for that matter any positive virtue, in allegorical form.

Even if not directly responsible for the revelation, Bronzino's Fraud indicates by her very presence that what is seen is false. We might consider renaming the painting: *"Fraude filia Temporis,"* or "Fraud daughter of Saturn" (Fraud being an aspect of *Venus Volgare* who is a daughter of Saturn). The entire painting, in fact, might be read, as Walter Kaiser has pointed out, as a parody of *"Veritas filia Temporis."*[74] We must keep in mind, however, that this is not a narrative painting. So it is appropriate to our allegory that what is seen, like a mirror image, exists only in the present. Significantly in Ripa's *Tempo* "del tempo solo il presente si vede e ha l'essere, il quale per ancora è tanto breve e incerto che non avanza la falsa imagine dello specchio" (Panofsky, "Father Time" n. 50) [only the present is visible and has being, which is still so brief and uncertain that it is no better than a false image in a mirror].

In another of Doni's descriptions, relevant to the Bronzino painting, *Tempo* and *Occasione* tyrannically manipulate the world. Lovers, they marry with two witnesses, *L'Arte* and *L'Inganno*: "Così con il braccio della Occasione e con la mano del Tempo fu posto la briglia a questa macchina et a tutte le cose sue" (*Le Pitture* 18f.)[75] [Thus the arm of Fortune and the hand of Time control the reins of this machine [e.g. the world] and all its business].

Resemblances between this scenario and the "plot" of Alain de Lille's *De planctu naturae* cannot be coincidental. It must have been in large part through the intermediary of Doni's *oeuvre* that such medieval personifications entered Bronzino's vocabulary of allegorical images. Certainly Doni's *Le Pitture*, in advance of Cartari, provided inventive descriptions of personified ideas intended as emblems for use by artists. It seems that Vasari made use of the same repertory of personifications in his ceilings and the same must have been true for Bronzino. Illustrations to *I Mondi* as well as Doni's text provide a link between Bronzino's pictorial style, contemporary literary satire, and emblematic mottos.

Two engravings from Doni's *I Mondi* represent a figure closely resembling the medieval description of Fraud: a woman bald and dressed in rags. One bears an inscription in Latin: QUOD MOLESTIVS, PATIOR, TACES (fig. 9); the other, in Italian, reads: QUEL CHE PIÙ MI MOLESTA ASCONDO ET TACCIO (fig. 10).[76] McTavish proposed Bronzino as the artist of these emblems (*Giorgio Vasari, cat.* : 200) which reappear as frontispieces in a variety of Marcolini publications. An obvious companion illustration (32) framed in a similar oval but heavier and undecorated (signifying the zodiac in other Marcolini illustrations) is a figure which appears to be Truth seated on a similar *broncone*, holding a down-turned torch which burns a mask. It carries the motto: QUEL CHE MI MOLESTAVA / ACCENDO ET ARDO (fig. 11).[77] These figures of "Truth" and "Falsehood" complement one another in pose and motto. Truth, saying: "That which disturbed me, I ignite and burn;" Falsehood saying: "That which most disturbs me I hide and keep silent."[78] Thus Truth destroys what it considers false, while Falsehood merely covers it up. Falsehood's mask is more than a disguise; as seen by Bing (310), it is a protective covering.[79] This view of falsehood, as well as the visual type utilized, lies behind the image of Fraud in the *Allegory*. Among the emblematically derived illustrations in Doni's *I Mondi* we also find an *Occasione* (Fortune or Chance) which imitates Alciati's emblem.[80] Given the relevant Doni texts quoted above and the popularity of contemporary images of *Occasione*, the forelock and bald head of Bronzino's Fraud might well have been adapted from a similar emblematic source.

From its beginnings Fortune as *Kairos* was considered a part of and often presented as a partner of Time. Like Venus and the Moon with whom she was allied, Fortune had two aspects: good and bad (Patch 118). Associated with love, Cartari described Fortune as "una donna cieca e pazza." Given their conceptual similarities, especially the idea that temporal fortune is deceptive, the assumption by Fraud of some of Fortune's features must have seemed an acceptable solution in Bronzino's search for a visual type. We are dealing with a composite figure, freely compiled from several sources, visual and literary, medieval and Renaissance. Doni, who owned a collection of medals, who sent his literary emblems to Marcolini to have them illustrated, and whose descriptions were borrowed by Cartari, would be a likely author of the ideas on which Bronzino's seemingly original personifications were based. It is unlikely that Bronzino himself was the inventor of the allegory behind his painting. The most prolific creator of such conceits for the Medici court at the time was Vincenzo Borghini, however, the anti-medicean bias which I find in the painting precludes having such a loyal subject as its inventor and suggests instead one of the more radical, satiric members of the academy, like Doni or Gelli.

Conclusion: The Allegorical Conceit

All Bronzino's figures, including their attributes, are antithetical to the "celestial" aspects of Cupid and Venus.[81] The idea that the *Allegory* was an inversion of a Holy Family was proposed by Levy (32) and mentioned in a footnote by Freedberg (700, n.13). A strikingly appropriate example of the religious paradigm is Raphael's so called *Holy Family of Francis I*, now in the Louvre (inv. 604), a work commissioned by Lorenzo de' Medici as a gift to the queen of France in 1518. The kiss of Cupid and Venus parodies that of the Christ Child and the Virgin Mary, with John the Baptist replaced by *Giuoco* and Saturn substituting for Joseph. St. Anne and *Invidia* are compositional counterparts. It is important for the style of the *Allegory* as well as for its content that these inversions reflect the ornamentalism of medieval rhetorical description.

Bronzino translates poetic dissimulation into visual form, employing, as he does in his writings, techniques of "moral inversion" found in allegorical prototypes, for example the *Roman de la Rose*. Just as in the *Roman*,[82] there is a disjunction between the painting's courtly style and its crude meaning; cool artifice discloses a shocking message (Fleming 73). The chill artificiality of Bronzino's *maniera* negates the possibility of a truly empathetic response. The viewer is seduced, but as a voyeur (Ginzburg 134). The painting plays with the spectator, urging through a disjunction of style and meaning that he draw from the image a message contrary to what he witnesses. Because the moral aspect of the painting, its didactic message, contrasts with the visual (or physical) statement, a reading of the image results which capitalizes on the effect of ambivalence transmitted. "Form wants to prevail over content, the letter contests the spirit," to cite Bergson's essay on the comic (43). Bronzino seduces the viewer using the techniques of painting, traditionally considered an "art of deception," a fact demonstrated in Ripa's dependant personifications of *Simulatione* (455) and *Pittura* (405).[83]

Our analysis of the images of Fraud and Saturn tells us that the external appearances of these personifications are disguises which at once conceal and reveal their true nature: conceal because they project a falsely beautiful image, reveal because we are given clues that all is not what it seems to be. This process applies directly to the image of Venus who embodies two different aspects of her nature in a single form. Viewed in isolation on the basis of attributes alone, she can be seen as either good or bad (witness the painting's conflicting interpretations). But the viewer or the art historian should not take this to mean that any interpretation is acceptable. The true nature of Venus can be determined only by placing her within a proper allegorical context.[84] In context she is Alain de Lille's "Venus monstrosa." Truth, at first obscured by a "bella menzogna" or beautiful lie (Hollander 30–31), becomes an ugly truth when exposed.[85] At first deceived by beauty, the observer soon notices the negative clues in the painting, such as the sting of *Piacere* or the thorns of *Giuoco*. As Doni says: "Si voleva aprir bene gli occhi" (*I Mondi* 52v) [You have to keep your eyes wide open!]. Finally, the viewer is asked to substitute a positive ideal for the negative one. At this point we might apply Freedberg's observation that "In Maniera the spectator, not the artist, may be regarded as the agent who effects a synthesis" (426).

In the burlesque *Capitolo* called "On the onion," Bronzino, following current literary theory, wrote: "Così la poesia di vestirsi usa / di favole e di giuocchi e dentro asconde / la verità ch'or ti loda, or t'accusa." [In this way, to clothe herself poetry uses fables and jokes, and underneath [the cloak] she hides the truth, which now praises and now blames you.][86] In Bronzino's allegorical scheme the mutable figure of Saturn controls the "veil of pretense." In this painting we are shown the lie—*in the guise of* truth: "La bugia sotto l'ombra della verità" as Doni says (*I Mondi* 52v). This is demonstrated most effectively in the image of *Piacere*, who we know from the festival description is another form of *Inganno*.[87] Like Dante in his allegory of False Pleasure (*Purgatorio* 19) in his mind's eye the viewer himself must transform the image and substitute a "new vision" (*Purgatorio* 19.56).[88] Even if, as Panofsky proposed, there once existed a companion piece to Bronzino's painting, Truth's conspicuous absence is significant; she must be called up, if only mentally, to effect a "reversal" of what we see. If the painting is understood as a "contrary," the obverse of a positive image, it must be seen as satirical, a parody of the traditional image of Venus.[89] The moral allegory to be drawn from the image (based on its implied converse) is that deception is the result of false perception. The spectator sees a false beauty (Venus) and a false love (Cupid) and extrapolates from this a moral message which warns against deception. Like Carnival itself, the transgressions enacted in the painting "remind us of the existence of the rule" (Eco 6).

NOTES

1 The major portion of this paper was presented in a lecture at the Harvard Center for Renaissance Studies, Villa I Tatti, Firenze, on April 17, 1986. My fellowship was funded by the National Endowment for the Humanities. Funds for photographs were provided by a Union College Faculty Development grant. I would like to thank both institutions and most particularly the library staff of the Biblioteca Berenson and my collegues at the Villa for their generous assistance, in particular, Maurizio Gavrioli for his technical assistance. In addition I thank the Institute of Fine Arts, N.Y.U. for the use of their computer facilities.
2 The bibliography on this painting has become too extensive to cite in full. Included in the bibliography at the end are those works relevant to specific points in my interpretation. A chronological list of previous publications can be found in Frangenberg (n. 1). As I was preparing this article for publication a new contribution by Cheney came to my attention.
3 *Passioni* is translated "torments" on the basis of the *Vocabolario degli Accademici della Crusca*.
4 Suggestions made by scholars for the discrepancies between the description and the painting, include Vasari's distance in time or place from the original and his confusing it with other works by Bronzino of similar subject. Among these works is a quite different version in Budapest which has no upper-register personifications and has been proposed as a companion piece to the London painting despite differences in size and style (Haraszti-Takàcs, Plate 2, *Venus, Cupid and Jealousy* and text opposite). The Budapest painting, sometimes suggested as representing the positive side of Venus, shares the two central figures and an iconographically more traditional *Invidia* with our Bronzino. A close copy of the London painting also exists in Budapest. I am grateful to Dr. Vilmos Ta'trai, Szepmuveszeti Muzeum, Budapest, for providing me with

a photograph of this version which may be a later copy of the London painting, despite its slightly amplified frame.

5 In 1545 Cosimo had Bronzino's *Pietà* sent to France as a gift to Granville, minister to Emperor Charles V. Cox-Rearick proposed that Henry II rather than François I may have been the recipient of the *Allegory* (1984 6–22; "La Collection" 40–1), a suggestion repeated by Cheney. The painting's whereabouts before the 18th century are not documented. Gould (43) believed it did not remain long at Fontainebleau and arrived only later to the Louvre. It came to the National Gallery, London via the Beaucousin collection (Paris 1860).

6 A similar uncertainty as to the road taken from Italy to the Louvre applies to two of Michelangelo's *Slaves*, a gift from the artist to the *fuoriuscito* Ruberto Strozzi who then shipped them to France. Strozzi represents only one link between Florence, Venice, Lyons and the court of France. In 1532 Antonio Mini in Lyons proposed selling Michelangelo's *Leda and the Swan* to François I (de Tolnay 3.106f, 190f; ills. 279, 280) making at least two copies for Florentine patrons in that city. Instead of the original, the king bought a copy made in Italy by Rosso Fiorentino. This may be the *Leda* now in the National Gallery, London, formerly in the collection of Hon. John Spencer, who also possessed a version of Bronzino's *Allegory* (Gould 44). The taste of the Florentines in Lyons suggests a predisposed appreciation for a mannerist style deriving from Michelangelo. Bronzino's *Allegory*, in fact, shares specific elements with the lost *Leda*, in particular the drape beneath and behind the sculptural figure (Barocchi, *Giorgio Vasari* 3.1105 ff.; 2.316). A large painting of *Venus, Bacchus and Cupid* in the collection of the Luxembourg Museum has been attributed to Rosso Fiorentino by Silvie Béguin of the Louvre who recently proposed that it was among the paintings done for the Galerie François I at Fontainebleau thus dating it before 1539 (Béguin 165). In verbal communication, Dr. Béguin expressed the opinion that Bronzino must have known the Rosso composition. Thus the style of our painting can be connected to Rosso and the decoration of the Gallery at Fontainebleau. Cf. Béguin, "New Evidence" 828–39.

7 Panofsky's interpretation was severely hampered by the desire to make of the painting a companion to the Bronzino tapestry entitled the "Vindication of Innocence" c. 1546 (Panofsky 91). It would seem that from technical considerations alone, the two were not meant to be paired. The dimensions of the London Allegory are 146x116, that of the tapestry 242x172 (Smyth, *Bronzino as Draughtsman* 88; figs. 20, 22); the difference in size could not be attributed to the lack of a border on the *Allegory*. Certainly there are stylistic affinities between the *Allegory* and the tapestries, for example in the corpus of poses and limbs collected in the representation of *Joseph and Potipher's Wife*, but the London painting's composition and iconography does not support pairing the two. On the Joseph series see the catalogue of the restoration of the Tapestries (*Gli arazzi*) and Smyth ("Cosimo I"). On the tapestry production for Cosimo

I, see Adelson.
8 Based on the classical phrase *Veritas filia temporis* (Saxl 197 ff.), it is thematically allied with the "Calumny," an allegory represented by Apelles, cf. Cast. Panofsky (90) compared compositional and figural relationships between the Bronzino tapestry cartoon and an emblem used by the printer Marcolini depicting this theme, in which Calumny or Falsehood takes the form of a fantastic siren-like figure. The Marcolini emblem, most likely invented by Anton Francesco Doni, also inspired Vasari (*Giorgio Vasari, cat.*: 26, 116) in the scene designs for Aretino's play *La Talanta*, published by Marcolini, in which the same image appears. On this see the entries of McTavish in the *Giorgio Vasari, cat.*: 112 ff. Connections between theatrical productions and the circle of Aretino in Venice would seem, then, to provide the background for Bronzino's subject and stylistic sources as well. Doni, in contact with Vasari, is allied with this Venetian circle after 1545. For additional bibliography on the emblem, see Frangenberg 384, n. 9.
9 On the advice of Walter Friedlaender, he renamed the painting *The Exposure of Luxury*, a title which has not gained general approval.
10 A discussion of the parallels between visual and literary allegory in the Cinquecento will be the subject of a longer study.
11 It is not possible in the limits of this study to discuss the other figures in detail with respect to these two; this will be treated elsewhere. The major theme and its elaboration via the other five figures is expressed in nucleo by Saturn and Fraud.
12 Castelvetro (2.126) is interpreting Aristotle's phrase (*Poetics* 1449a.31): "Che il vizio, in quanto muove riso, è soggetto della rassomiglianza comica." [That vice, insofar as it elicits laughter, is the subject of comic affinity.]
13 Because no two scholars have seen the painting in the same way, in order to make clear my view of the work it is necessary to present a brief description of its contents. Since no description can be completely objective, the order and organization of the painting therefore reflects my interpretation.
14 This drape also appears in the engraving after Michelangelo's *Leda and the Swan* copied by Rosso Fiorentino, as well as engravings from the School of Fontainebleau on the theme of the Loves of the Gods, some of which are attributed to Rosso. A similar drape appears in Perino del Vaga's design for a *Doris and Neptune* also from a series of the Loves of the Gods (Bartsch 28; old 15, pt. 1: 88). Thus, the painting can be linked both thematically and compositionally with Rosso's early work for François I at Fontainebleau and other works on the same theme. On Bronzino's use of prints see Smith, "Bronzino's use." Both the Michelangelo and the Perino derive from antique reliefs, the Perino from a relief of Mars and Venus. One can only speculate on a common source for the series (Michelangelo?). Similar drapery behind figures of the Gods appears on numerous sarcophagi (Bober and Rubenstein figs. 38, 38ii, 21–2, 11, 69–70, as well as the Renaissance drawings after them

such as 70a). I believe that the imitation of sculpture is meant to be recognized as such in both the painting and the related prints.

15 Variously identified as Truth, Night, Fraud (Levey), Oblivion (Hope 239–43) and most recently Chastity (Cheney), see below (n. 65).

16 An earlier example of this pose is Parmigianino's *Cupid Carving his Bow*. See Barolsky (90, fig. 5–14) on "Buchismo."

17 Cf. also Quintilianus (*Inst. Or.* 9.4.113,) on *emblema* as a rhetorical ornament, noted by Miedema. I am grateful to Julian Kliemann for this reference. The exactly contemporary interest in Alciati's *Emblema* (Green), combined with close relationships in composition between the painting and the earliest emblem illustrations, especially those for the Lyons edition (Russell 535), confirms Bronzino's knowledge of the genre. A connection between Bronzino's painting and emblems exists thematically via Moschus's epigram on Cupid, translated by Varchi (see nn. 21 and 80), available in the fonts of the *Anthologia Greca* and utilized for various *emblemata* of Amor. The 1540 French edition of the *Emblema* by Gilles Corrozet, entitled *Hécatomgraphie*, recommends itself as a source for fantasies for tapestries: "Prendre en ce livre aulcune fantasie, Comme ilz feroient d'une tapisserie" (Miedema 247). This may be taken figuratively or literally, but suggests a design which is ornamental, concentrated and possessing the stylistic qualities found in our *Allegory*. Such shared decorative qualities may also explain why Panofsky considered the painting to be a tapestry cartoon.

18 Cf. Danto (3; 119) on interpretation and the role of context. A title implies the artist's intended structuring of the separate elements of his work. This assumes that in any painting there is a guiding structural (compositional) principal which is connected to its meaning. By identifying the central element, a whole set of emanations which depend on and elucidate it are identified. Conversely Danto believes that "the structure of the work undergoes transformation, in accordance with differences in interpretation" (120). In Bronzino's painting, though the subject of "love" is self-evident because of the identities of the central pair, the absence of a defining title enables us to question not only the subject but the focus and intention of its treatment. Had an original title or motto come down to us the picture would undoubtedly lose much of its problematic nature. It is conceivable, however, that Bronzino's work would retain the ambivalent character of its affective readings regardless, because of the pictorial/allegorical techniques he employed.

19 The sculptural sources, both antique and contemporary, on which these figures depend will be the subject of a separate study. Clearly the marble quality of the figures contributes to the conflict between the sensuality of the pose and the lack of emotion evoked. On the ability of statues of Venus to elicit love (*agalmatofilia*) see Varchi's *Due Lezzioni* (Barocchi, *Scritti* 538; see also Mendelsohn 120 and Carlo del Bravo, on Bronzino's use of Cinquecento sculptural models).

20 In a popular Renaissance source text such as the *Allegoriae Poeticae* of Albricus, the image of Venus derived from *epygrama* is traditionally linked with that

of Saturn (doves included). It is likely that Bronzino, or whoever composed the program of the *Allegory*, referred to allegorical source works such as this (cf. the lengthy mythographic citations on Venus and Saturn in *Mythologiae*), or directly to the epigrams themselves for descriptions of personifications, as well as to contemporary poets and writers in the Accademia Fiorentina.

21 This is the description of Saturn according to Abu Ma'sar (Klibansky 130).

22 This is not the only occasion in which Bronzino used suggestive sexual allusions, for example in the *Orpheus* and in the *St. Sebastian* (Cox-Rearick, "A St. Sebastian" 161). On the pose of Cupid, cf. Barolsky 90. On visual references to sodomy in the Renaissance, cf. Saslow. Coded references to sodomy are ubiquitous in satirical writings by members of the Accademia Fiorentina, in particular *burleschi* by Anton Francesco Grazzini, known as il Lasca, and in Bronzino's own *Rime in Burla*. A glossary of "double entendres" is given by Toscan, vol. 4. Among the key words are: *Giuoco, fraude* and *riso* (Plaisance 187 ff.). This humor depends stylistically on the 'inverted' humor of popular carnival songs. In the *De Planctu Naturae* of de Lille, cited here as a source for the painting, subtitled on the Florentine mss. "prosa & carmine contra Sodomiae crimen," sodomy is equated with idolatry, *Lussuria* and excessively ornate rhetoric. For a fuller treatment of the references to sodomy and their meaning for the painting, see my forthcoming contribution in *L'Arte del Cinquecento in Toscana* (1992).

23 In Cicero (*De Natura Deorum*: 3.57 ff.) there are four forms of Venus and three of Cupid; each of these has a separate and distinct identity, not, as in later interpretations, two natures within one form. On Cupid's duality see Varchi's *Lezzioni* on Petrarch's *Triumph of Love* (21). Among the personifications Pleasure simultaneously displays her true, hidden nature so that it can be seen by the spectator on close examination of the painting. A source for this figure in Castiglione's *Cortegiano* was discussed in a lecture I delivered at the Annual AAIS Convention in Pittsburgh (April 1985), entitled "La Bella Menzogna: Ambiguity and Duplicity in Bronzino's London Allegory."

24 *Gioco* or Cruel Joke, appears in Classical illustrations as an old, dwarfed man who hides behing a youthful mask (Cartari 478). See also the drawing usually called "Truth," (Battista Franco, attr. after Michelangelo, Uffizi) in which a figure who might be called Fraud or Venus rather than Truth is accompanied by a small figure hiding behind a large grotesque mask (Chastel, "Masque" fig. 108).

25 A mask is found similarly placed beneath the foot of Jupiter-Diana in the etching after Rosso depicting *Jupiter seducing Callisto in the guise of Diana* in the series of the Loves of the Gods painted for François I at Fontainebleau, dated by Zerner c. 1534 (Zerner fig. pm. 4).

26 Bronzino illustrates the negative aspect of the vice, which in its self-destructive image resembles the description of the Desperate Man and carnival figure of Desperation described below. See Smith, "Jealousy" 250 ff., on the relationship

between the two forms of *Invidia*.
27 Uranus or *Cielo* ("Sky" or "Heavens") holding the canopy is found on the Cuirass of the Augustus of the Prima Porta. *Cielo*, who appears in the decorations of the Palazzo Vecchio, links the Planetary Saturn to Time in ways which parallel the political and personal iconography Cosimo I adapted in imitation of Augustus (Davis, but also Rousseau 328-30 who sees the fresco as the castration of Saturn rather than Caelus).
28 (Vasari, *Vite* 6.283); Caruggi was known as the "Mons Saturnius" (Rousseau 301).
29 (Allegri 105 ff.; Frey 30.1, 31.412-5; Vasari 8.45). On Bartoli and Vasari see Davis. In the Sala di Opi, the geneological references make Saturn the Father of Cosimo I and Opi (both wife and sister of Saturn), his mother. Elsewhere Saturn's reign is compared to that of Cosimo even though the implication is that as the Son of Saturn, Cosimo is actually Jupiter. The Saturn of the Terrace, though later, is based on Vasari's designs of 1541-2 for the "apparato dei sempiterni" scenery for the carnival performance of Aretino's *La Talanta* in Venice, published by Marcolini (*Giorgio Vasari, cat.*: 112 ff.). Along with Mercury and Janus, Saturn forms an important part of the frieze at Poggio a Caiano, in this context, related to the theme of Time but in the role of a positive, agricultural god (Landi fig. 11, where the right arm of Saturn is extended in a way which is recalled later in the Bronzino). One is tempted to hypothesize a common (classical?) prototype. The frieze is attributed to Andrea Sansovino and Bertoldo by Landi. Cox-Rearick (1984 132, n. 52) finds Saturn in a similar astrological-agricultural context in Pontormo's lunette at Poggio a Caiano.
30 Also the sign of Charles V (Cox-Rearick, 1984 276 ff.). See Pontormo's drawing of a Saturn on a goat (in Capricorn), Uffizi 6510F. The sign of Capricorn is also connected to Venus. In Cartari, Venus on a goat signifies *Piacere Honesto*. Cf. the drawing known as Venus in Capricorn, Paris, Louvre, Cabinet des Dessins 10396, discussed in Cox-Rearick, "Master" 8, 4, 371, 372, entry 344a, attributed to Pontormo by Shearman and published by Cox-Rearick in the 2nd edition of *The Drawings of Pontormo*. The drawing is there connected to Cosimo Primo's wedding decorations described by Giambullari (1539) as well as to the pose of the Venus of the *Allegory*. Cox-Rearick ("addenda" 372) denies the drawing's connection to either the Palazzo Vecchio or the Villa Castello decorations dating it c. 1540.
31 (Vasari, *Vite* 8.11 ff.). *I Ragionamenti*, a dialogue between Prince Ferdinando dei Medici and Giorgio Vasari (1588), is a retrospective description and explanation of the meaning of the decoration of the Palazzo Vecchio from the time of its occupancy by Cosimo I in 1537. In Vasari's explanation Cosimo and his wife Eleonora are identified with the two deities. To explain the Sala degli Elementi we are given a series of positive virtues such as Clemenza, Sapienza, Grazia etc., simple personifications with positive meanings. To the Prince, questioning the planetary meaning of the sphere in relation to Saturn,

Vasari replies: "Quello, come sa V.E., è un corpo cosmo, che così è nominato dalli astrologi il mondo, che è dritto il nome del duca nostro signore, che è fatto patrone di questo Stato; e Saturno, suo pianeta, tocca il Capricorno ascendente suo, e mediante i loro aspetti fanno luce benigna alla palla della terra, e particolarmente alla Toscana, e, come capo della Toscana, a Firenze, oggi per Sua Eccellenza con tanta iustizia e governo retta" (*Ragionamento Secondo* 43 ff.). Explaining the Triumph of Saturn: "*Questo è il padre Saturno, cioè il Tempo*, [emphasis mine] che d'ognuno trionfa consumando ogni vita, ma non già così ogni memoria; . . . ed avendo domo le cose terrene e gl'inganni, vola nel cielo con le penne delli scrittori, o alle divine cose, che Crono, con le cronache che ha in mano, ha segnato negli annali i gesti gloriosi, per lasciare a quelli che nascono le grandezze fatte da lui. Le quattro Stagioni, consumate a piè del carro, mostrano che non à perdonato a occasione, che sia venuta d'ogni tempo, per accrescere, magnificare, ed ingrandire questa illustre casa, riducendola a quella suprema altezza che oggi noi vediamo col fine dell'ultima Parca." The image of Time-Saturn as the chronicler of the Medici may have been inspired by Doni. While Vasari cites the usual negative qualities of Time-Saturn, his overall symbolic intention is positive. In the *Ragionamento terzo*, explaining the frescoes in the Sala di Opi, Vasari compares Cosimo and Saturn in "aministrando giustizia, tenendo i populi in pace." The author of this program was probably Cosimo Bartoli. On viewing the scenes of Venus in the Sala di Opi of the Palazzo Vecchio Ferdinando exclaims in an ingenuous vein: "O che pensieri, o che immaginazioni! le fanno venir voglia d'innamorarsi" (Vasari, *Vite* 43 ff.).

32 Alanus ab Insulis, *Anticlaudianus* 4.8, Migne, *PL* vol. 210, col. 528, including such oxymorons as: "obscurus lucet" and "iuvenisque senescit." Compare the same author's description of Cupid: "Does not Desire, performing many miracles, to use antiphrasis, change the shapes of all mankind. Though monk and adulterer are opposite terms, he forces both of these to exist together in the same subject . . . . Deceit, trickery, fear, rage, madness, treachery, violence, delusion, gloom, find a hospitable home in his realm. Here reasonable procedure is to be without reason, moderation means lack of moderation, trustworthiness is to not be trustworthy. He offers what is sweet but adds what is bitter. He injects poison and brings what is noble to an evil end. He attracts by deceiving, mocks with smiles, stings as he applies his salve, infects as he shows affection, hates as he loves" (9.5; Sheridan 149).

33 A Medici theme which begins in the Quattrocento. For other examples see Gombrich; Rousseau ch. 2, and Cox-Rearick, 1984 261 ff.

34 The dialogue is between *Giove* and *Anima*. See also the world under Time, below (n. 38).

35 On Doni's works and those of other *poligrafi*, see Grendler 49 ff.

36 Klibansky 157: "Poimandres says that after death the soul frees itself of the bad qualities acquired on earth, leaving in the sphere of Saturn its lurking lies."

37 Lucian's Momus, from the dialogue "Jupiter Tragoedus," lines 7–17, is a common source for both Doni and Leon Battista Alberti (see the edition of *Momo o del Principe*).

38 "He held three great mirrors in front of his face looking now in one, now in the other; depending on what he saw in them he changed his appearance now happy, now neutral, now sad, his left side sad, his right side happy." The members of Time's cortege included "War and Peace, Life and Death and Love and Hate" and other "powerful figures." These always looked him in the face, obeyed his orders ("cenni") and sent to earth this or that great power. At his feet were seated Fate (*Fato*) holding a book on to which *Fortuna* and *Sorte* kept throwing cards. Time made Fate write down everything that was decided by him. The description (*I Mondi* 16–17) includes the idea of the futility of attempting to overcome Time's power.

39 Apparently Time was painted in the Venetian Academy by a member with the nickname *Pigro*: "Fu bella invenzione ancora quella del Pigro a far dipingere nell'Accademia il *Tempo, capace d'ogni inganno e d'ogni frodo*, e la Morte orribile a vedere, che giocavano insieme a scacchi . . . questi due tiranni del mondo pieno d'errori e padroni della vita nostra infelice . . ." *Pitture del Doni*, Padova: 1564 (Barocchi). The description of Time and Death continues: "Ecco il Tempo e la Morte, che sono i nostri padroni. Che han da fare i duchi, che gli imperador, che' signori, del fatto nostro? . . . di *questi due crudelissimi diformi e brutti personaggi*, i quali nel colmo delle mortali grandezze a nessuno la rispiarmano, sien begli, sien brutti, sien pazzi, savi, dotti, ignoranti, ricchi, poveri, buoni o cattivi." Time creates, Death destroys (i. e. they are contraries). "Così quello mantiene la generazione, e quella la corruzione, discordi del fare e d'accordo nel disfare. . . ." Doni quotes both Ovid and Petrarch on Time (Petrarch, *Rime* 355.1–4: "O tempo, O ciel volubil, che fuggendo / Ingannì i ciechi e miseri mortali, / O dì veloci più che vento e strali, / Ora *ab experto* vostre frodi intendo"), strongly associating time with deception.

40 "E aburattandomi in questa baia, mi sopragiunse un uomo grande, bello, con un barbone, un certo figurone come il Moisè di Michel Agnolo in Roma, ch'è alla sepoltura di Giulio secondo, e mi dice: — Tribolo, lascia dormire il tuo corpo un pezzo, e andiamo a spasso in questo mezzo; poi tornerai a destarlo, finito le comedie. MOSCHINO. Chi era cotestue? TRIBOLO. Il Tempo. E tutti due andavamo di compagnia, caminando per aere senza muover piedi, ma solo con quella volontà, sì come fareste voi adesso con la fantasia ad andare di qui a casa vostra, di qui [Firenze] a Prato o altro luogo più lontano. . . . Per la via, andando a mezz'aere, egli cominciò a dirmi come egli era il più antico che uomo e che sapeva ogni cosa." Tribolo asks Tempo a series of questions: 1) "Qual è la più bella cosa che voi abbiate mai veduta? . . . . Egli mi dice: — Il Mondo." 2) "Qual è la maggior cosa che si trovi? — Io sono — disse egli — che consumo e ricevo in me ogni cosa; io ne son padrone, son sempre in tutti i luoghi, sono stato presente a quanto s'è fatto e mi ritroverò a ciò che si farà."

3) "Chi è colui che più sa di tutti?.... Madesì!—egli rispose subito—chi sa più di me? chi più di me è intelligente?.... Non udite voi che 'l Tempo è quel che sa? ... (*Opere di Pietro Aretino e di Anton Francesco Doni* 737–9).

41 Bronzino, *Il Piato* 17.4.205–16, Firenze, Biblioteca Nazionale Centrale, Fondo Magl. 7.115 (Nardelli 244). In cap. 3, lines 79–81 (Nardelli 234), Bronzino refers to Kronos the castrator, a Tempo which increases to occupy a large space. Nardelli also sees a relationship between the figure called "Tempo" in the painting and in the tapestry of Innocence and Time, the theme of "Verità daughter of Time" and the lines cited (cf. her notes for 17.4.428, nn. 6, 9).

42 If we use Toscan's glossary, the references to sexual practices, particularly sodomy, are ubiquitous in this poem. A sonnet by Bronzino dedicated to Michelangelo utilizes the same image of the veil: "squarciò l'indegno e tenebroso velo,/ che men chiaro render / l'Empirea Corte" (Baccheschi 9).

43 "e il carro camminar sotto le ruote / e 'l punto aver le tre dimensioni / e le ragion del cubo esserne vote. / E vidi in questa tresca i savi e' buoni / esser gli sciocchi e' tristi e l'allegrezze / dolori e in somma tutti rovescioni." Bronzino, *Il Piato* 17.4.31–6. Cf. Nardelli 238 ff.

44 "... humor in oculis concretus, unde lippitude venire solet" (*Pictorius*: fol. 7v Cap. 7). Sources used by this author include Macrobius, Cicero, Lactantius, Isidorus, Servius and Ovid's *Fasti*. From Macrobius he takes the description of Saturn with "canis capillis, barba et concretis oculis" (fol. 8) and the union of Kronos with Time: "planet dari Saturno falcem veluti messis insigne."

45 Bernardus Silvestris, quoted in Klibansky 185.

46 The problem of the relationship between the two prologue figures has, along with the identity of the "female," frequently been argued in the literature. A major question being whether or not they act in unison or in opposition to veil or to unveil the scene below.

47 Pope-Hennessey, plate 118, 119 Museo Nazionale (Florence), cast in 1546, chased and gilded in 1547. Cosimo preferred the "impassive Mask" of Bandinelli (ibid. fig. 68).

48 Inv. 1472 (Uffizi catalogue 188) and Langedijk (vol. 1): on the Medici children, their dates of birth and their portraits, see also Becherucci. Cambell, reviewing Langedijk, suggests the possibilty that the portrait was executed after the death of the child in 1542 (*Burlington Magazine* 987 (May 1985): 388.)

49 It is tempting to read the other personifications in the *Allegory*, at least in part, as Children of Saturn, "the unhappiest of mortals" (Klibansky 148). That is, they seem to partake of the temperament of *Melancholia*, even to resembling known illustrations of these, such as the engraving by Dürer known as *The Man in Despair*. The engraving has been discussed in relation to melancholic types, similar but not identical to the "choleric Melancholic" who is "terribilis in aspectu" and tormented by "furores and maniae" (Klibansky 403–5). Schultz discusses the print in connection with a possible lost *écorché* bozzetto by Michelangelo in his study (34). A study for the hands of *Gelosia*, at-

tributed to Bronzino by Mario di Giampaolo, recently appeared on the art market (Sotheby's Montecarlo, 20 June 1987, lot 33). While connecting the engraving with the so-called figure of *Gelosia* and also with Michelangelo, Tietze-Conrat makes no mention of the Saturnian allusion (but cf. Klibansky, appendix). On another occasion Doni used Dürer's image of *Melancholia*, a copy of which he probably owned, as a model for his description of Scultura in his dialogue *Il Disegno* (Venice, 1549). Operating on the same allegorical level as parody, i.e. contemporary-historical, the *Gelosia*, according to Conway, is a reference to syphilis. In the first decade of the sixteenth century in Germany the "nuova malatia," also known as the "morbo gallico" or the French Disease, was considered one of the signs of the second coming. Its representation by Dürer had already been given a political meaning relating to the Emperor Maximillian (Warburg 351–60). Since *Gelosia* was described as incurable ("al cui grave male Remedio alcun di medico non vale") by Cartari (416–7), the historically equivalent disease might well have been seen as symbolizing the contemporary French threat. The *volgare* description of the vice of Invidia taken by Cartari (416) from Virgil, in fact, reads like the medical description of the disease, and therefore may be the common source for both. Further historical-political implications of the image of Saturn in Bronzino's *Allegory* undoubtedly exist but cannot be discussed here.

50 While probably not by the hand of Bronzino, the Wallace portrait must depend on his model and is certainly a court product. Objections to representing Eleonora as a lustful Venus in a Medici Commission are certainly sustainable. Nevertheless in a Carnival context where the ultimate message of the image is the same as that of the Wallace portrait it might be considered justifiable. The use of Medici family portraits is not uncommon in other contemporary works by Bronzino. Cox-Rearick ("Les dessins" 8–22) proposes (ibid. 20, n. 72) a portrait of Maria de Medici in the *Allegory*, "qui ressemble à sa mere [Eleonora] d'une façon frappante" as *Piacere*. She also sees a portrait of Eleonora appearing in the center of the nearly contemporary *Pietà* for the Chapel in the Palazzo Vecchio (ibid. 20 and figs. 21–2), and recently, in discussing the *Crossing of the Red Sea*, sees a pregnant Eleonora to the left of Moses. Since the drawing of a female head for *Moses Striking the Rock* (her fig. 17), also resembles the so-called Eleonora of the *Pietà*, especially around the mouth, allusions to Eleonora would seem ubiquitous in the Chapel. On portraits in Bronzino's religious paintings and sixteenth century criticism of them as lascivious, see Gaston. On Cinquecento portraits of women see Mendelsohn, "Boccaccio" 323–34.

51 A ms. in the BNF (Biblioteca Capponi, "Il diario di Firenze dal 26 Gennaio 1536–55," attributed to Antonio da San Gallo) describes a *bufola*, in which Cosimo himself participated (24 March 1546). Cf. Manetti 198, on *bufole*: "Ciascuna mascherata si presenta come un vero e proprio *Tableau vivant* al cui complesso allestimento avevano collaborato i migliori esponenti delle arti

minori e dell'artigianato fiorentino."
52 For example, "Il Vituperio carnale cacciato dalla Castità." Cf. Bronzino's drawing in Oxford, Christ Church n. 1340, on this theme (ill. *Il Primato* 88 no. 34).
53 G.B. Busini, in a letter to Benedetto Varchi c. 1550, testifies: "non so altro di certo, se non che l'Asino d'oro era da lui figurato per Luigi Guicciardini e di lui si doleva spesso. L'altre bestie di Circe erano tutti gli amici dei Medici, ma non so partitamente quali" (Varchi, "Lezione" 2.71–3). On parody in Cinquecento literature with reference to painting see Barolsky 104 ff. The relationship of the satiric style of the *Allegory* to comic theater can only be touched upon in this article but will be given fuller treatment elsewhere.
54 A second manuscript, another copy of the same text, Capponi 105, seems to be calculated from Jan. 1 and thus March 1546 would be 1546 rather than 1547. Ms. 91 is probably sixteenth century. The copyist of 105 is, in the opinion of Gino Corti, 17th century.
55 The *lacunae* indicated by the copyist make it impossible to ascertain whether Duke Cosimo appeared in the guise of Death, but this seems unlikely to me. Another manuscript describing the same event (Capponi 105) omits the three dots and instead repeats the word Death in their place. This manuscript is, however, in general a less accurate transcription of what must be a lost master original. Manetti in her article accepts the reading of mss. 105, while citing 91, suggesting that Cosimo appeared as Death. In Doni's *Pitture*, quoted below, Death and Time are paired, thus Cosimo might have appeared as a Time-Saturn similar to our allegorical figure. Besides six *bufolate*, the pageant consisted of a float or *carro*, in the form of the earth on which were represented, among others, the crippled ("zoppi") and deformed ("malfatti").The three days of festivities also included the performance of a Comedy entitled the Death of Ginevra (BNF Capponi 91.70). The theme of the Carnival *mascherata* as stated in the Cinquecento description is strikingly close to Doni's *I Mondi*. It should also be noted that the 4th *bufola* was said to include slaves "alla bronzina."
56 It is tempting to utilize the phrase "alla Bronzina" to connect Tribolo's three-dimensional figures with our artist, but the gender of the word makes this problematic. "Alla Bronzina" may refer to a type of bearing used for mechanical stage *apparati*, indicating that the figures, realized as sculpture, may have been moveable (*Vocabolario degli Accademici della Crusca* 1866, 2.286). The possibility that the statues were painted to simulate bronze cannot be excluded (cf. *Vocabolario*, s.v. "Bronzino": "Di colore di bronzo . . . "), even though the word is masculine in gender. It has been suggested to me that the word "maniera" may be understood.
57 Though holding a flower and a knife, rather than the honeycomb and sting which we see in the painting, the two images, one three-dimensional (possibly the earlier of the two) reflect two very similar conceptions of Deceit. Although Smith proposed that the so-called *Piacere* was in fact Fraud, I would not change

the painting's nomenclature on the basis of the description of the statue. As I have already stated, all the figures are forms of deception. Within the painting itself, one aspect of deception may well be called *Piacere*. If so this is surely a *Piacere Dishonesto*.

58 Vasari (6.87 ff.) mentions that Tribolo was responsible for decorating festival *carri*. Unfortunately, the *carro* of the Temple of Discord described was burned accidentally during the *bufola*. Sculptural vestiges of this or a similar program may survive in two Seicento statues by Susini from the Boboli. One statue surviving, of Fraud, now in the Pitti, was probably originally paired with a statue of Saturn by Silvani. Cf. Pizzorusso 57–8. The dependance of Bronzino's style on sculptural precedents has been frequently noted (Smyth; Del Bravo; Mendelsohn).

59 Mamone ("Feste" 223, and n. 59) has pointed out the use of the *tableau vivant* in French *fêtes* et *entrées* and their gradual eclipse in favor of *quadri dipinti* under Italian influence. *Quadri dipinti* made for French patrons may well have taken on the characteristics of the *tableau*.

60 On Medici festivals see essays in *Toscana dei Medici nell'Europa del '500*: Mitchell 2 and 3.995–1004; Tofani 2.645–61; Ruffini 138 ff. (on "gli ornamenti della sala," for a performance of la *Calandria*). Cf. also articles by Mamone, Manetti on *le bufolate*; Testaverde Matteini and Molinari, in *Quaderni di Teatro*, 7 dedicated to "Il teatro dei Medici." The Matteini article in particular documents a connection between Don Vincenzo Borghini and the French author Du Choul, important for Borghini's 1565 decorations for the wedding of Francesco de' Medici, as well as connecting ephemeral festival decoration with antique medals and *imprese*. Although these references for the most part post-date Bronzino's painting, earlier examples may well have existed. There is good reason to suppose that the Academia Peregrina, sponsors of Doni's *I Mondi*, composed and performed theatrical works as did the Intronati di Siena in their production of *Gl'Ingannati*, published in 1538.

61 The association of this painting, like the later *Allegory of Happiness* (Smith, "Bronzino's Allegory"), with epithalamic paintings of the Cinquecento may provide the connecting link with theater. While the *Allegory* resembles the Lotto *Venus and Cupid* of 1513–26 (Christiansen ill. 9), the *Triumph of Chastity* takes itself more seriously and might compare to the hypothetical missing 'serious' or positive representation of the theme suggested by Panofsky. If the *Triumph of Chastity* is the 'high' version of the theme, the *Venus and Cupid*, like the *Allegory*, would correspond to a 'popular or low' style comparable to *Canti carnascialeschi* or *Strambotti* in poetic form. An example of this might be Machiavelli's "De' diavoli iscacciati di cielo" sung by masked figures on the theme of the "passioni d'amore" (Machiavelli 66–8).

62 Shearman proposed that the two major pantings for the Gallery of François I in Fontainebleau, around which the other decorations for the room evolved, had some other prior function: "I think we should face the possibility that the whole

decoration of the Galerie was arranged round two pre-existing, independent paintings, not made for this purpose" (Shearman, "The Galerie" 8). As Sylvie Béguin has shown, one of these two paintings for the Gallery, the one now in Luxembourg, was probably known to Bronzino (see n. 6).

63 The function of these two figures can be compared to the prologue dialogues that preceded Latin comedies and their sixteenth century imitations such as those by Doni quoted above. On this see Castelvetro's *Commentary on Aristotle*: "the Roman poets invented the type of prologue peculiar to Latin comedy to set the argument before the audience and so prepare it for understanding an action of which it knew nothing" (Buongiorno 210). In a representation of Ruzante's *Anconitana*, Tempo, "dopo aver recitato il prologo, sedeva in disparte a simulare l'arresto del proprio corso per tutta la durata della rappresentazione" (Zorzi 99).

64 One might note a vague resemblance to Cellini's "Victory holding a Torch," a decoration for the Porte Dorée of the Chateau of Anêt now known only through a plaster in the Louvre (Pope-Hennessey: plate 83, 140, 141).

65 *Pace* Hope's proposal of Oblivion, first suggested by Shearman in a footnote in *Mannerism*, later (1981) changed to Deceit, and Panofsky's Night, both of which share qualities of Fraud without having her malevolence. I do not agree with Cheney's proposal of Chastity although finding the origins of the allegory in the *Psychomachia* is surely correct. In the London *Allegory*, however, there is no apparent positive presence and if there were it would have to be far more prominent and made instantly visible, to become an opposing force. A close comparison of the actual painting with photographs and X-rays before, during and after the Dec. 1957 restoration at the London National Gallery (at which time it was cleaned and damages retouched) lead me to conclude that damage to the canvas obscured part of the original figure which probably accounts for the loss of laurel leaves. Some evidence for the presence of leaves in the area above the ear is found in the Budapest copy which is an extremely accurate one in a slightly larger format. Certainly made before the cleaning but perhaps later than the sixteenth century, in this copy the billowing drapery that frames her head is both more readable and more ample and is clearly attached to a patch of curls connected to the mask-like face. The treatment of this patch of false hair is close to the treatment of the hair on the chin of the male mask. The edge of the forehead in the radiograph (22–1–58) and the Infra Red photos (19–6–58), taken during and after cleaning respectively, do suggest a mask. On the other hand, an ear, though cut off, exists.

66 Among the Latin vocabulary related to fraud we have numerous variants, such as *fraudulentia*, *fraus*, *Fraus*, and *fraudare*. The last appears frequently in Ovid and includes the meaning *to steal, embezzle* or *withdraw a thing from a person*.

67 Bandini 3.449, cod. 21 (Palatina): Alani Magni de Insulis Doctoris Parisiensis . . . *De Complanctu Naturae Liber* 10.90, Sup. Cod. 21. The book is inscribed as belonging to Angeli Zenobi de Gaddi de Florentia 92. Another exists in Rimini in the Biblioteca Civica, ms. D 2.20 (I am indebted to Arthur Field for

this information).
68 A comparison of this text with the painting raises interesting questions about the relationship between painted and literary allegory, and between Medieval and Renaissance allegorical style which I will discuss in a separate article. De Lille also offers the most satisfying explanation for the presence of *Giuoco*, illegitimate son of Venus and Antigamus. Associated with Cupid in Horace (*Odes* 1, 2, 3, 4), *Giuoco* is named "Cruel Joke" (*Acronis* 1.127-8).
69 In his *Distinctiones* (Migne 210.783c), de Lille says that in a fabula the entire narrative is false "in verbo et non in facto."
70 The situation in *De planctu* is described as that which occurs "when brotherly love is afflicted with fraud and the right hand lies to its sister" (Sheridan 167). Loss of virtue results in degeneracy and this is symbolized by homosexuality: "man, no longer man-like . . . unmans himself and deserves to be unmanned." If one applied this oddly prefreudian description to Bronzino's painting one might rename it the "Unmanning of Cupid" in view of his disarming by Venus. Considering Bronzino's burlesque poetry, for example "Il Penello" (Del Bravo 87 n. 56), one can easily see here a visual-verbal pun.
71 Similarly in *I Mondi*, Momus proposes two ways to change the world. One is to place a veil over it which would obscure the truth, the other is to use false eyeglasses which distort the truth. Momus chooses instead to switch souls and bodies, that is, to place inappropriate "animae" in bodies of different temperaments, classes and intellectual levels. The "strattagemma" perpetrated on the world results in the kind of chaos described in *De Planctu* (*I Mondi* 53v). "O il male venne sotto i panni (come dir sotto coperta) del bene, & la buggia sotto l'ombra della verità, & rimase ingannato: io me sono accorto di poi. Si voleva aprir bene gli occhi, potrò sempre dir io, perché t'ho fatto l'intelletto, la vista, & perché t'ho io dato la ragione se no perché tu sappi il fatto tuo bene bene . . ." (52v). It is also possible to read this according to the vocabulary of Toscan as a reference to sodomy.
72 McCorquedale's analysis of the gestures of Time and Fraud (89) agrees in large part with my own except that Time and Fraud are not, in my opinion, necessarily in conflict.
73 The problem of the "veil" has been treated by Frangenberg (377), who reads the action as Time preventing Fraud from covering the scene. One might also read the gesture as an attempt on the part of Fraud to cover herself. The cloth seems to be both drape and veil, but its function may relate to the theater, perhaps to the display of figures in an *intermezzo*. Another possibility is that it is connected to the display of statues of the Gods, as in Michelangelo's *Leda* (see n. 14, re the etchings by Rosso and Perino).
74 An observation that would seem the logical conclusion to my interpretation of the painting but one which had escaped me until Prof. Kaiser's critical reading of my paper.
75 Their two children, brothers, Il Tuo and Il Mio, who are enemies, resemble the

two children of Venus and Antigamus in de Lille's *De Planctu*. The dialogue continues in a vein close to the medieval source: "Febo, il qual non puo mirar torte cose diritte, né torte con diritti occhi, vedde che il Tempo si signoriva di questi dominii terreni artificiosamente e con malizia; fece a Giove et a gli altri Dei intendere come avevano il reame della terra perduto, e che il Tempo e la Occasione la tiraneggiavano e voltavano maria e montes a lor *Piacere* sotto e sopra. Laonde sdegnati le lor deità levaron via di terra, per mezzo d'Apollo e Nonne Muse, il *Piacere* (i panni del quale trovò il Dis*Piacere*, perché, salendo di terra in cielo nudo come dovea, gli lasciò e così il Dis*Piacere* se gli messe in dosso,) et ordinarono nella maestà del lor concilio che mai più il Tempo signor delle terrene cose potesse tornare in cielo. Per ciò in cielo non vi è Tempo, se ben vi è Giove, padre del Tempo, con la virtù del Tempo; non v'è né ora né punto, né giorno né notte."

76 Doni, *I Mondi*, Venice, Marcolini: 1552. In this edition, used with the kind permission of the Biblioteca Berenson, Villa I Tatti, Firenze, the smaller version of the figure, framed in a cartouche, is found opposite p. 110, while the larger figure, posed somewhat differently and in a harder linear form and framed in a simple oval, appears on p. 18 introducing the "Comparationi dal piccolo al gran mondo, del dubbioso et dello sbandito academici peregrini. Ragionamento primo." Cf. *Giorgio Vasari, cat.*: 199–200, and Bing.

77 Bing introduces an engraving illustrating the idea that man is prevented from seizing opportunity by Time. "Time is a Janus figure who pulls man violently away from Occasion and has covered man's eyes." George Reverdy, who executed the engraving was born in Lyons and worked there and in Italy between 1531 and 1564. Bing further notes that in Doni's writings both Fortune and Truth are "fickle handmaidens of Time." Other links between Time and Fortune (Occasion) are discussed by Wittkower (313 ff.).

78 Published under the auspices of the Academia Peregrina of Venice, the "libro primo" is dedicated to Ruberto Strozzi, elected "Principe" of the academy. Ruberto, son of Filippo Strozzi, leader of the anti-Medici faction and *fuoriuscito*, as a youth in Venice was a pupil of Benedetto Varchi, and was at this time probably a resident in Lyons. To Ruberto's brother Pietro, *Defensore* of the academy, Doni (*I Mondi* a. 2) dedicated the *Libro delle Historie chiamato Teatro de valorosi capitani d'Italia*; the fourth volume of *I Mondi* he says is dedicated to Pietro Strozzi "Padre della Patria, Padre vostro," and the entire collection of *I Mondi* is written in praise of the Casa Strozzi (see n. 6). On the imitation of Florentine ritual in Lyons see Mitchell, "Firenze."

79 Cf. Ripa's (455) figure of Simulatione, a woman "with a mask over her face in such a way that she reveals two faces . . . holding the mask over her face, covering the truth to make visible the false." ["E il nascondere con doppiezza di parole & di cenni anima & core proprio; però tiene la maschera sopra il volto, ricoprendo il vero per far vedere il falso."]

80 In the "annotatione" (Cartari 570) it is said that Cartari's image of Fortune

derives from an "inventione" of Doni. Thus Alciati probably provided the ultimate source. An illustration of Fortune (albeit on a swan with a sail) resembles in reverse, with blowing forelock, the head of Bronzino's Fraud. Cf. *Andreae Alciati Emblematum libellus*, Paris, 1534 (Green 20), ill. "In Occasionem," describing a statue by Lysippus. Vasari's companion drawing to his Time, Truth and Falsehood is an image of Virtue, Fortune and Envy, utilized for his house in Arezzo (summer 1548) (*Giorgio Vasari, cat.*: 26 and *Vite* 7.686). Deriving from his Venetian theater decorations, these employ the same cast of characters as the Bronzino.

81 A technique which resembles the literary alternation of the medieval polarities *Caritas* vs *Cupiditas*. On antithesis see Summers 344 ff., 347 n. 60a, 350 n. 73.

82 This is an example of the way in which medieval French allegory supports the method employed by Bronzino.

83 Ripa's illustration of "Imitazione" (Venice: 1669: 2.273) holding a mask and a bunch of paint brushes, obviously lies behind both the personifications of "Simulatione" (see above n. 79) and "Pittura" (404 ff.). All three hold masks. The use of deception to convey a moral message calls to mind Plutarch's saying (*De Gloria Athen.* 5.348) attributed to Gorgias: "Tragedy, by means of legends and emotions creates a deception in which the deceiver is more honest than the non-deceiver, and the deceived is wiser than the non-deceived."

84 The ambiguous nature of symbols and their use is discussed by St. Augustine in Book 3 of *De doctrina cristiana*, where "context" provides the means of determining whether a sign is "boni" or "mali."

85 The idea that Bronzino employs this technique was presented in my lecture delivered at the meeting of the AAIS in Pittsburgh, Spring 1985.

86 Capitolo terzo, "Della cipolla" 1.157–9, ed. Nardelli 144.

87 For a fuller treatment of literary and visual sources for this figure see my article cited above n. 22.

88 On reason and vision as the means by which this is achieved see above n. 71, Frangenberg 382 and n. 44.

89 Only Barolsky (147) has recognized the element of satire as central to the painting. Frangenberg, while discussing satirical sources, does not see the painting itself as a satire. In this context we should consider the possibility that Venus appears in her role as the goddess of comedy with her companion *Giuoco* who signifies laughter, a characteristic of lasciviousness (Cartari 478).

WORKS CITED

Adelson, C. "The decoration of Palazzo Vecchio in Tapestry: The 'Joseph' Cycle and other precedents for Vasari's decorative campaigns," in *Giorgio Vasari, tra decorazione ambientale e storiografia artistica. Convegno di Studi. Arezzo, 8–10 ottobre 1981.* Ed. Gian Carlo Garfagnini. Firenze: Olschki, 1985.

———. *The Tapestry Patronage of Cosimo I de' Medici: 1545-53.* (Unpubl. diss.). New York University, 1990.

Albricus. *Allegoriae Poeticae seu de veritate ac expositione poeticarum fabularum libri quatuor Alberico londonensi Authore nusquam antea impressi.* Paris: 1520. Rpt. *The Renaissance of the Gods.*

Allegri, E. and A. Cecchi. *Palazzo Vecchio e i Medici.* Firenze: S.P.E.S., 1980.

Baccheschi, E. *L'Opera Completa del Bronzino.* Milano: Rizzoli, 1973.

Baldini, B. *Discorso sopra La Mascherata della Geneologia degl'iddei de' Gentili.* Firenze: Giunti, 1556. Rpt. *The Renaissance of the Gods.*

Barocchi, P. *Giorgio Vasari. La Vita di Michelangelo nelle redazioni del 1550 e del 1568.* 5 vols. Milano-Napoli: Ricciardi, 1962.

———, ed. *Scritti d'Arte del Cinquecento.* Vol. 3. *Pittura e scultura. La letteratura italiana, storia e testi.* Milano-Napoli: Ricciardi, 1971. (Torino: Einaudi, 1978).

Barolsky, P. *Infinite Jest: Wit and Humor in Italian Renaissance Art.* Columbia: U of Missouri P, 1978.

Bartsch, A. von. *The Illustrated Bartsch. Italian Masters of the Sixteenth Century.* Eds. S. Boorsch, J. Spike. 28 New York: Abaris Books, 1985.

Becherucci, L. *Manieristi Toscani.* Bergamo: Istituto italiano d'arti grafiche, 1944.

Béguin, S. "La Galerie François I[ier] au Château de Fontainebleau: le programme mythologique." *Revue d'Art* 16–7 (1972): 165–72.

———. "New evidence for Rosso in France." *Burlington Magazine* (Dec. 1989): 828–39.

———. *Bacchus, Vénus et l'Amour, Redécouvert d'un tableau de Rosso Fiorentino, peintre de François I[ier].* Luxembourg, 1989.

Bergson, H. *Le Rire.* Paris: Presses Universitaires de France, 1983. (Italian trans. *Il Riso.* Ed. F. Sossi. Milano, 1990.)

Bing, G. "Nugae circa Veritatem: Notes on Anton Francesco Doni." *Journal of the Warburg and Courtauld Institutes* 1 (1937): 304–12.

Bober, P. and R. Rubinstein. *Renaissance Artists and Antique Sculpture.* London-New York: Oxford UP and Harvey Miller, 1986.

Bragantini, R. *Il riso sotto il velame. La novella cinquecentesca tra l'avventura e la norma.* Firenze: Olschki, 1987.

Bronzino, A. *Rime in burla.* Ed. Franca Petrucci Nardelli. Roma: Treccani, 1988.

Buongiorno, A., trans. *Castelvetro on the Art of Poetry, an abridged translation of Lodovico Castelvetro's Poetica d'Aristotele Vulgarizzata et Spostata.* Binghamton: Medieval and Renaissance Texts and Studies, 1984.

Cartari, V. *Le Vere o Nove Imagini de i Dei de gli Antichi.* Venezia: Marcolini,

1556. (Facsimile of Padua: PP. Tozzi, 1615, rpt. *The Renaissance of the Gods*, London: Garland, 1979).

Cast, D. *The Calumny of Apelles. A study in the humanistic tradition.* New Haven: Yale UP, 1981.

Castelvetro, L. *Poetica d'Aristotele, Vulgarizzata e Sposta*. Ed. Werther Romani. Bari: Laterza, 1978.

Chastel, A. "Le Myth de Saturne dans le Renaisssance italienne." *Phoebus* 1 (1946): 125-34.

——————. "Masque, mascarade, mascaron." *Fables, Formes, Figures*. Vol. 1. Paris: Flamarion, 1978: 249-58.

Cheney, I. "Bronzino's London *Allegory*: Venus, Cupid, Virtue, and Time." *Source* 6.2 (Winter, 1987): 12-8.

Christiansen, K. "Lorenzo Lotto and the Tradition of Epithalamic Painting." *Apollo* (Sept. 1986): 166-73.

Comitis, Natalis. *Mythologiae*. Venezia, 1567. Rpt. 1627 ed. *The Renaissance and the Gods*. New York & London: Garland, 1976.

Consolo, R., ed. *Leon Battista Alberti, Momo o del principe*. Genova, 1986.

Conway, J. "Syphilis and Bronzino's London Allegory." *Journal of the Warburg and Courtauld Institutes* 1.49 (1986): 250-55.

Cox-Rearick, J. "A St. Sebastian by Bronzino." *The Burlington Magazine* 79.1008 (March 1987): 155-62.

——————. *Dynasty and Destiny in Medici Art: Pontormo, Leo X and the Two Cosimos*. Princeton: Princeton UP, 1984.

——————. "The Drawings of Pontormo: addenda." *Master Drawings* 8.4 (1970): 363-78.

——————. *The Drawings of Pontormo*. New York: Hacker, 1981.

——————. "Les dessins de Bronzino pour la chapelle d'Eleonora au Palazzo Vecchio." *Revue d'Art* 14 (1971): 7-22.

——————. "La Collection de Franois I[ier]." *Les dossiers du département des peinture, Musées du Louvre* 5 (1972): 40-1.

——————. "Bronzino's Crossing of the Red Sea and Moses Appointing Joshua: Prolegomena to the Chapel of Eleonora di Toledo." *Art Bulletin* 69 (1987): 45-67.

Davis, C. "The Pitfalls of Iconology or how it was that Saturn gelt his Father." *Studies in Iconography* 4 (1978): 79-94.

Daly, P.M., V.W. Callahan, S. Cuttler. *Andreas Alciatus. Emblems in translation*. Vol. 2. Toronto: U of Toronto P, (c. 1985).

Danto, A. *The Transfiguration of the Commonplace*. Cambridge, Mass.: Harvard UP, 1981.

Del Bravo, C. "Dal Pontormo al Bronzino." *Artibus et historiae* 12 (1985): 75-87.

De Lille, Alain. *Anticlaudianus*. Vol. 4.8. *Patrologia Latina*.

——————. *De Planctu Naturae. Patrologia Latina*.

——————. *The Plaint of Nature*. Trans. and ed. James J. Sheridan. Toronto:

Pontifical Institute of Medieval Studies, 1980.

―――――. *The Complaint of Nature by Alain de Lille*. Trans. Douglas M. Moffat. New York: Henry Holt, 1908.

De Tolnay, C. *Michelangelo*. Princeton: Princeton UP, 1943.

Doni, A. *Il Disegno*. Venezia, 1549.

―――――. *I Mondi*. Venezia: Francesco Marcolini, 1552.

―――――. "Pitture del Doni academico pellegrino. (La Pittura del Tempo)." Padova, 1564. *Scritti d'Arte del Cinquecento*. Vol. 3. Milano-Napoli: Ricciardi, n.d.

―――――. *Opere di Pietro Aretino e di Anton Francesco Doni*. Ed. Carlo Cordié. *La Letteratura Italiana, storia e testi*. Milano-Napoli: Ricciardi, 1976.

Eco, U. "The Frames of Comic Freedom." In *Carnival!* Eds. Thomas Sebeok and Marcia E. Erickson. Berlin, N.Y. & Amsterdam: Mouton, 1984. 1–9.

Fleming, J. *The Roman de la Rose, a study in allegory and iconography*. Princeton: Princeton UP, 1969.

Foster, K.W. "Metaphors of Rule: Political Ideology and History in the Portraits of Cosimo I." *Mitteilungen des Kunsthistorisches Instituts in Florenz* 15 (1971): 65.

Frangenberg, T. "Der Kampf um den schleier zur Allegorie Agnolo Bronzino in der National Gallery London." *Wallraf-Richartz Jahrbuch* 46–7 (1985–6): 377–85.

Freedberg, S. *Painting in Italy 1500–1600*. Tennessee, 1979. (Harmondsworth: Penguin, 1971).

Frey, K. *Der literarische Nachlass Giorgio Vasaris*. Munich: Muller, 1923.

Gaston, R. "Iconography and Portraiture in Bronzino's 'Christ in Limbo.' " *Mitteilungen des Kunsthistorischen Institut in Florenz* 26 (1983): 41–72.

Giambullari, P. *Apparato e feste nelle nozze del illustrissimo Signor Duca di Firenze*. Firenze: Giunti, 1539.

Ginzburg, C. "Tiziano, Ovidio e i codici della figurazione erotica nel Cinquecento." *Miti emblemi spie*. Torino: Einaudi, 1988.

Giorgio Vasari, cat. mostra. Arezzo 1981. Firenze: Edam, 1981.

Gli arazzi della Sala dei Duecento, studi per il restauro, cat. mostra. Firenze. Modena: Panini, 1985.

Gombrich, E.H. "Renaissance and Golden Age." *Norm and Form*. London: Phaidon, 1966. 29–34.

Gould, C. *London, National Gallery: The Sixteenth Century Italian Schools (excluding the Venetian Schools)*. London: Publications Dept., National Gallery, 1975.

Green, H. *Andreae Alciati Emblematum Fontes Quatuor*. London: Brothers and Trubner, 1870.

Grendler, P.F. *Critics of the Italian World (1530–1560) Anton Francesco Doni, Nicolo Franco and Ortensio Lando*. Madison: U of Wisconsin P, 1969.

Haraszti-Takàcs, M. *The Masters of Mannerism*. Budapest: Corvina, 1968.

Hollander, R. *Allegory in Dante's Commedia*. Princeton: Princeton UP, 1969.
Hope, C. "Bronzino's *Allegory* in the National Gallery, London." *The Journal of the Warburg and Courtauld Institutes* 45 (1982): 239–43.
Horace. *Odes*. Ed. F. Harthal. *Acronis et Porphyrionis commentarii in Q. Horatium Flaccum*. Amsterdam: n.f, 1966.
Il Primato del disegno, cat. Firenze: Electa, 1980.
Klibansky, R., E. Panofsky and F. Saxl. *Saturn and Melancholy: Studies in the History of Natural Philosophy, Religion, and Art*. London: Thomas Nelson, 1964.
Landi, F. *Le temps revient. Il fregio di Poggio a Caiano*. Firenze: Landi Editore, 1986.
Langedijk, K. *The Portraits of the Medici: 15th–18th Centuries*. Firenze: Studio per edizioni scelte, 1981.
L'Arte del Cinquecento in Toscana. Conference in honor of Sylvie Béguin at the Kunsthistorisches Instituts Florence, Oct. 1989. Ed. Monika Cämmerer. Munich: Forschungen des Kunsthistorisches Institut in Florenz, 1992.
Levey, M. "Sacred and Profane Significance in Two Paintings by Bronzino." *Studies in Renaissance and Baroque Art Presented to Anthony Blunt on his 60th Birthday*. London: Phaidon, 1967. 30–3.
Machiavelli, N. *Opere*. Ed. Mario Bonfantini. Milano-Napoli: Ricciardi, n.d.
Mamone, S. *Il Teatro nella Firenze Medicea*. Milano: Mursia, 1981.
―――――. "Feste e spettacoli a Firenze e in Francia per le nozze di Maria de' Medici con Enrico IV. " *Il teatro dei Medici. Quaderni di Teatro, rivista trimestrale del Teatro Regionale Toscano* 7 (March, 1980): 206–28.
Manetti, D. "Una festa ai tempi di Cosimo de' Medici: le buffolate." *Quaderni di Teatro, rivista trimestrale del Teatro Regionale Toscano* 7 (March 1980): 195–205.
Mazzotta, G. *The World at Play in Boccaccio's Decameron*. Princeton, N.J.: Princeton U.P., 1986.
McCorquodale, C. *Bronzino*. New York: Harper & Row, 1981.
Mendelsohn, L. *Paragoni: Benedetto Varchi's Due Lezzioni and Cinquecento Art Theory*. Ann Arbor: UMI Research Press, 1982.
―――――. "Boccaccio, Betussi e Michelangelo: Ritratti delle Donne Illustri Come 'Vite Parallele.' " *Letteratura Italiana e Arti Figurative, Atti del XII convegno di studi di lingua e letteratura Italiana. (Toronto, Hamilton, Montreal, 6–10 May 1985)*. Ed. Antonio Franceschetti. Firenze: Olschki, 1988.
Miediema, H. "The Term *Emblema* in Alciati." *The Journal of the Warburg and Courtauld Institutes* 31 (1968): 234–50.
Minor, A.C. and B. Mitchell. *A Renaissance Entertainment. Festivities for the marriage of Cosimo I, Duke of Florence*. Columbia: U of Missouri P, 1968.
Mitchell, B. "Firenze illustrissima: L'Immagine della Patria negli apparati delle nazioni Fiorentine per le Feste di Lione del 1548 e di Anversa del 1549." *Firenze e la Toscana dei Medici nell'Europa del '500*. Firenze: Olschki, 1983.

995–1004.
Monbeig-Goguel, C. "Salviati, Bronzino et 'La Vengence de l'Innocence.'" *Revue d'Art* 31 (1976): 33–7.
Panofsky, E. "Father Time." *Studies in Iconology*. New York: Torchbook edition, 1962. 69–91.
Patch, H.R. *The Goddess Fortuna in Mediaeval Literature*. Cambridge, 1927.
Patrologiae cursus completus, Series Latina. Ed. J-P. Migne. Paris: n.p., 1844–96.
Pictorius, Georgius. *Theologia Mythologica*. Antwerp, 1532. Rpt. *The Renaissance and the Gods*.
Pizzorusso, C. *A Boboli e altrove, sculture e scultori fiorentini del seicento*. Firenze: Olschki, 1989.
Plaisance, M. "Reécriture et écriture dans les deux commentaires burlesques d'Antonfrancesco Grazzini." *Reécritures, Commentaires, Parodies, Variations dans la Litterature Italienne de la Renaissance*. (CNRS) vol. 1. Paris: Université de la Sorbonne Nouvelle, 1983. 185–223.
Pope-Hennessey, J. *Cellini*. London: Macmillan, 1985.
Richelson, P. *Studies in the Personal Imagery of Cosimo I de' Medici*. Diss. 1973. New York: Garland Press, 1975.
Ripa, C. *Iconologia*. Roma, 1603.
Rousseau, C. "Cosimo Primo De Medici and Astrology: The Symbolism of Prophecy." Ph. D. Dissertation. New York: Columbia University, 1983.
Ruffini, F. *Teatri Prima del Teatro: visioni dell'edificio e della scena tra Umanesimo e Rinascimento*. Roma: Bulzoni, 1983.
Russell, D. "Alciati's Emblems in Renaissance France." *Renaissance Quarterly* 34.4 (Winter 1981): 534–54.
Saslow, J.M. *Ganymede in the Renaissance: Homosexuality in Art and Society*. New Haven: Yale UP, 1986.
Saxl, F. "Veritas Filia Temporis." *Philosophy and History, essays presented to Ernst Cassirer*. Eds. R. Klibansky and H. J. Paton. New York: Harper and Row, 1936. 197–222.
Schultz, B. *Art and Anatomy in Renaissance Italy*. Ann Arbor: UMI Research Press, 1985.
Segni, B., trans. *Rhettorica e Poetica di Aristotele*, Firenze: Torrentino, 1551.
Shearman, J. *Mannerism*. Harmondsworth: Penguin, 1967.
——————. "The Galerie of Franois Premier: a case in point." *Miscellanea Musicologica: Adelaide studies in musicology* 2 (1980): 1–15.
Smith, G. "Jealousy, Pleasure and Pain in Agnolo Bronzino's Allegory of Venus and Cupid." *Pantheon* 39 (1981): 250–58.
——————. "Bronzino's Allegory of Happiness." *Art Bulletin* 66.2 (Sept. 1984): 390–98.
——————. "Bronzino's use of Prints: some suggestions." *Print Collector's Newsletter* 9 (1978): 110 ff.
Smyth, C H. *Bronzino as Draughtsman: an introduction*. Locust Valley: J.J.

Augustin, 1971.

———. "Cosimo I and the Joseph Tapestries for Palazzo Vecchio." *Renaissance and Reformation* 6.3 (Aug. 1982).

Summers, D. "Contrapposto: Style and Meaning in Renaissance Art." *Art Bulletin* 49 (1977): 336–61.

Testaverde Matteini, A.M. "Una fonte iconografica francese di don Vincenzo Borghini per gli apparati effimeri del 1565." *Il teatro de' Medici. Quaderni di Teatro* 7 (March 1980): 135–44.

Tietze-Conrat, E. "A Lost Michelangelo Reconstructed." *The Burlington Magazine* 68 (1936): 163–70.

Toscan, J. *Le Carnaval du Language. Le lexique erotique des poets de l'équivoque de Burchiello a Marino (XVe–XVIIe siècles)*. Lilles: Presse de Universitaires, 1981.

Varchi, B. "Lezione sopra quei versi del Trionfo d'Amore del Petrarca 'Quattro destrier via più che neve bianchi . . . '" *Opere di Benedetto Varchi*. Milano and Trieste: Lloyd austriaco, 1859. Vol. 2: 489–96.

Vasari, G. *Le vite de' più eccellenti pittori, scultori ed architettori*. Ed. G. Milanese. Firenze: Sansoni, 1881.

———. Ed. Paola Barocchi & Rosanna Bettarini. Firenze: Sansoni, 1966.

Warburg, A. *La rinascita del paganesimo antico*. Ed. Bing. Firenze: La Nuova Italia, 1980.

Whitman, J. *Allegory, The Dynamics of an Ancient and Medieval Technique*. Oxford: Clarendon Press, 1987.

Wittkower, R. "Chance, Time and Virtue." *The Journal of the Warburg and Courtauld Institute* 1 (1937): 313–21.

Zerner, H. *The School of Fontainebleau*. New York: Abrams, 1969.

Zorzi, L. *Il Teatro e la città, saggi sulla scena italiana*. Torino: Einaudi, 1977.

FIG. 1: **Bronzino**, *Allegory of Love*, 146x116 cm., oil on panel. Figures 1–8, courtesy London, National Gallery

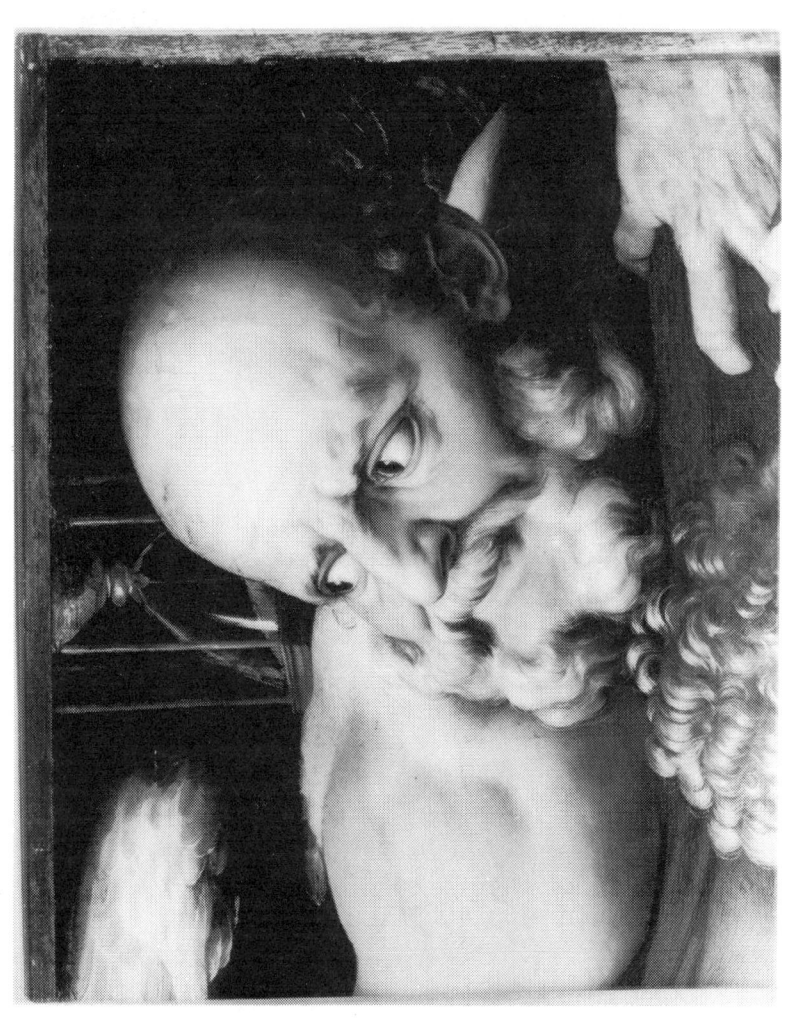

FIG. 2 detail, head of Time-Saturn.

FIG. 3: *detail*, head of *Fraude*.

FIG. 4: *detail*, head of *Giuoco*.

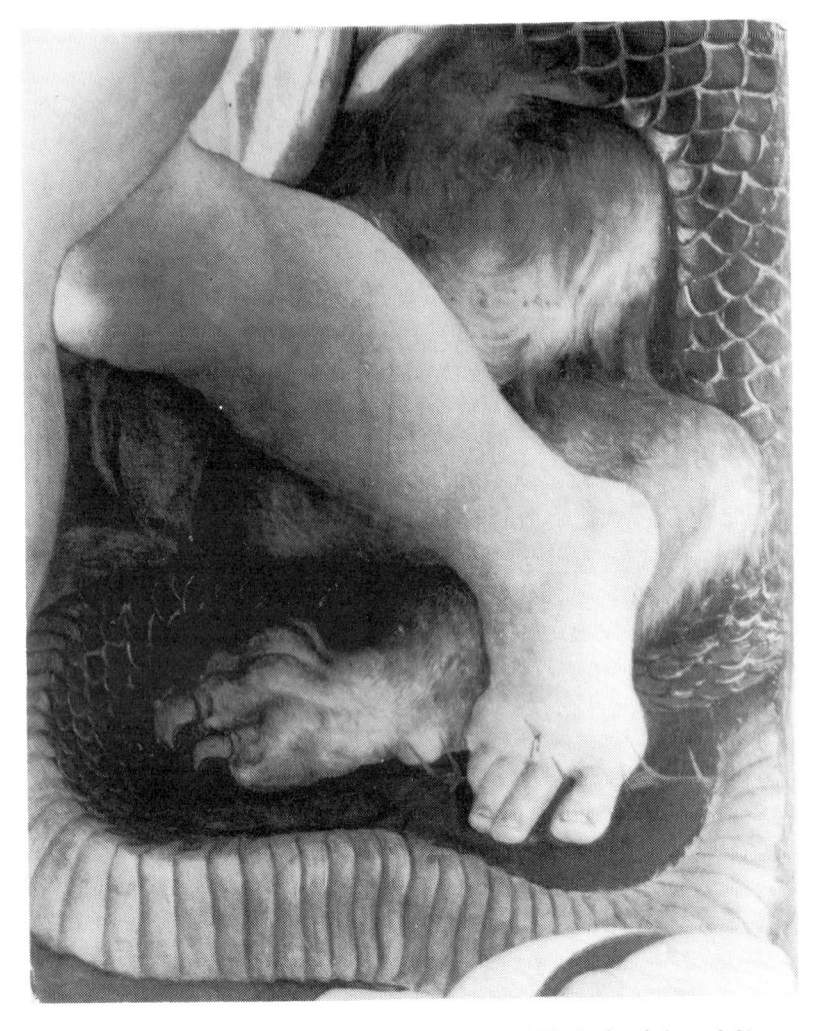

FIG. 5: *detail*, foot of *Giuoco*.

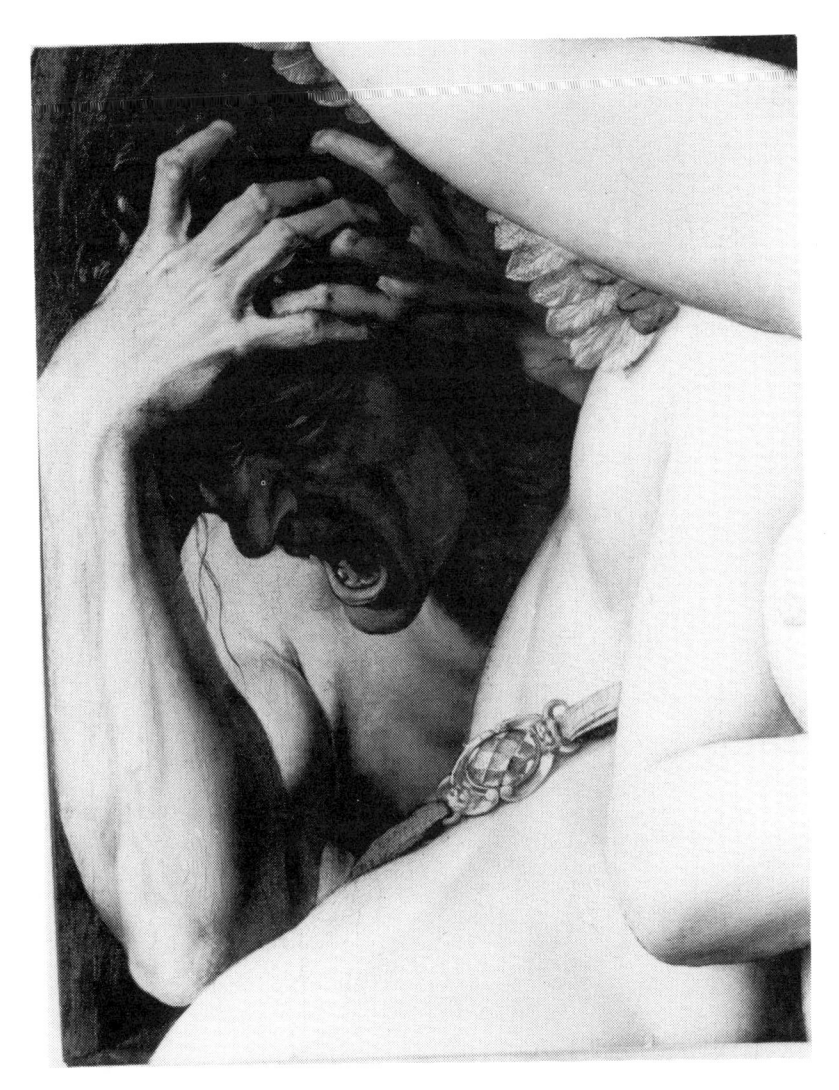

FIG. 6: *detail,* **head of** *Gelosia.*

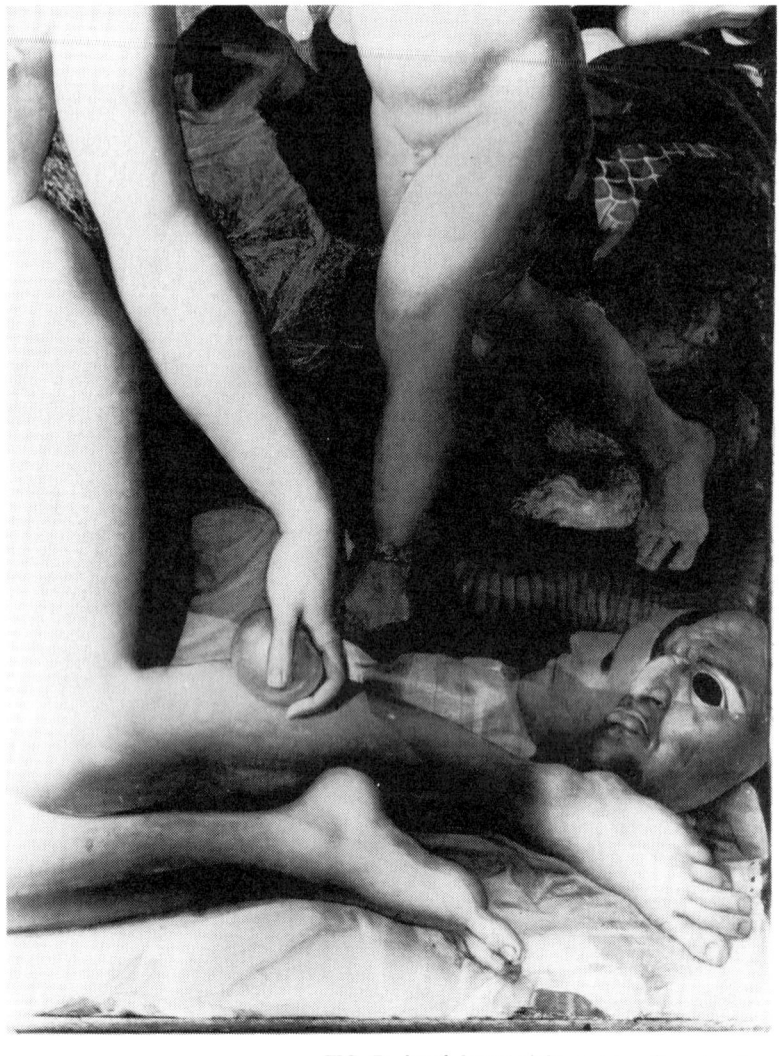

FIG. 7: *detail*, **lower right corner after cleaning.**

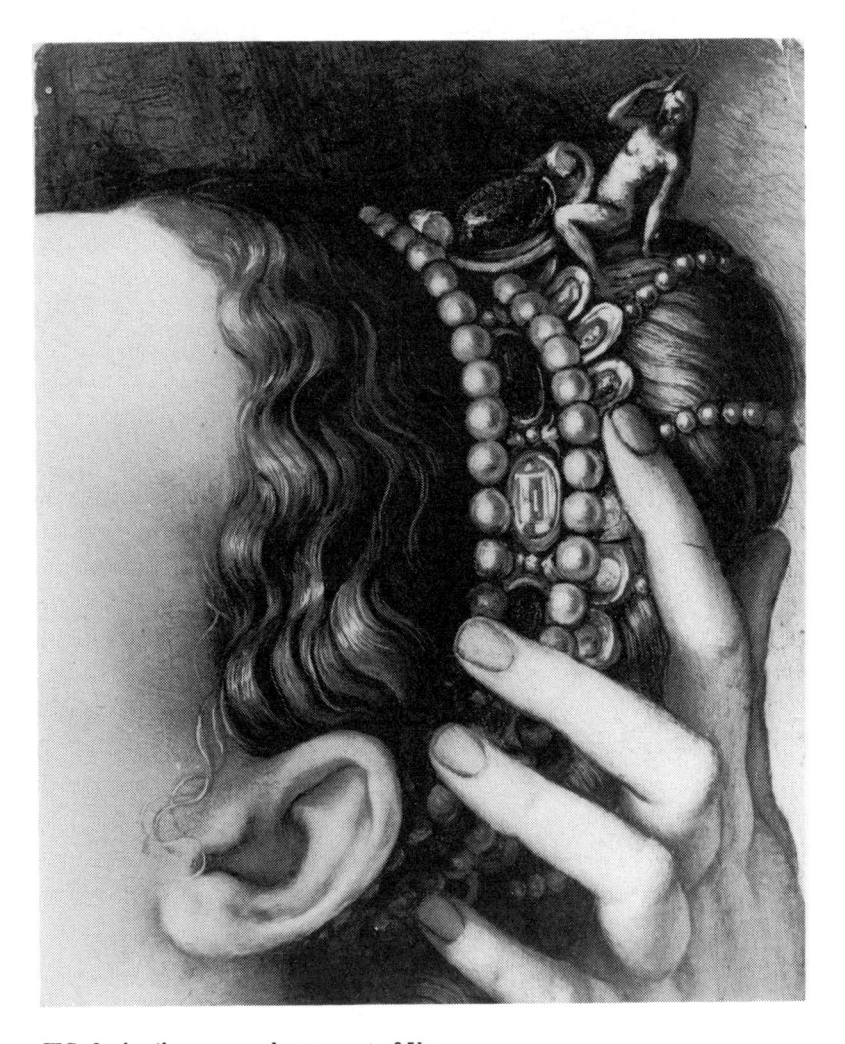

FIG. 8: *detail,* **crown and ornament of Venus.**

FIG. 9: **Fraud 1** *illustration*, Doni *I Mondi*, engraving.

FIG. 10: **Fraud 2** *illustration*, Doni *I Mondi*, engraving.

FIG. 11: **Truth,** *illustration*, Doni *I Mondi*, engraving.

Frederick A. de Armas

Saturn in Conjunction: From Albumasar to Lope de Vega

An inquisitional trial held in the late 1570's resulted in an order to disband the scientific brotherhood of the Segreti. Its leader, Giambattista della Porta, was also commanded to refrain from practising the occult arts. Louise George Clubb adds that: "As a parting shot, the Neapolitan tribunal commanded him to write a comedy" (16). In all likelihood, *L'Astrologo* was the result of this order. This play can be seen as a palinode where della Porta satirizes astrology, necromancy and magic in general, thus offering "proof" of his reformation to the Holy Office and to his public. The play was published many years later, in 1606. On March 9th of 1614, Thomas Tomkis presented an adaptation of this work before "the Kings Maiestie at Cambridge" (71). He entitled it *Albumazar*, utilizing the name of della Porta's main character, an astrologer. The play's success is attested by its revival in 1668, for which John Dryden wrote a prologue, claiming that Ben Jonson's *The Alchemist* was actually inspired by Tomkis' play. Performances ran from February 2nd to the 22nd, further evincing its popularity, although Samuel Pepys records in his diary that he did not see "any thing extraordinary in it" (Tomkis 55).

In the intervening years between the Italian and the first English version of *L'Astrologo*, that is, between 1580 and 1614, the Spanish playwright Félix Lope de Vega Carpio included the name of Albumasar in at least four of his *comedias*: *La difunta pleitiada* (1593–95), *El primer rey de Castilla* (1598–1603), *El secretario de sí mismo* (1604–06) and *La desdichada Estefanía* (12 November, 1604).[1] Referring to this last *comedia*, Frank Halstead explains: "Albumasar seems to have been one of Lope's favorite astrologers, and is, apparently, the only famous diviner who ever appeared as a character in Lope's surviving works" (217). Faced with Albumasar's presence in the theaters of Naples, Spain and England at the close of the sixteenth and the beginning of the seventeenth centuries, it may be well to inquire who this Albumasar was and why he was chosen as the epitome

151

of the astrologer. This information will then be used to understand better the celestial context of Lope de Vega's four *comedias*. This study will focus on the influence of Saturn, for this seventh Ptolemaic planet was deemed to be the most powerful by the Arabic astrologer, and was also greatly feared by Lope de Vega.

David Pingree laments that "there is, as yet, no authoritative treatment of Abu Ma'shar's life nor even a reliable list of his works" (*Thousands* 2). We know that he was born in Balkh on August 10, 787 (Abu Ma'shar, *De Revolutionibus* 5). He studied in Baghdad, and was a contemporary of the philosopher Al-Kindi. Having devoted himself to the study of Islamic traditions, Abu Ma'shar is said to have turned to astrology at the age of forty-seven. However, Pingree presents evidence that he delved into this occult science long before the year 834 (*Thousands* 20). He died in Wasit, almost a centenarian, in 886.

His impact on medieval and Renaissance Europe was such that it stands in striking contrast to his present day obscurity. Richard Lemay claims that: "During the thirteenth century, the authority of Abu Ma'shar on astronomy-astrology, and on cosmology disputed the first place with Aristotle himself" (36). Lemay shows how twelfth-century translations of Abu Ma'shar "became an important and hitherto unnoticed channel through which Aristotelian natural philosophy entered the West some twenty years before any specific work of Aristotle's natural philosophy was actually translated into Latin" (40). Much of this knowledge came through the *Introductorium Maius in Astronomiam* written in 848. This *Greater Introduction* was first translated into Latin by John of Seville in 1133 and then by Hermann of Corinthia in 1140. It was the second version that was printed in the Renaissance, first in Augsburg (1489) and later in Venice (1506). Hermann, who "detested the prolixity of the Arabic language" (Lemay 29), made cuts to the original, including passages that would have shown the extent of the Arabic astrologer's fatalism, as when he claims that: "The planets . . . indicate that man will choose but what is implied in planetary motion" (Albumasar, *Introductorium* 4.3; Lemay 128; Wedel 58).

The emphasis on astral determinism is coupled with a defense of astrology as the highest branch of the science of nature. Abu Ma'shar, following Aristotle, states that the motions of the heavenly bodies are the basis for all activity in the physical world and explains how entities and objects in this inferior realm have an innate disposition to receive influences from the heavens (Albumasar, *Introductorium* 1.2; Lemay 49; North 53–4). This influence can come through an invisible intermediary as in the case of the magnet whose attractive force is carried by air (Lemay 63; North 54). A clear example of influence is found in the doctrine of the tides developed in the *Greater Introduction*. For Pierre Duhem, "c'est dans ce livre, peut-on-dire, que tout le Moyen Age latin a appris les lois du flux et du reflux de la mer" (2.369) [it is in this book, one might say, that the entire Latin Middle Ages learned the rythm of the ebb and flow of the sea]. Abu Ma'shar claims that the moon not only governs the tides, but also certain animals and plants and even discusses Luna's effect upon illnesses (Duhem 2.368).

The influence of the Moon and of all seven planets is exercised, as noted, through motion. Celestial bodies move in circular or perfect orbits, and these revolutions also include circular epicycles: "The epicycle itself is moved along an eccentric circle, the which in turn revolves in the inclined path of the Ecliptic" (Lemay 97). Using Aristotle's *De Caelo* and Ptolemy's *Almagest*, Abu Ma'shar is able to show the intricate and "thrice modified" motion of the planets which results in *fortuna* or *infortunium*. As for the nature of these planets, they are made of a fifth essence. He thus argues against the general astrological opinion of his time and affirms that their color is not directly related to their nature. Relationships between the color and nature of these celestial bodies would lead to error since, for example, "it would make Saturn and Mars evil, the which on the contrary are productive of life and growth by their assimilation on other grounds to fire and earth" (Lemay 97). In rejecting the color theory, Abu Ma'shar is also negating what was to become one of the more common links in the Middle Ages and the Renaissance, the relationship between planets, elements and humors through their corresponding qualities and colors. Abu Ma'shar argues that coloration belongs only to mixed bodies such as the four humors. Black is the color of melancholy and is also linked to Saturn. This does not prove they are of the same nature, for the planets are not mixed bodies, but partake of the fifth essence. Abu Ma'shar also rejects the relationship between Mars and choler, Jupiter and the sanguine humor and the Moon and phlegm. Both Al-Kindi and Alcabatius would defend such links.

In spite of this polemic, Abu Ma'shar repeats the notion that Saturn's nature is "fuscus et niger" (Klibansky *et al.* 128), and that it is cold and dry. Perhaps he means that these qualities exist only *virtually* in the planets: "Saturn, for example, would not be cold to our touch, since it does not actually possess the quality of coldness; rather, it has the capacity to produce the effect of coldness. . . . Thus, the qualities and properties assigned to the planets were based largely on their alleged capacities to produce certain effects on terrestrial bodies" (Grant 287). In spite of previously objecting to the image of an evil Saturn, Abu Ma'shar's description of the seventh planet is for the most part negative:

> With regard to Saturn his nature is cold, dry, bitter, black, dark, violent and harsh. . . . He presides over . . . avarice and bitter poverty . . . over far, evil journeys; over blindness, corruption, hatred, guile, craftiness, fraud, disloyalty, harmfulness (or harm); over being withdrawn into one's self; over loneliness and unsociability; over ostentation, lust for power, pride, haughtiness and boastfulness; over those who enslave men and rule, as well as over every deed of wickedness, force, tyranny and rage. (Klibansky *et al.* 130–31)

Abu Ma'shar continues his list with "affliction, hard life, straits, loss, death" sounding very much like the more extreme astrologers who seldom praised Saturn and considered it as the most malefic of planets. However, it does present a few positive qualities such as the association with farming, estates and wealth. A rather ambivalent, but much repeated trait, is its association with secrets and magic.

It would appear, then, that Abu Ma'shar is part of that long tradition that considers Saturn the most powerful and the most malefic of planets, a tradition that is constantly undergoing revision as opponents try to emphasize the bi-polarity and even the sublime gifts of the seventh planet. This is a tradition that is even alive today in popular astrology as in Liz Greene's *Saturn: A New Look at an Old Devil*. It is also a tradition that Lope knew well, since he studied this occult science under Luis Rosicler, who was arrested by the Inquisition in Toledo in 1605 for casting horoscopes. Rosicler, a Frenchman, was married to one of Lope's sisters, Isabel del Carpio. He cast the playwright's horoscope and must have instilled in him a fear of Saturn that is reflected in a number of poems and plays. Lope's texts often oppose the amorous and benefic Venus to the cold and malefic Saturn. The seventh planet is seen as the cause of misfortunes in love: "mi suerte impía / te dió a Saturno, con que helada y fría / de tu rigor la causa persevera" (de Armas, *Saturn* 68) [my unfortunate fate / gave you to Saturn, with whom you continue frozen and cold / and Saturn remains the cause of your rigidity].

In *La Dorotea*, where Lope alludes to his astrology teacher and to his own horoscope, nothing is said of Abu Ma'shar. The astral knowledge evinced here is derived in part from Marsilio Ficino. Indeed, when Lope decided to try his hand at translation of astral mythology from the Latin, and chose to begin it with a description of the feared Saturn, he did not select the Arabic astrologer as his source. Instead he began a translation of "Las imágenes de los dioses como las escribió Albrico, clarísimo poeta y filósofo" [The images of the gods as Abricius, most famous poet and philosopher, prepared them]. Joaquín de Entrambasaguas assumes that the translation comes from the twelfth-century Albricus. However, as Jean de Seznec has pointed out, there are in reality two writers by that name. The second wrote the *Libellus de imaginibus deorum* which, far from being an early medieval work, is inspired by Petrarch and by his friend Pierre de Bersuire, author of the *Ovide Moralisé*. It is from this second Albricus that Lope translates descriptions of the gods, beginning with Saturn:

Saturno, el primero de los dioses, se ponía y pintaba como un hombre viejo, cano, prolija la barba, corcovado, triste, pálido, cubierta la cabeza y de color melancólica, en la mano derecha tenia una guadaña en que también estaba la imagen de una culebra, que él propio mordía por el extremo; en la siniestra tenía un pequeño hijo, que también parecía devorarle. . . . (Entrambasaguas 2.517; Seznec 176)

[Saturn, the first among the gods, was made and drawn like an old man with white hair, a great beard, hunched over, sad, pale, his head covered and of melancholy colour, his right hand holding a scythe as well as the image of a snake whose tail he was biting; on the left, he held a small son whom he was also seemingly devouring. . . .]

In spite of Lope de Vega's utilization of this astrological and mythical text, he must have been aware of Abu Ma'shar's centrality on the Saturn question. One of the key sources for the transmission of the pagan gods to the Renaissance was Boccaccio's *Genealogia Deorum*. In his presentation of a mainly malefic astrological Saturn, Boccaccio gives Albumasar as his only reference. Indeed, he even ascribes to the Arabic astrologer the link between Saturn and melancholy (137v). Following his lead, Lope may have thought that Abu Ma'shar was a major source for both the medical and the astrological presentations of Saturn.

Another clue as to Lope's interest in Abu Ma'shar is found in his lengthy imitation of Tasso, an epic poem entitled *Jerusalén conquistada*. In a note of his own to the puzzling verses in book eight: "Estaba en la primera Decanoria / De la Virgen la blanca Adrenedefa" (343) [The white Adrenedepha was in the first decan of the Virgin], Lope explains: "Adrenedefa es una estrella que nace en la primera parte del signo de Virgo. Albumasar" (503) [Adrenedepha is the star that rises in the first part of the sign Virgo]. Discussing the sign Virgo, Richard Hinckley Allen reports that the Arabs "adopted the Greek figure, and called it Al'Adhra'al Nathifah, the Innocent Maiden, remains of which are found in the medieval titles Eladari, Eleadari, Adrendesa, and in the Adrenedesa of Albumasar"

(464). The name, then, appears to be synonymous with Virgo. But Lope had also mentioned "la primera Decanoria." Albumasar divided the signs of the zodiac into three parts each, thus creating thirty-six decans with distinct images. In the *Greater Introduction* he describes the first decan of Virgo as "a maiden fair and chaste and pure, with long hair, and a lovely face, having two ears of wheat in her hand, and she sits on a canopied throne and nourishes a child, giving him whereof to eat, dwelling in a place which is called Abrie; and a certain people calls the name of that child Jesus" (Renaker 221). The relationship between Virgo and the Virgin Mary as depicted in the first decan of the sign according to Abu Ma'shar became a most popular topic in medieval and Renaissance Europe.[2] Marsilio Ficino, for example, explains in *The Book of Life*: "In the first face of Virgo, a beautiful virgin seated, holding twin spikes in her hand, and feeding a child. And the rest, which Albumasar describes and certain others" (145).

The certain others could well be Roger Bacon, Albertus Magnus and Pierre d'Ailly. Roger Bacon interpreted Abu Ma'shar to mean that: "The Blessed Virgin had a figure and image within the first ten degrees of Virgo, and that she would nurture her son Jesus Christ in the land of the Jews" (Shumaker 61). Albertus Magnus in his *Speculum Astronomiae* considered Abu Ma'shar's statements to refer to the horoscope of Christ and not to Mary's astrological chart. He proposed that Jesus' ascendant sign was the eighth degree of Virgo, in other words, the first decan, where the Virgin feeds the child in Abu Ma'shar's system. Lope de Vega's *Jerusalén conquistada* utilizes this particular decan to pinpoint the time in which the moorish king Aliberbey of Valencia decides to massacre a group of Christian children. Lope may well be implying that their horoscope is akin to Christ's. Although the Spanish playwright gives Abu Ma'shar as his source, he must have been well aware of the controversies raging over this particular horoscope, which eventually led Girolamo Cardano to have difficulties with the Inquisition.

In the controversy over the horoscope of Christ, Pierre d'Ailly took issue with Albertus Magnus, claiming that the first decan of Virgo was not ascending at Christ's birth, but at the time of the "'great and almost unparalleled' conjunction of Jupiter and Saturn that occurred six years, four days and seven hours before Christ's birth" (Renaker 223). D'Ailly's daring assertion does not go as far as the speculation of some astrologers who claimed that the star of Bethlehem was the result of such a conjunction (Vernet 22). D'Ailly's clever substitution shows a deeper knowledge of his original source, Abu Ma'shar, for the Arabic astrologer proposes, according to Eugenio Garin, "a close connection between celestial phenomena—relative positions of the planets—and the great changes in the history of humanity" (16). In *The Thousands* Abu Ma'shar promulgates his own system of the Great Year or complete cycle of creation and destruction of the world. For him, a cycle begins with a Great Conjunction of all the planets at zero degrees of Aries. David Pingree, who has studied his system and compared it to others such as the Indian *yugas*, accuses Abu Ma'shar of having elaborated a legend to add credibility to a system that must compete with others that seemed as appealing such as Masha'Allah's *Astronomical History*, a work that also contains a horoscope of Christ's nativity (8, 46). In the legend, King Tahmurath of Persia, on being informed by his astrologers of the imminence of a universal flood, deposited the books of scientific knowledge in a special building call Sarawiya so that they would survive the catastrophe. Abu Ma'shar thus claims to be in possession of antediluvian wisdom, which was considered then as almost superhuman knowledge.

But the conjunction of all planets in Aries is different from the type of configuration proposed by d'Ailly as a signal for the birth of Christ. Abu Ma'shar's *The Indications Given to Superior Beings*, translated into Latin by John of Seville as *De magnis coniunctionibus et annorum revolutionibus ac eorum profectionibus* had a much greater impact on the West than *The Thousands*. The work was published in Augsburg in 1489 and in Venice in 1515. Krzystof Pomian labels it a *chronosophy* since it incorporates past and future in a theology of history "looking for the sufficient reason of its course outside the world humans are living in" (38). *De magnis coniunctionibus* proved more popular than *The Thousands* since the astral events involved in it could be tried and measured by the people within their own historical perspective. In this work, Abu Ma'shar establishes a "hierarchy of celestial events the top of which is reserved for conjunctions of Saturn and Jupiter" (Pomian 36), the highest and oldest planets which "are jointly responsible for religion, prophecy, empires, kingdoms, dynasties" (37). Conjunctions of these planets are thus key indicators of changes in these areas. They are the makers of history. The magnitude of the change brought about has to do with the type of conjunction. Abu Ma'shar divides them into three types: major, middle and minor. The minor conjunctions occur every twenty years, and they are always found in the same triplicity. Triplicities are divisions of the twelve signs of the zodiac into four categories of three signs each. The four triplicities correspond to the four elements. For example, the fiery triplicity includes Aries, Leo and Sagittarius (Albumasar, *Flores* 6). The two highest Ptolemaic planets will meet in one of these three signs every twenty years, creating minor conjunctions. At the end of 240 years, the conjunctions will pass to the earth triplicity (Taurus, Virgo and Capricorn). The first conjunction in this new group will be a middle conjunction. After 960 years, Saturn and Jupiter will once again return to the fiery triplicity, having passed through earth, air and water. The first conjunction here will be a major or grand conjunction and will signify drastic changes in religion and / or politics.

Cardinal Pierre d'Ailly in the *Elucidarium* (1414) believes he has discovered a major conjunction of Saturn and Jupiter as signal for the greatest event in world history for the Christian believers, that is, the birth of Christ. The malefic Saturn has taken on a new role as herald of Christ, companion of Jupiter and key to the political and religious transformations of the world. D'Ailly's interest in Saturn-Jupiter conjunctions led him to compose several treatises relating historical events to these astral meetings. In early studies, he agrees with other writers in the dating of one such conjunction in Aries two years before the biblical flood. Later in life he reconsiders the matter, and writes yet another treatise on the conjunction changing his conclusions (Thorndike 4.109). The Cardinal's works stand as a clear indication of Abu Ma'shar's impact on western thought. His popularity and authority remained virtually unchallenged until the end of the fifteenth century. Many would still invoke him as an authority well into the seventeenth century. Robert Burton's *Anatomy of Melancholy*, for example, cites Abu Ma'shar among those who "define out those great conjunctions of Stars, with Ptolomaeus, the periods of Kingdoms, or Religions, of all future Accidents, Wars, Plagues, Schisms, Heresies . . . " (930). It is Abu Ma'shar's reputation as prophet of historical and religious transformations that made him into the epitome of the astrologer.

The earliest threat to this position came in the Simon de Phares affair. This seeker of knowledge reportedly traveled "from Scotland and Ireland to Alexandria and Cairo" (Thorndike 4.546) and eventually settled in Lyons where he gained fame as an astrologer. It was here that he received a visit from Charles VIII. Simon de Phares soon moved to Paris and became the French King's astrologer. The move was also triggered by the archbishop of Lyons, who had forbidden him to practise his art. Once in Paris, he appealed to the Parliament. But this body was not satisfied with the King's confidence in Phares. They submitted his books to the faculty of theology at the university. The Parisian process lasted from June 14, 1491 to February 19, 1494. Phares was prohibited from practising divinatory astrology, but could delve into astronomy "which conjectures certain natural effects of the planets probably and prudently in a general way" (Thorndike 4.548). Curiously, out of the many books in the library of this sage, the faculty selected only eleven to be burned, including various works by Albumasar.

The Spaniard Pedro Ciruelo was in Paris at this time studying theology and was affected by this process. He returned to Spain some years later, obtaining a *cátedra* at the University of Alcalá in 1510. In the *Apotelesmata* of 1521, he criticizes the theologians at Paris who censured books without having a knowledge of astrology. Ciruelo, as both astrologer and theologian, takes it upon himself to separate the licit branch of astrology from the vain and forbidden. This attempt is made both in the *Apotelesmata* and in his most popular work, *Reprouación de las supersticiones y hechizerías* (1530). In the latter he considers that the astrologer who claims he can tell someone what will happen on the road or in gambling "deue ser castigado como medio nigromantico" [ought to be castigated as only half a necromancer]. Nor is it the role of the astrologer to discover "los secretos del coraçon y voluntad del hombre" (57–8) [the secrets of man's heart and will]. On the other hand, it is true that the heavenly bodies "con sus mouimientos y luzes alteran el ayre y la mar y la tierra" (56) [with their motions and lights alter the air and the sea and the earth]. Furthermore, "ansi los cielos causan en nuestros cuerpos diuersas calidades: complexions passiones, y enfermedades: diuersas inclinaciones: y abilidades y muchas artes y ciencias" (56) [thus the heavens cause in our bodies several qualities, temperaments, passions and illnesses; several inclinations and abilities; and many arts and sciences]. The type of *juicio* that clarifies these influences, be it in medicine, weather or natural philosophy, is licit. Of course, there is quite a range from divination to "natural" astrology. A horoscope, for example, can tell a person's physical and mental traits, but not the actions of an enemy — that would be divinatory. Interestingly, Ciruelo cites Albumasar frequently in *Apotelesmata*, although he prefers Ptolemy. He even approves of the doctrine of conjunctions, but disapproves of Albumasar's works on this and other subjects (Thorndike 5.277), perhaps reflecting the condemnation by the Paris theologians.

Pedro Ciruelo had an ideal occasion to test the theories of conjunctions, for in 1524 there occurred one of the most notable astral events of the times, which triggered over one hundred and thirty-three publications from more than fifty-six authors: the conjunction of all the planets in the sign Pisces during the month of February. In his treatise, Ciruelo takes issue with what was perhaps the most famous of the writings on this conjunction,

De falsa diluvii prognosticatione (1519) by Agostino Nifo, a native of the kingdom of Naples. Nifo's alleged purpose is to allay public fears of a universal deluge. However, his intricate arguments and his use of Albumasar's theories of conjunctions coupled with Ptolemy's theories on eclipses leads him to declare that an excess of waters is predicted. Ciruelo rejects Nifo's connection between conjunction and eclipse since they do not occur close enough chronologically. Although he predicts much rain in Spain, he asserts that there is no danger of cities being submerged (Thorndike 5.211). The panic created by astrologers who predicted a deluge in 1524 is clearly evinced in Ciruelo's advice not to sell all of one's possessions, but to pray to God to mitigate the coming catastrophe.

Other Spaniards also wrote concerning this conjunction. Fernando Encinas, for example, composed a treatise against the predictions, claiming that there would be no deluge (Hurtado Torres 139; Thorndike 5.209); while Tomás Rocha defended Abu Ma'shar against Encina's attack (Thorndike 5.209). Finally, the bishop of Barcelona, Martín García, uses Abu Ma'shar in a sermon to show the coming extinction of Islam:

> Según dice Albumasar en el libro *De magnis coniunctionibus* diferencia septima 'la secta mahometana durará 875 anos.' Si acepto lo que dicen sus sabios no debe durar en ningún caso mil años . . . Granada fue conquistada por nuestro rey Fernando en 1491, la secta de Mahoma empezó en 616 y si según Albumasar ha de durar 875 años, la suma de 616 y 875 da 1491, o sea el año de la conquista de Granada. Aquí empezó el principio del fin de los agarenos que se extinguirán en el año de 1524, pues según los astrólogos, en ese año, en el mes de febrero, han de cambiar extrodinariamente todos sus reinos, pues ocurrirán mas de veinte conjunciones. . . . (Vernet 23)
>
> [As Albumasar states in his book *De magnis coniunctionibus*, chapter seven, "the moslem sect will last 875 years." If I accept what their wise men say, it should certainly not last one thousand years . . . Granada was conquered by our king Fernando in 1491, the moslem sect began in 616, and, if according to Albumasar it should last 875 years, the sum of 616 and 875 equals 1491, that is, the year of the conquest of Granada. This marks the beginning of the end of the descendants of Agar who will disappear in the year 1524, since, according to the astrologers, in that year, in the month of February, all their kingdoms will undergo change, since more that twenty conjunctions will take place.]

Abu Ma'shar's theories on conjunctions are certainly at the forefront of astrological discussions in the early sixteenth century. Astral speculation did not abate as the century progressed, for even though dire predictions were not fulfilled, the heavens held humanity's attention with new and even rarer phenomena.

In 1572, the Danish astronomer Tycho Brahe observed the appearance of a new star in the Cassiopeia constellation. According to Lynn Thorndike, this event was more of a shock to Europe than Copernicus' theories (6.68). After all, there was supposed to be neither generation nor corruption in the sphere of the fixed stars and yet this shining apparition of 1572 slowly faded and finally disappeared in 1574. Astrologers, philosophers, and theologians argued about its nature. They called it a new star, a new divine creation, a comet, and a meteor in the ethereal regions. Tycho Brahe gained fame with his treatise *De nova stella* where he cited Albumasar. The Arabic astrologer had also seen a "comet" in the ethereal regions more specifically, beyond the sphere of Venus. He also reported sightings of other comets beyond Jupiter and even Saturn (Vernet 16). The Spanish astronomer Jerónimo Muñoz also observed this star and also stated that it was a comet in the regions above the moon, where no generation or corruption is to take place. In fact, he placed it beyond the sun, and like Brahe, he cited Albumasar's observations (Vernet 15).

Tycho Brahe became the astrologer of the Emperor Rudolf II in 1599. He was joined in Prague by an assistant, Johann Kepler, who, on Brahe's death in 1601, became Court Mathematician and Astronomer. While observing the sky around Sagittarius, where yet another conjunction of Saturn and Jupiter was taking place, he noticed that the two highest planets were joined by Mars. Furthermore, a brilliant star, never seen before, suddenly emerged in the region of the conjunction, Serpentarius. According to Kepler's computations, this particular conjunction can only take place every 800 years, so that previous ones corresponded to the crowning of Charlemagne and the birth of Christ. As for the brilliant star that appears in its midst, it may well be the one that the magi saw 1600 years before, the star that led them to Bethlehem: "Perhaps he [God] even . . . placed it in the spot to which the magi most especially directed their eyes because of the triple planetary conjunction, as was likewise done in the case of this modern star of ours" (Renaker 227). Kepler's book on the *nova* of 1604, *De stella nova in pede Serpentarii*, was as popular as Brahe's treatise on the new star of 1572. All of Europe became obsessed with deciphering this double portent. Max Caspar explains that "there were many interpretations. There was talk of a universal conflagration, of the Day of Judgement, of the overthrow of the Turkish kingdom, of a general revolution in Europe, of the appearance of a great new monarch: *Nova stella, novus rex*" (155). Spain did not escape this new furor either. Tommaso Campanella, for example, believing that Spain was destined to expand its rule into a universal empire shortly before the end of the world, wrote a treatise on how and why Spain was to accomplish this. He points to this Saturn-Jupiter conjunction as one of the signs that reveal such a destiny since the Great Conjunction takes place in Sagittarius, which is the constellation of Spain. He adds that this event "will discover many secrets" upon which he will discourse at a later time.

When della Porta composed *L'Astrologo* in the 1570's, Abu Ma'shar was at the center of astrological controversy. Although no significant effects had been felt from the 1524 conjunction, some argued that such influences often took many years to manifest. The *nova* of 1572, however, seemed to restore faith in Abu Ma'shar since it corroborated his statement that new stars or comets could exist above the moon, in contradistinction to Aristotle's notion that generation and corruption are purely sublunary phenomena. Della Porta thus takes the name of one of the most controversial astrologers, one whose books had been burned in Paris, and applies it to his central character who is nothing more than a charlatan and a thief. This new Albumasar pretends to wisdom and utilizes astrological terminology in order to cheat his clients with the help of two thieves. In Tomkis' adaptation of della Porta's play, Albumasar is sufficiently aware of astral mythology to label the thieves who help him as people of Mercury and has enough knowledge of recent inventions to speak of a *perspicill* or telescope (Tomkis 75, 81). Although Galileo was the inventor of this instrument, della Porta claimed to have discovered it first (Clubb 42–3). His fascination with this instrument is attested by the fact that in 1614, the year of Tomkis' adaptation, della Porta "was constructing a new kind of telescope which would penetrate the Empyrean" (Clubb 53). The passage on the telescope, although included by Tomkis in order to satirize Galileo's findings announced in the *Sidereus Nuncius* of 1610 (Dick 544–48), can ironically refer back to della Porta. But there is little serious discussion in either della Porta's text or Tomkis' version—talk of telescopes in the 1614 play gives way to the presentation of an *otacousticon*, a pair of asses' ears that can help the person hear what is being said far away (Tomkis 82). Nor are any of the astrological details particularly accurate. Albumasar, for example, claims that since the moon proceeds from Capricorn to Aquarius and to Pisces, the subject in question has been drowned and has been eaten by fishes (Tomkis 88).

The fictional Albumasar's notions of astrology have little to do with universal cycles, decans or conjunctions. The astrologer claims that the world "is a theater of theft" (Tomkis 76), and indeed this drama centers on ways in which astrology can be used to cheat others. Curiously, the action focuses on astral magic, and particularly on the transformation of one person into another using the powers of Jupiter and Sol (Tomkis 88) through a ceremony that calls upon the Moon (Tomkis 96). Such metamorphoses are more the subject of treatises ascribed to Apuleius than of Abu Ma'shar's works. The classical writer was reputed to have translated the *Asclepius*, a key hermetic text. However, his fame rests on a fictional work, as Frances Yates notes: "He is famous for his wonderful novel, popularly known as *The Golden Ass*, the hero of which is transformed by witchoo into an ass and after many sufferings in his animal form, is transformed back into human shape after an ecstatic vision of the goddess Isis. . . . The whole mood of the novel with its ethical theme . . . its ecstatic initiation or illumination, its Egyptian colouring, is like the mood of the Hermetic writings" (9.10). Both della Porta and Tomkis parody this process, substituting the realization of being cheated for the ecstatic initiation. Indeed, Apuleius' work is cited during the false metamorphosis (Tomkis 112).

Della Porta and Tomkis have thus produced dramas that point to the dangers of credulity. References to the Moon and Pisces do not an astrologer make. Furthermore, the central beliefs questioned are not those of Abu Ma'shar, but are elements of astral magic at its most extreme which are found in the fictions of Apuleius. Della Porta's dramatic palinode may have served to assuage the Inquisition, but it cannot be construed as an attack on astrology itself, only on impostors and extremists in the art. Certainly, della Porta never abandoned his own beliefs and was known to consort with people of questionable orthodoxy such as Galileo and Campanella. Indeed, by having a charlatan take on the name of Albumasar in order to deceive, della Porta and even Tomkis may well be paying homage to the authority of this ancient astrologer whose mere name imparts respect.

In Lope de Vega's earliest play which refers to Abu Ma'shar, *La difunta pleitiada*, Manfredo, the central character, calls his slave Celín a new Albumasar for suspecting that his master loves Isabela:

>Del alma astrólogo fuiste
>fuiste un nuevo Albumasar,
>que pronosticas tan bien
>el nacimiento a mi bien
>y principio a mi pesar.
>
>(*Obras*, N. 4.545)

[You have been the astrologer of my soul.
You have been a new Albumasar,

who predicts so well
the birth of my happiness
and the beginnings of my sorrow.]

But the Albumasar in this play is not the slave Celín, but the lover Manfredo. His astrological and magical know-how is intended as part of a *burla* in order to gain Isabela's love. Indeed the *comedia*'s reference to the Arabic astrologer is particularly fitting since Manfredo will dress as a Moor in order to enter Isabela's house. Once inside, Isabela corrects the belief that Celín, the slave, is an astrologer, by labeling Manfredo as a true practitioner of this art:

(Con qué vana astrología
por las rayas de mi frente
juzgaste tan locamente
la liviandad fácil mia?

(R. A. E. N. 4.555)

[With what vain astrology
based on the lines of my forehead
are you judging so rashly
my supposed capriciousness?]

Curiously, both della Porta and Tomkis had also portrayed their sage as an expert in metaposcopy or reading the lines of the forehead. Tomkis had actually amplified upon della Porta by referring to Saturn's mark (Tomkis 89). In his *Anatomy of Melancholy*, Robert Burton explains: "Thaddaeus Haggesius, in his Metoposcopia, hath certain Aphorisms derived from Saturn's lines in the forehead by which he collects a melancholy disposition" (182). Burton follows this statement by a reference to della Porta: "and Battista della Porta makes observations from those other parts of the body, as if a spot be over the spleen; or in the nails, if it appear black, it signifieth much care, grief, contention and melancholy" (182). Thus, divination by looking at specific aspects of the physiognomy was an art much admired by della Porta, whose own studies were condemned by the Inquisition (Thorndike 6.150). Perhaps della Porta's reference to metaposcopy in *L'Astrologo* is a grudging admission of his guilt. Tomkis would expand upon it by finding the source of the statement in Hagacius. But, why would Lope de Vega include such a reference? Could he have known della Porta's *L'Astrologo*?

In addition to the reference to Albumasar and to metaposcopy, there are other clues that might indicate that the Spanish playwright could have been aware of the Italian text. Calixto, an *escudero* in Isabel's house, opposes Manfredo's desires, thus reflecting an astral battle between Venus and Saturn (de Armas, *Callisto*). The lover, however, wishes to transform this malefic influence of Calixto-Saturn into a positive one:

> ese Calixto, que mi sol eclipsa,
> haré le yo mi estrella, norte y polo,
> como se mira la estrellada imagen:
> Calixto en la tierra y Elice en el cielo.
>
> (*Obras*, N. 4.550)
>
> [That Calixto, who is eclipsing my Sun,
> I will make into my star, my polestar,
> in the manner one sees the celestial constallation.
> Calixto on earth and Ursa Major in the heavens.]

In the astral myth to which Manfredo alludes, Callisto is transformed by the goddess Diana into a bear. She is then placed in the heavens as Ursa Major, the Great Bear, thus becoming the "Elice en el cielo." This constellation, as Manfredo reminds us, points to the North Star. The lover is thus confident that he will be guided by the *escudero* as mariners are guided by the Pole Star. Mention of the North Star as guide would immediately bring to mind the lodestone. For most Renaissance writers, the magnet was magical. It represented proof of the link between stars and stones. Giambattista della Porta devotes one of the twenty sections of his *Magiae naturalis* (1558; rev. 1589) to this stone, since it best exemplifies the occult forces in nature. Abu Ma'shar, like della Porta, was fascinated by magnetism. John D. North explains that the Arabic astrologer "likened celestial influence to magnetic power, acting as it seems to do without contact" (71). Lope de Vega could well have included these references to the Pole Star to point to his guiding sources, della Porta and Abu Ma'shar.

Although astrology is constantly invoked in both *L'Astrologo* and *La difunta pleitiada*, both plays go beyond it to focus on astral magic. The false transformation of a servant into a man who was supposedly dead is echoed in Lope's play in the transformation of a dead woman into a living one. Isabel, on marrying Leandro, swoons and dies. Manfredo goes to see his dead beloved at the church and miraculously brings her back to life. At this point, the audience may recall Fulgencia's suspicions on seeing Isabela in her death bed:

> Tambien pienso si Manfredo
> algun hechizo le dió. . . .
> Si él la mató no me toca
> decillo, ni en ello hablar
>
> (*Obras*, N. 4.568)

[I wonder if Manfredo
gave her a talisman. . . .
If he killed her, it is not up to me
to reveal it or talk about it.]

Has some *hechizo*, some talisman been used by Manfredo-Albumasar to cause the apparently deathly illness so that he can bring her back to life? Manfredo's Neapolitan origins further confirm his role as *magus*, since at the time this *comedia* was written, Naples was at the forefront of occult pursuits through the writings of Giordano Bruno, Tommaso Campanella and Giambattista della Porta. The third act shows how Manfredo takes his beloved to Naples to wed her there, further pointing out the origins of the plot and of the magic. References to metaposcopy, the pole star, metamorphosis, and the raising of the dead through astral magic may all be ways in which Lope pays tribute to one of the foremost magicians of the times, della Porta, who was also a dramatist like Lope. Manfredo as Albumasar takes up the admiration of the Neapolitan author for the Arabic astrologer, bringing it to fulfillment.

El secretario de sí mismo also utilizes an Italian background. On arriving in Rome, Feduardo witnesses how the governor of that city, Fabio Colonna, rewards a poet named Valerio for having identified an ancient statue as Venus:

. . . estas prisiones
que a los pies la acompañan, muestran claro
que las pone el deleite a los mortales.
Tal la pinta la misma astrología
si Albumasar y a Guido y otros lees.

(*Obras, N.* 9.314)

[. . . these chains
that are by her feet are clearly the result
of mortal delights.
This is how she is pictured astrologically,
if you read books by Albumasar, Guido and others.]

Valerio uses as his sources Guido Bonatti, a thirteenth-century astrologer whom Dante placed in the eighth circle of hell, and Albumasar. Since Bonatti was known as a diviner and a practitioner of astral magic, it may be that Albumasar is also considered in this category. Feduardo amazes the governor and the poet by rejecting the attribution to Venus and proving that the statue is Truth.

While *La difunta pleitiada* and *El secretario de sí mismo* present a

Saturn in Conjunction: From Albumasar to Lope de Vega   167

positive portrayal of Abu Ma'shar in the context of a Renaissance search for wisdom, the other two plays that include this figure are more critical since they focus on Abu Ma'shar as a representative of Arabic culture which is at war with Christian Spain. In *El primer rey de Castilla*, Audalla, the moorish king of Toledo, has fallen in love with Teresa, sister to the king of Leon, Alfonso V. Such is his love for the Christian woman that he promises Alfonso free passage through his land as well as six thousand moorish soldiers so that the Christian king can attack Almanzor. Alfonso agrees to the marriage not only because of its political advantages but also because Audalla is a wise ruler, who is versed in many sciences:

> Medicina, Astrología
> Sabe con estudio tanto
> Que Albumasar y Avicena
> No son en los dos tan sabios.
>
> (*Obras* 8.46)
>
> [Medicine, Astrology
> he knows so well
> that Albumasar and Avicenna
> are not as wise in these two fields.]

Teresa, however, is of a different opinion. She refuses to submit to her new husband, and prays to the Christian God to be delivered from his advances. An angel appears in response to her prayer and leaves Audalla mortally wounded. In this *comedia* the wisdom of an Albumasar and of an Avicenna are no match for a Christian angel. This heavenly being can wound in a manner that cannot be cured by a physician even if he were wiser than Avicenna. This angel can also surprise an astrologer more learned than Albumasar.

La desdichada Estefanía includes a character named Albumasar, who is a moorish astrologer of great renown:

> (Sabes que astrólogo soy
> no sólo en Fez y Marruecos
> conozido, donde estoy,
> mas que a España con los ecos
> de mi fama y nombre doy?
>
> (116–17)
>
> [Do you know that I am a well known
> astrologer not only in Fez and in Marocco
> where I live,
> but also in Spain, which echoes
> with my name and fame?]

An audience of the period may have thought that this was the true Abu Ma'shar, although the historical figure never went to Morocco, and the chronology would be mistaken. This fictional creation by Lope advises a poor worker that he is to become a great ruler:

> Si entendieras el camino
> de aquestas causas secretas,
> vieras su curso divino
> y el fabor de los planctas
> de aspecto dichoso y trino.
>
> (117)

[If you understand the way
of these secret causes, you would see the divine course
and the favour bestowed by the planets
who are in favourable aspect and in trine.]

Abdelmón is to lead a rebellion against the present ruler and become the leader of the Almohades. He will then invade Spain:

> Rey del Africa serás
> a España con gente yrás;
> tu frente espera un laurel . . .
>
> (118)

[You will be King of Africa,
and you will go to Spain with many followers.
Your forehead awaits a laurel. . . .]

Albumasar should have spoken of a grand conjunction, for only the meeting of Saturn with Jupiter would yield a change in dynasties and a continental invasion. The play refrains from discussing this situation, perhaps because such a clear allusion to a contemporary astral event could have led to censorship. The *comedia* was written in 1604, a year when the *nova* which had followed a Saturn-Jupiter conjunction was creating much speculation. Instead of a conjunction, the fictional Albumasar simply speaks of planetary aspects in Abdelmon's own horoscope, mentioning specifically Jupiter and Sol, two benefic celestial bodies often associated with leadership and kingship:

> - O si del sol entendieras
> y de Júpiter el bien
> que por su respeto esperas!
> - Tú has de ser Rey!
>
> (117–18)

[If you only understood
the benefits and respect
you will receive from Sol and Jupiter!
You will be King!]

Albumasar's prediction is one that would lead to the triumph of the Almohades over Christian Spain. As in the previous play, Lope shows that the assistance of the Christian God transcends any Arabic prophecy: at the conclusion of the *comedia*, Alfonso VII captures Abdelmon, but sets him free when he swears that he and his army will return to Africa (204–5).

From this overview of Abu Ma'shar's impact in Western Europe, and particularly in Spain, it can be seen that this neglected figure was often at the forefront of astrological and scientific discussions. John D. North is not exaggerating when he claims that: "Fashions came and went, in astrology, but he [Albumasar] seems to have been read and quoted constantly from the time of the translations of John of Seville and Hermann of Carinthia in the twelfth century to the decline of the subject in the seventeenth" (52). It is thus fitting that della Porta, Tomkis and Lope de Vega utilize this name as the epitome of the astrologer. Lope de Vega presents two opposing portrayals of Abu Ma'shar. As a sage revered by Renaissance seekers of knowledge, the Arabic astrologer stands as a figure of great wisdom and the source of many revelations including astral magic, transformations, metaposcopy and the power of life over death. In this sense he is akin to Saturn, the planet of the highest wisdom, since this astral body rules secrets, magic and the power over death. If Lope de Vega learned from Marsilio Ficino to fear Saturn and yet strive for its gifts, the Florentine Platonist learned some of this planet's traits from Albumasar, consoling his readers in *The Book of Life* by telling them that the Arabic astrologer confirms that "Saturn does not harm those in his house, his domestics, but only outsiders" (166). Lope thus viewed Abu Ma'shar as a figure akin to Ficino and della Porta. Indeed, by using the name of Albumasar, the Spanish playwright may be referring to the famed dramatist and philosopher from Naples who wrote a play featuring an astrologer by that name. In this sense, *La difunta pleitiada* can be seen as a tribute to the author of *L'Astrologo*. In *El primer rey de Castilla*, Lope sees Abu Ma'shar mainly as a representative of Islam and, as such, a figure that must be humbled. Even though the astrologer in *La desdichada Estefanìa* comes close to presenting the theory of conjunctions as a key to historical events, Lope stops short of mentioning this aspect, allowing his audience to ponder on the *nova* and the Saturn-Jupiter conjunction of

1603–4, while at the same time comforting them with the notion of Christianity's triumph. Lope de Vega's dual view of Abu Ma'shar is akin to the prevalent conception of Saturn. The bi-polar astral body represents the highest wisdom for the platonists, just as Abu Ma'shar is praised for his knowledge in *La difunta pleitiada* and *El secretario de sí mismo*. For the astrologers, Saturn is most often malefic, bringing death and disaster. This is the figure of Abu Ma'shar the Moor in *El primer rey de Castilla* and *La desdichada Estefanía*. It is fitting that Lope's portrayal of Abu Ma'shar should coincide with that of Saturn, for the Seventh planet was said to rule astrology, and it was also considered the most important celestial signifier by the sage from Baghdad.

Pennsylvania State University

NOTES

1 The dates listed for Lope de Vega's *comedias* refer to their probable date of composition as found in Moreley and Bruerton. The date for *La desdichada Estefanía* appears in the manuscript.
2 Virgil's *Fourth Eclogue*, where he sang of a goddess and a child, triggered the association between Astraea-Virgo and Mary, mother of Jesus. This association persisted through the Middle Ages and the Renaissance (de Armas, *The Return of Astraea*).

WORKS CITED

Albumasar. *Flores Astrologie*. Venezia: n. p., 1506.
───────. *De magnis coniunctionibus et annorum revolutionibus ac eorum profectionibus*. Augsburg: Erhard Ratdolt, 1489.
───────. *De revolutionibus nativitatum*. Ed. David Pingree. Leipzig: G. B. Teubner, 1968.
───────. *Introductorium in astronomiam*. Augsburg: Erhard Ratdolt, 1498.
───────. *The Thousands of Abu Ma'shar*. Ed. David Pingree. London: The Warburg Institute, 1968.
Boccaccio, G. *De la genealogie des dieux*. Paris, 1531. New York: Garland, 1976.
Burton, R. *The Anatomy of Melancholy*. Eds. Floyd Dell and Paul Jordan Smith. New York: Tudor, 1948.
Campanella, T. *Thomas Campanella an Italian Friar and second Machiavel. His advice to the King of Spain for attaining the universal monarchy of the world*. London: Philemon Stephens, 1660.
Caspar, M. *Kepler*. Trans. C. Doris Hellman. New York: Abelard Schuman, 1959.
Ciruelo, P. *Reprouación de las supersticiones y hechizerías*. Ed. Alva Ebaersole. Valencia: Albatros-Hispanófila, 1978.

Clubb, L.G. *Giambattista della Porta, Dramatist*. Princeton: Princeton UP, 1965.
De Armas, F.A. "Callisto's Saturnine Star: Astrological Imagery in Lope de Vega's *La difunta pleitiada*." *Studies in Honor of William C. McCrary*. Lincoln, Nebraska: Society for Spanish and Spanish-American Studies (1986): 115–36.
──────. *The Return of Astraea. An Astral-Imperial Myth in Calderón*. Lexington: The UP of Kentucky, 1986.
──────. "The Saturn Factor: Examples of Astrological Imagery in Lope de Vega's Works." *Studies in Honor of Everett W. Hesse*. Eds. William C. McCrary and José Antonio Madrigal. Lincoln, Nebraska: Society for Spanish and Spanish-American Studies (1981): 63–80.
Dick, H.G. "The Telescope and the Comic Imagination." *Modern Language Notes* 58 (1943): 544–48.
Duhem, P. *Le système du monde. Histoire des doctrines cosmologiques de Platon à Copernic*. Paris: Librairie Scientifique A. Hermann, 1915. Vols. 2 and 3.
Entrambasaguas, J. de. *Estudios sobre Lope de Vega*. 3 Vols. Madrid: Consejo Superior de Investigaciones Científicas, 1946.
Ficino, M. *The Book of Life*. Ed. and trans. Charles Boer. Irving, Texas: Spring Publications, 1980.
Garin, E. *Astrology in the Renaissance: The Zodiac of Life*. Trans. Carolyn Jackson and June Allen. London: Routledge and Kegan Paul, 1983.
Grant, E. "Cosmology." *Science in the Middle Ages*. Ed. David C. Lindberg. Chicago: U of Chicago P, 1978.
Greene, L. *Saturn. A New Look at an Old Devil*. York Beach: Samuel Weiser, 1976.
Halstead, F.G. "The Attitude of Lope de Vega Toward Astrology and Astronomy." *Hispanic Review* 7 (1939): 205–19.
Hurtado Torres, A. *La astrología en la literatura del Siglo de Oro*. Alicante: Instituto de Estudios Alicantinos, 1984.
Klibansky, R., E. Panofsky, and F. Saxl. *Saturn and Melancholy*. London: Thomas Nelson, 1964.
Lemay, R. *Abu Ma'shar and Latin Aristotelianism in the Twelfth Century*. American University of Beirut, Oriental Series 38. Beirut, 1962.
Lope de Vega Carpio, F. *La desdichada Estefanía*. Ed. Hugh W. Kennedy. University of Mississippi: Romance Monographs, 1975.
──────. *Jerusalén conquistada*. Ed. Joaquín de Entrambasaguas. 3 Vols. Madrid: Consejo Superior de Investigaciones Científicas, 1951.
──────. *Obras de Lope de Vega publicadas por la Real Academia Española*. Madrid: Sucesores de Rivadeneyra, 1898. Vol. 8.
──────. *Obras de Lope de Vega publicadas por la Real Academia Española (Nueva Edición)*. Madrid: Tipografía de Archivos, 1917 and 1930. Vols. 4 and 9.
McCready, W.T. "Lope de Vega's Birth Date and Horoscope." *Hispanic Review* 28 (1960): 313–18.

Masha'Alla. *The Astrological History.* Ed. David Pingree. Cambridge: Harvard UP, 1971.

Moreley, S.G. and C. Bruerton. *Cronología de las comedias de Lope de Vega.* Madrid: Gredos, 1968.

North, J.D. "Celestial Influence—The Major Premise of Astrology." *Astrologi Hallucinati, Stars and the End of the World in Luther's Time.* Ed. Paola Zambelli. Berlin: Walter de Gruyter, 1986. 45–100.

Pomian, K. "Astrology as a Naturalistic Theology of History." *Astrologi Hallucinati, Stars and the End of the World in Luther's Time.* Ed. Paola Zambelli. Berlin: Walter de Gruyter, 1986. 29–43.

Porta, G. della. *Natural Magic.* New York: Basic Books, 1957.

Renaker, D. "The Horoscope of Christ." *Milton Studies* 12 (1978): 213–35.

Seznec, J. *The Survival of the Pagan Gods.* Trans. Barbara F. Sessions. Princeton: Princeton UP, 1972.

Shumaker, W. *Renaissance Curiosa.* Binghamton: Medieval and Renaissance Texts and Studies, 1982.

Thorndike, L. *A History of Magic and Experimental Science.* 8 Vols. New York: Columbia UP, 1923–58.

Tomkis, T. *Albumazar: A Comedy.* Ed. Hugh G. Dick. Berkeley: U of California P, 1944.

Vernet, J. *Astrología y astronomía en el Renacimiento.* Barcelona: Ariel, 1974.

Wedel, T.O. *The Medieval Attitude Toward Astrology.* New Haven: Yale UP, 1920.

Yates, F. *Giordano Bruno and the Hermetic Tradition.* Chicago: U of Chicago P, 1964.

Massimo Ciavolella

Saturn and Venus

The conjunction of Venus and Mars in the dignity of Saturn will lead me to concentrate with such intensity in venereal things that I will find no peace. . . . I am constantly tortured by the thought of sex; and that pleasure that I was not allowed to reach completely, or that I was ashamed to obtain when I could, I have artificially created [within myself] with the constant application of my thought . . . from the dominance of Luna and Saturn and from the mixing of their rays, I have derived a profound yet lascivious mind, hence my inclination to a shameful and obscene libido.[1]

With these words Girolamo Cardano, renowned scholar, mathematician, physician, and astrologer (Pavia 1501–Rome 1576) defines his character and personality in a lengthy horoscope written about himself—one of several he published during his long and tormented life.[2]

The ambiguity of such a peculiar inborn inclination, forever torn between the pursuits of the mind and the call of the flesh, did not escape Robert Burton, the most profound student of melancholy of the seventeenth century. The above quotation from Cardano derives from the third book of his *Anatomy of Melancholy* devoted to the study of "Love-melancholy," Section 2, Member 2, subsection 1: "Causes of heroical Love, Temperature, full Diet, Idleness, Place, Climate, etc." Burton, however, unlike Cardano professes to be skeptical of the influence of the stars: "Of all causes [of heroical love] the remotest are stars." But then he proceeds to discuss the opinion of some among the most influential authors of the Renaissance, who believed in the opposite view: "Ficinus, *cap.* 19, saith they are most prone to this burning lust, that have Venus in Leo in their horoscope, when the Moon and Venus be mutually aspected, or such as be of Venus' complexion. . . . Those who, in the moment of their birth, had Venus in the masculine sign and in the house of Saturn or in opposition to Saturn, are more apt to masculine coitus. . . . Ptolemy in the Tetrabiblos has numerous and extraordinary aphorisms on this very argument . . . in the Astrology, Campanella gathers many aphorisms, and among these, many that explain erotic madness" (58–59).

The passage relative to the effects of "Venus in the masculine sign in the house of Saturn" at the time of birth is an almost verbatim quotation from Ficino's *Commentary on Plato's "Symposium" on Love*, Speech VI, chapter 14, "Whence comes love for males, whence for females," where Ficino discusses the causes of sexual attraction between male and female:

But since the reproductive drive of the soul, being without cognition, makes no distinction between the sexes, nevertheless, it is naturally aroused for copulation whenever we judge any body to be beautiful; and it often happens that those who associate with males, in order to satisfy the demands of the genital part, copulate with them. Especially those at whose birth Venus was in a masculine sign and either in conjunction with Saturn, or in the house of Saturn, or in opposition to Saturn. (135)

Venus and Saturn are traditionally considered by the astrologers as enemies of each other; it is indeed an axiom that Venus and Saturn are planets with opposite properties: Venus is hot and humid, Saturn cold and dry. And yet their influence, while unreconcilable at a purely astrological level, finds a common ground at the purely somatogenic level. Ancient, medieval, and Renaissance science — and by science I mean that branch of philosophy and medicine which went under the name of natural philosophy or *physica* — considered the influence of Venus and Saturn as being inextricably, yet fatally, connected. That is to say that those born under the sign of Saturn, and as a consequence more prone to the ill effects of *melancholia*, share certain fundamental characteristics with those born under the sign of Venus (especially if in conjunction with Mars and/or Luna) — who are more predisposed to the stimuli of the flesh. Indeed, such are the *vincula* between *melancholia* and *lussuria* at their most acute degree, that the boundaries between the two conditions remain blurred, to the extent that one condition can turn into the other, even be confused with the other. And vice versa. I shall contend that it is also because of the unyielding influence of the rays of Saturn and Venus on the human being that lovers can turn melancholic, and melancholics can see their feelings of longing heightened to an unbearable level. Thus the state of erotic superexcitation is an objective correlative of melancholy, and the passionate lover lives under the menacing sickle of Saturn, at the mercy of the darker side of his nature.

Let's go back to the words of Girolamo Cardano: the two salient characteristics of his personality that he wants to impress in the mind of the reader are the profundity of his mind — that is to say his intelligence, his capacity to concentrate, his obsession with study — and his overwhelming passionality—that is to say his obsession with his own sensuality, and with the objects of his erotic desires. It is in this very element of obsessiveness that we find the common ground between the saturnine and the venereal temperaments. The current concept of obsession has assumed a very specific meaning dictated by psychoanalysis. In Renaissance thought, obsession took the name of "fixation of the imagination," and it carried other connotations, lost to the modern reader.

For Ficino, for Cardano, for Burton, for Campanella, and for their contemporaries, *amor* — love — and *melancholia* — melancholy — are caused by a perverted imagination, that is to say of a "fixed imagination." The meaning of "imagination," it goes without saying, has also undergone a radical transformation: "fancy, creative faculty of the mind" (*The Concise Oxford Dictionary*, s.v.). Until the seventeenth century, however, the term *imaginatio*, imagination, referred to a specific function of a very precise, albeit at times confused and confusing, physiological and psychological system which supposedly explained the nature and the behaviour of the human being. This system hides the roots of the concepts of eros and melancholy, and the explanation of Girolamo Cardano's words.

Marsilio Ficino, at the beginning of the seventh book of his *Commentary on Plato's "Symposium" on Love*, shifts his discussion on love from the level of moral philosophy to that of natural philosophy—Ficino, as we all know, considered himself not only a moral philosopher, but also a *physicus*. In Speech VII, chapter 3, "On bestial love, that is a kind of insanity," he writes:

We think that the madness by which those who are desperately in love are afflicted is, strictly speaking, caused by a disease of the heart, and that it is wrong to associate the most sacred name of love with these. But lest perhaps we seem to be too wise against the many, for the sake of this discussion let us too use the name love for these. (158)

Later, in the seventh chapter, Ficino explains why " Vulgar love is a disturbance of the blood":

That this passion is in the blood there is evidence in the fact that this kind of heat has no periodic break. Any fever which is continuous is located by natural philosophers in the blood; one which gives six-hours of rest, in the phlegm; one which gives one day, in the bile, and one which gives two, in the humor of black bile. Therefore, we are right in placing this fever in the blood; in blood, that is, which is melancholic, as you have heard in the speech of Socrates. Fixation of thought always accompanies this kind of blood. (164)

Even the four kinds of divine madness spring from a "fixed and profound thought." He whose mind is trained in the art of philosophy can be overcome by erotic furor, alias divine madness, inspiration: "For we achieve neither poetry nor mysteries, nor prophecy — Ficino writes — without vast zeal, burning piety, and sedulous worship of divinity. But what else do we call zeal, piety, and worship, except love? Therefore all exist through the power of Love" (171–72). Man, however, can also inherit at birth a physiological disposition towards melancholy and love — Ficino and all his followers at the Florentine Academy considered themselves children of Saturn. This is to say that at birth certain physiological conditions are created, mainly within the constitution of the blood and in that of the receptacle of imagination, which foment the melancholy temperament.

The nature of the melancholic's and of the lover's condition can be explained only in terms of the physiology of the brain itself, that is to say in terms of the nature and disposition of the internal sense, that body of internal functions of the human being which oversees sensation, perception, and intellection.[3] Very briefly, the frontal lobe of the anterior ventricle of the brain is occupied by the common sense, whose task is to receive from the eyes the form of the object of sensation. This form, once the object of perception is no longer present, is preserved by the power of fantasy (the Greek *phantasia*, which corresponds to the Latin *imaginatio* or retentive imagination), located in the dorsal lobe of the anterior ventricle of the brain. The impressions retained within fantasy are separated from each other or combined, if they belong to the same genre, by the power of imagination, called *virtus cogitativa* in man, which is physiologically located in the anterior lobe of the middle ventricle of the brain. The dorsal part of the same ventricle is occupied by *virtus aestimativa*, that is to say the power that perceives the non-sensitive intentions within the single objects of sensations. These non-sensitive intentions perceived by the power of estimation are preserved by memory *virtus conservativa et memorialis*, located in the posterior ventricle of the brain. In other words, memory parallels, at a higher level, the power of fantasy, which preserves the sense impressions received from the common sense. The highest power, which oversees all other activities of the soul from the citadel of the brain, is reason. This is the summary given of this psychological process by the great Arab philosopher Ibn Sina (Avicenna) in his *De anima*:

> The similitude [of the object of perception] is fused with the spirit that carries the power of vision . . . and it penetrates into the spirit that is located in the first ventricle of the brain. It is then imprinted upon the spirit, which is the one that carries the power of the common sense. . . . Then the common sense transmits the

form to the neighbouring spirit, imprinting it with the form, and thereby places the object in the imaginative power, that which creates forms. ... Then the form that is in the imagination enters into the posterior ventricle of the brain and unites itself with the spirit that carries the power of estimation ... and the form that was in the *imaginativa* imprints itself upon the spirit of the power of estimation. ...[4]

According to natural philosophy, the first cause of the obsession which torments lovers and melancholics is to be found in the corruption of the faculty of estimation, the power which should separate the good from the harmful intentions within the objects of sensation. However, if the desire for an object of perception is too strong and persistent — an aberration which can be caused by a variety of causes, such as a diet of fat foods combined with a sedentary life, a hot and humid climate, or the influence, at the time of birth, of the planet Venus in conjunction with Mars and Saturn, as in the case of Girolamo Cardano — the power of estimation can become confused, leading the subject to believe that harmful things are good, and unattainable things are attainable. Arnald of Villanova (d. ca. 1313), one of the most esteemed professors of medicine of the School of Montpellier with whose works Marsilio Ficino was well acquainted, sums up this condition with the following words in *De amore heroico* 46–47:

Because of the violent desire, he [the subject] retaines the form [of the object of perception] imprinted upon his mind by the fantasy, and because of memory, he is constantly reminded of the object. From these two actions a third follows: from the violent desire and from the constant recollection arises compulsive cogitation. The lover dwells on how and through which methods he will be able to obtain this object for his own pleasure so that he may come to the enjoyment of this destructive delight that he has formulated in his psyche.[5]

The object of desire becomes an obsessive idea which polarizes thought itself, while the corruption of the power of estimation brings about the derangement of the remaining faculties of the soul, since their state depends from the well-being of the the *virtus aestimativa*. In time, this obsession can darken and overpower reason itself, driving the subject to seek the gratification of his bodily impulses against all sense and good judgement.

Because of their very nature, however, the internal senses of the soul cannot undergo change, and therefore any false judgement on their part must depend on the instruments that the faculty of estimation employs to carry out its functions: the middle cavity of the brain and the spirits (pneuma) it contains. The spirits provide the essential link between the powers of the soul and the body. It is this link that gives the human being his capacity to reason, and therefore to raise himself above all other species. Writes Marsilio Ficino, summing up this process:

The entire attention of a lover's soul is devoted to continuous thought about the beloved. . . . Moreover, wherever the continuous attention of the soul is carried, there also fly the spirits, which are the chariots, or instruments of the soul. The spirits are produced in the heart from the thinnest part of the blood. The lover's soul is carried towards the image of the beloved planted in his imagination, and thence towards the beloved himself. To the same place are also drawn the lover's spirits. Flying out there, they are continuously dissipated. Therefore there is a need for a constant source of pure blood to replace the consumed spirits, since the thinner and clearer parts of the blood are used up every day in replacing the spirits. On that account, when the pure and clear blood is dissipated, there remains only the impure, thick, dry, and black. Hence the body dries out and grows squalid, and hence lovers become melancholic. For from dry, thick, and black blood is produced melancholy, that is, black bile, which fills the head with its vapors, dries out the brain. . . . (121)

It is not within the scope of the *Commentary on Plato's "Symposium" on Love*, however, to describe the complex psycho-physiological process which leads to the growth of passion and melancholy; Ficino is satisfied in outlining its basic traits. Therefore, he does not describe the essential physiological interplay between the heat created by passion and the coldness produced by melancholy. For this, we must go back to the more traditional medical texts.

When a pleasing object captures the attention of a person and reaches the internal powers of the soul — these texts tell us — the sudden pleasure that arises causes a rapid multiplication of the spirits which overheat and spread throughout the body, thereby overheating the entire organism. The receptacle of the faculty of estimation, the dorsal portion of the middle ventricle of the brain, being in contact with the burning spirits coming from the heart, also becomes inflamed, and from this state of inflammation the permanence of the phantasms of perception occurs.

The faculty of estimation controls the *imaginativa*, and the permanency of memories (from Plato onward the recurring image is that of the imprint of a seal upon wax) is in direct relation with the level of heat and dryness of the encephalic cavity in which memory is localized. The excessive heat of the spirits which, being overheated, move towards the *egemonikòn*, overheats the other encephalic cavities and the spirits with which it comes in contact, causing an evaporation of the radical humour. The overheating of the spirits and of the receptacles of imagination and memory causes the image of the object of desire, its *phantasma*, to remain firmly implanted in the organ of memory. The successive evaporation of the radical humour and the growth of black bile, cold and dry, fix the phantasm upon the organic substance of the brain, just like the imprint of the seal remains in the wax when it cools and dries. The image of the object of desire thus remains the only datum obsessively present to the consciousness of the lover, an *idée fixe* which engenders endless torments. It is this obsessive presence of the phantasm that is the cause of that pathological condition known as *complexio venerea*, or better as erotic melancholy.

The symptoms of the psycho-physiological condition we have described as erotic melancholy correspond to those assigned to the saturnine temperament: a fixation of thought occasioned by the coldness and dryness of the brain. Those who are born under the sign of Venus, having a warm and moist temperament, can easily fall prey to the snares of love, and eventually turn melancholy and mad. Conversely, those who are born under the sign of Saturn are prone to obsessive behaviour because of their cold and dry temperament. The influence of the combined effect of the two planets at the time of birth can only be a fatal one. As a consequence, those who were born with a temperament that predisposes their imagination towards the permanent retention of images, that is to say, towards obsessive behaviour, will also undergo a parallel clinical course. We should not be surprised, therefore, if Marsilio Ficino, in his *Book of Life* insists that the melancholics to whom he addresses his book — namely the scholars and the philosophers — should follow a psychological and physiological diet which is almost a copy of the one prescribed by physicians for the cure of erotic melancholy, or if he suggests moderate sexual exercise as a valid therapy against the dark phantasms of a melancholic temperament. Nor should we be bewildered by Giordano Bruno's statement, in his *De vinculis in genere*, that "as a consequence of their temperament, melancholics are more prone to the ties of indignation, sadness, volupty, and love. Being in fact more impressionable, they imagine pleasure with a greater intensity. For the very same reason they are most disposed towards contemplation and speculative thought, and in general they are moved and agitated by more vehement passions. Thus, for what concerns Venus, their end is more their personal pleasure than the propagation of the species" (163).

Giordano Bruno's comments on the relationship between melancholy and erotic passion, and his precise reference to the fact that the images of pleasure remain more firmly impressed within the imagination of the melancholics, corraborates Girolamo Cardano's description of his own peculiar temperament in the eighth nativity of the supplement to his commentaries on Ptomely's *Treatise on Heavenly Body*, the text with which we opened our discussion. Cardano remained convinced throughout his entire life that the numerous ills he suffered, and in particular his overwhelming libido and his inability to engage in sexual activities, as he himself tells us in *The Book of My Life*: "from my twenty-first to my thirty-first year I was unable to lie with women, and many a time I lamented my fate, envying every other man his own good fortune" (5) were caused mainly by the conjunction of Saturn and Venus at the moment of his birth on September 24, 1501, at 6:40 a.m. Girolamo Cardano was aware that the disease from which he suffered had tormented men of genius since Socrates first spoke about it. And just like Giordano Bruno a few decades later, he knew that his conception of the relationship between eros and melancholy was part of the scientific heritage of his own age, and that despite the many treatises written on this tragic passion, for those born under the signs of Saturn and Venus there could be no respite from *amor hereos*, as it was universally called:

> At times I have been tormented by a tragic passion so heroic [sic: *laboravi interdum etiam amore heroico*] that I planned to commit suicide. I suspect that this has happened to others also, although they do not refer to it in their books. (25)

University of Toronto

NOTES

1 The passage is quoted by Robert Burton in his *Anatomy of Melancholy* in Cardano's original Latin.
2 The horoscope is the eighth of twelve horoscopes, *Liber XII geniturarum*, appended to his commentary on Ptolemy's *Quadripartitum*, and written "for the usefulness of scholars of astrology."
3 Since this paper was first delivered, the following discussion concerning the psychophysiology of love was expanded and included in D. Beecher's and M. Ciavolella's introduction to Ferrand's treatise 70–82.
4 Quoted in Ferrand 80.
5 Translated by D. Beecher and M. Ciavolella in Ferrand 79.

WORKS CITED

Avicenna (Ibn Sina). *De anima*. Venetiis: apud Juntas, 1546. Rpr. Westmead: Gregg International Publishers, 1969.

Arnald of Villanova. *De amore heroico*. In *Opera medica omnia*. Ed. M.R. McVaugh. Barcelona: Universitat de Barcelona, 1985.

Bruno, Giordano. *De magia. De Vinculis in genere.* A cura di A. Biondi. Pordenone: Edizioni Biblioteca dell'Immagine, 1986.

Burton, Robert. *The Anatomy of Melancholy.* In 3 vols. Vol. 3. London: J.M. Dent, 1932.

Cardano, Girolamo. *The Book of My Life (De vita propria liber).* Trans. J. Stoner. New York: Dover Publication, 1962.

⸺. *De vita propria liber.* Amstelaedami: apud Joannem Ravesteinium, 1654.

⸺. *Opera omnia.* Lugduni: Sumptibus Ioannis Antonii Huguetan et Marci Antonii Ravaud, 1663.

Ferrand, Jacques. *A Treatise on Lovesickness.* Trans. D. Beecher and M. Ciavolella. Syracuse: Syracuse UP, 1990.

Ficino, Marsilio. *Commentary on Plato's "Symposium" on Love.* Trans. S. Jayne. Dallas, Texas: Spring Publications, 1985.

⸺. *The Book of Life.*Trans. C. Boer. Dallas, Texas: Spring Publications, 1980.